THE TECHNO PAGAN OCTOPUS MESSIAH

IAN MUIR WINN

The Techno Pagan Octopus Messiah by Ian Winn.
First published in 1999 by I.M.P Fiction. Reprinted 1999.
This 20th Anniversary 3rd Edition and e-book published in 2018 by
Ian Winn.
ISBN: 978-1-9806-6126-9

This work is Copyright © Ian Winn 2018
The right of Ian Winn to be identified as the author of this work
has been asserted by him in accordance to the Copyright, Designs
and Patents Act, 1988

All rights reserved. No portion of this book may be reproduced,
stored in a retrieval system, or transmitted in any form or by any
means, electronic, mechanical, photocopying, recording or
otherwise, without the prior permission of Ian Winn, the copyright
owner. For permissions please contact:

www.octopusmessiah.com

Author photo: Bjarte Johannesen

Cover Art by Lala

TO MY PARENTS

for their love and words

TABLE OF CONTENTS

I	Chepren	6
II	India	60
III	The Yoga of Rishikesh	81
IV	Naga Baba	105
V	The International Silly Straw Experience	136
VI	Beginnings	202
VII	The Journal Inverse	254
IX	The Redemption of English Al	276
X	The Dream	309
XI	The Serpent	322

AUTHOR'S NOTE

The poems inside are transcripts of spoken word pieces I wrote in India and have since performed across Britain and the United States. They are meant to be heard, preferably near open flame, which is why I have made (hopefully redemptive) audio recordings of certain poems freely available on <u>octopusmessiah.com</u>. I recommend you listen to them first. To do so, please go to the Shouting *page and enter the password, because octopuses have: 3hearts*

PROLOGUE

Namaste, traveller, come sit by the fire
With the Techno-Pagan Octopus Messiah
Chosen by the powers that burn
Willing to teach if you're willing to learn...
You want the whole story from the beginnin'?
It's a long one filled with dreams, crystals and women
But don't let me stray from the point which is:
When I was twelve I dreamed of the pyramids
Where I found a crystal the color of good
And this was the most vivid dream of my childhood
But like most dreams I put it aside
Got into biology, the study of life
Which says that the ultimate nut is the gene
Describes the flesh perfect, don't touch on the dream
But half being half I got my degree
In straight-up marine cephalopodic biology
'Cause octopus, man, they're smarter than cats
The sharpest invertebrate mind, how 'bout that?
Their brains in a non-localized neural net
(My octopus, Clyde, was more roommate than pet)
Communicate by color and posture, believe
Wear what they're thinking on their eight sleeves
Which, if you think about it, sounds like telepathy
Could this be the next totem of humanity?

Now dig, I was born one Ian Muir Winn
Named after the naturalist John Muir, heard of him?

Created Yosemite National Park?
Climbed redwood trees during storms in the dark?
And like John, I feel most at home in the wild
So I got me a job on a small, desert isle
Teaching marine science and being in charge
Of the wetsuits and kayaks for Naturalists at Large
Nurturing children's innate curiosity
Earth Mother Native American philosophy
But something felt empty, you know what I mean?
And that's when I discovered...
Dimethyl tryptamine.

Met a man by the name of McKenna
An author, a scholar, a psychonaut — you betcha!
Some people call him an ethnopharmacologist
But ask him yourself and he'll say he's an alchemist...
Turned me on to the drug DMT
Jokingly called it "Three dimensional spirituality"
Now, I've gone and played with some dangerous drugs
(The worst ones were television and keg-beer from mugs)
Tried ecstasy, opium, acid and speed
I hit the base pipe and smoked my share of weed
Even did heroin once accidentally
But nothing prepares you for DMT mentally...

DMT can't be found on your basic black market
Can't eat it without Bannisteriopsis —
What the Amazon tribes call the Ancestor's Vine
It inhibits a certain digestive enzyme
So you smoke what a chemist has grown in a lab
And it stimulates nerves in your pineal gland
An organ Descartes called the seat of the soul

Between the two halves of the brain I've been told
And the pineal gland appears, no deception
At forty-nine days after conception
Inside a developing fetus' head
And in the Tibetan Book of the Dead
Forty-nine days is the same time it takes
A dead person's soul to reincarnate...
Now you're beginnin' to see what I mean
When I tell you watch out for dimethyl tryptamine…
And no one knows more about DMT
Then this man McKenna and it must be destiny
The day after he left it was offered to me
By a woman I'd never before or since seen...

When a spaceship lands in your fuckin' backyard
You got a choice and that choice is damn hard
Do you jump on that ship and go for a ride
Or run to your house, lock yourself inside?
They promise they'll bring you right back and with ease
But the crux of the issue is you have to leave...
And if that ship left without me? My life would be hell
Years of what-ifs and kicking myself
And so I lay down on that woman's couch
Put the evil base pipe in my mouth
And the smoke is foul — ssssp!
Like molten plastic — ssssp!
The act is ugly — ssssp!
Suckin' the glass dick
And I reached a membrane after three hits
Took one more — ssssp! — and busted right through it
Sped through the wormhole of the land In Between
Popped out at the Pyramids, just like my dream
And above me floated… hell, I don't know

I guess you'd call it a damn UFO!
Filled with the Gods of heaven and earth
Only recognized Shiva, the one I saw first
And the Gods, they expected somethin' from me
And I felt like a guest with no gift at a birthday party
So I reached back to my voice, fell to one astral knee
And said, "How can we reconcile wilderness with technology?"
Without hesitation the Gods answered me
By slamming my mind with a tidal wave of beauty
Oh, and the colors, man, it was awesome
Fractal, unfolding, crystalline lotus blossoms
Like the pixels that make images on TV
These mandalas constitute all that we dream
At their center is light the color of good
No one can describe them, I wish that I could
And I woke on that couch and I took a deep breath
And said, "Man, I sure feel better about death…"

I. CHEPREN

November 30, 1997, London Heathrow

Nothing has the air of finality like the retraction of a 747's landing gear. As the empty plane banks out of London toward Cairo, I pick up the *International Herald Tribune* and sober myself with the front page headlines. I'm nervous and still a bit ragged from Amsterdam where I stayed up all night in a Dutch karaoke bar failing to seduce a beautiful blonde baker, though she did hook me up with some excellent strudel.

I landed in London this morning at nine, hoping to take in the city during my eight-hour layover only to find that hippies with dreadlocks and open-toed shoes aren't allowed anywhere near English crowds when they're flying *from* Amsterdam *to* Egypt during an international travel advisory. This condemned me to spending the day in an airport bar sharing confidences with a group of Irish nationals on their way to sell psychedelic mushrooms in Tokyo because, apparently, the Japanese can't get enough of the stuff and none of the security dogs know the scent.

"Oh hell no," I told them. "I'm not afraid. I mean, no one's going to bother killing just *me*. I figure as long as I stay away from big groups of white people, ha-ha — yeah, I think I *will* have another Guinness, thank you very much — anyway, like I was saying, when the State

Department says it's not safe to go somewhere 'cause of terrorism, you know you won't have a problem with crowds or finding a decent hotel."

The *Herald* does little to boost my confidence. To review, two weeks ago in Luxor, six gunmen dressed like police herded two bus-loads of foreign tourists into the Temple of Hatshepsut's main courtyard, emptied automatic weapons into their legs, reloaded, fired into the writhing pile, finished off the survivors with knives, took a few noses and ears as mementos and, allegedly, touchdown-danced on the dead. The terrorists were killed in the ensuing gun battle. According to the *Herald*, followers of blind, batty Sheik Omar Abdel-Rahman — currently banged-up in a US prison for masterminding the '93 bombing of the World Trade Center in New York — claimed responsibility for the massacre, demanded the immediate release of the sheik and ended with the troubling remark they were sorry not to have killed any Americans or Jews.

I, of course, happen to be both, as does my friend Moorlock who's joining me in Cairo — and he'd better have shaved off his pink sideways mohawk 'cause that shit was cute in the coffee shops of Amsterdam but in Egypt it's a dare to kill tourist fifty-nine... So yes please, Arabian stewardess woman I'd *love* another beer, don't wake me for the meal, I'm just going to stretch out on these four seats here, and I'll say one thing for terrorist massacres, they sure make it easy to sleep on the plane.

Moorlock. The wild card. The tech-manual writer for embedded-systems programmers — something to do with the interface on microwaves. I met him buck naked in a hot tub at Esalen while attending Terrence

McKenna's "Primer for a Descent into Novelty" conference. To be there, I'd thrown down a week's teaching wages — as opposed to Moorlock's two hours writing code, something we both thought was pretty ridiculous — and still had to chop vegetables and sleep on the floor of the conference room to make the nut. Our first conversation concerned McKenna's time-wave theory, a shamanic, fractalized version of the King Wen sequence of the I Ching which supposedly charts a river of novelty that ends, along with the Mayan Calendar, on December 21st, 2012 precisely. While Moorlock and I both admired McKenna for his near-scientific approach to psychedelia, not to mention his legendary tolerance of psilocybin, we weren't all that keen on this whole time wave nonsense.

"Seems more like an elegant card trick than anything," Moorlock had said.

Right away I'd known we were meant to be friends.

He arrives without luggage on a direct flight from Amsterdam and my first thought is *Jesus H. Christ, he looks Jewish*. Six-foot-two, hooked schnoz, hard blue eyes, walking proud like he just made it back from extinction. His head has been shaved to the quick like I'd asked, only now there's an ear-to-ear stripe across his scalp from where the mohawk dye has discolored his skin. I'm trying my best not to act paranoid but we're like the only white people in the terminal and his head looks like a scimitar target.

I introduce Moorlock to a guy named Mohammed — the first tout who'd taken my hand off the plane — and inform him that Mohammed smokes between five and seven packs of Marlboros a day and that anyone with those kind of death-wish credentials lives life to the fullest and therefore can be trusted.

"Sounds reasonable," says Moorlock.

Next thing we're speeding north into Cairo, following the chain of events like a rosary and it suddenly flashes my mind like sheet lightning: *Holy Mother of God, I'm doing this*.

We arrive at the base of the Akbar Hotel, a fifteen-story, soot-covered high-rise. When the cab door opens, three uniformed Arab porters leap to our service, nodding in welcome and smiling insanely.

I've never met strangers so happy to see me which only increases my cultural whiplash. Yesterday I spent sixty guilders — which is thirty American dollars which is eighteen English pounds which is ninety-odd Egyptian pounds — for a squalid little room I shared with four pasty computer geeks in a city where you can legally purchase pure, powdered nicotine, snort the shit in a public toilet, roll a store-bought doobie the size of a Magic Marker then stumble into the Van Gogh museum with a freshly-pierced nipple and two Swiss sister whores on your arms, stare at the *Sunflowers* and go, "Dude, that guy could paint." Today I'm throwing down seven bucks a night, which is fourteen guilders which is twenty —oh fuck it, it's peanuts —to have freakin' *porters* carry my backpack to a marble-floored room overlooking the crown jewel of the African continent — and all the chickens, filth, camels and honking taxis *that* entails — where the women are hiding in headscarves and veils instead of strutting behind one-way glass in spandex fuck-suits and Moorlock and I aren't immune to the fact that we ate fresh strudel in Amsterdam this morning and now we're possibly the only tourists in a 5-star hotel that isn't even *in* my

Stupid Tourist Handbook and all of it makes me so manic and excited I can't even punctuate sentences

The porters set our packs at the foot of our beds then whisk us up the elevator to the rooftop restaurant. There we meet Mahmoud, who prefers to be called George, the hotel manager.

George is a robust, mustached man in his early forties with tightly-coiled red hair and light-brown, freckled skin — an odd complexion for an Arab. He seems more concerned for our peace of mind than he does about getting our deposit and passport numbers. We sit like kings at gilt-glass tables and when George claps his hands above his shoulder, a waiter in a tuxedo rushes over with a silver tray bearing three glasses of steaming, bright-red liquid.

"*Karkadeh*, Egypt's nationality beverage," says George.

He verifies my suspicion that Moorlock and I are the only tourists in the hundred and fifty room hotel.

"These people who kill the tourists in Luxor," George says. "Stupid people! Egypt is not like that. Egyptian people not tell them to kill tourists, Allah not tell them to kill tourists, Muslims not tell them. Small, small, small group of these stupid people tell them and now the governments of Swiss, America, English tell people not safe to travel to Egypt. You will look and see with your own eyes this week. You will know. You will see."

The waiter reappears with two, three-foot-tall hookahs called *sheesha* pipes which he proceeds to load with apple-flavored tobacco. I pucker my lips over the mouthpiece and take a beautiful, bubbling draw. Moorlock and I are soon toking away, drinking our hot hibiscus juice and starting to relax. The *sheesha* hits our heads like fishing weights — the kind you use to fish for giant flounder — and, what the hell? We reserve our room for all five nights. After that, Moorlock will head home to find another job and repair his reputation — he got busted and jailed for passing out pamphlets detailing the proper way for kids to burn down schools — while I take a train to the Valley of the Kings to tourist-trip sail up the Nile by fellucca. That, and to pay my respects to the slain at Hatshepsut's Splendor of Splendors.

George is so happy to have paying guests — "Americans also, and Jewish!" — he's beaming. After the paperwork is taken care of, he sits down next to us and says:

"You will die on the streets of Cairo. You will die on the streets of New York. You will die of old age, of a bullet, of sickness. You will get hit by car. Allah knows your fate. When it's your time to die, he will take you. So tomorrow? You will go into Cairo and you will not worry. You will be here and see Egypt."

December 1, Cairo

The cacophony awakens us just after nine. Our room overlooks the main Cairo train station, a magnet for car horns, street vendors and schoolchildren. We now understand why our room is on what George calls "the noisy side of the building." We dress then head upstairs for *karkadeh*, fresh falafel and another one of those wonderful *sheesha* pipes where the waiter tongs hot coals onto the bowl and it feels like the first time you buzzed off a cigarette. I warn Moorlock, who doesn't smoke, to be careful otherwise he'll puke. He flips me the bird, takes an extra-long draw, gets to his feet and turns green. It passes.

We head downstairs to meet our driver, Mohammed — different one — hop in his battered '61 Peugeot and hit the left side of the road toward the pyramids. Moorlock sits in the seat-of-death up front while I'm in the back without a proper seat belt. No one signals, the biggest vehicle gets right-of-way, dead pedestrians don't sue and whereas in Amsterdam you can get a ticket for honking unnecessarily, here the horn is applied with greater force and frequency than the brakes. I learn from my latest-edition *Stupid Tourist Handbook* that breathing Cairo air for one day is the equivalent to smoking thirty cigarettes. This is excellent news. Four roll-ups plus *sheesha* won't make a lick of difference.

Our first stop is to obtain student ID cards which will entitle us to untold benefits and discounts. Sadly, the veiled receptionist at the Egyptian Scientific Center is not impressed with my six-years-expired student ID or, for that matter, Moorlock's ministerial badge from the Cult of the Subgenius — even thought it's laminated. I do, however, manage to wangle a more status-filled Teacher ID card by showing the woman my Scuba license.

Back in the Peugeot, Moorlock bemoans the loss of his job — he couldn't claim county jail as vacation, apparently — and how two weeks before he'd left on this trip he'd hooked up with a nineteen-year-old AWOL-Navy nymphomaniac. On purpose, to his mind, she'd *slightly* overdosed him on morphine, lifted his wallet and stolen his Jeep which is why he'd gone straight to our mobbed-up friend Stanos whose pit-bull, Clockwork, uses a bowling ball as a chew toy. They'd tracked her down to a local Denny's and slapped her around until she'd brought them to the car.

"It was the first time I'd had an excuse," Moorlock says. He stares out the window, working his jaw. "She couldn't have weighed more than a hundred pounds, her arm in a cast from an unrelated beating... I dunno, man, I'd been kind of looking forward to it — the first act of justifiable violence in my life? But after it happened and she was just lying there? There's no satisfaction in beating a crack ho."

We enter a papyrus shop and drop five hundred Egyptian pounds on hieroglyphic wall hangings just because we can.

Trip-wise my finances are looking pretty good. I've got five grand to last six months, an outdoor ed contract lined up for the summer and an around-the-world ticket that lets me fly east. The world, as they say, is my octopus. After Egypt, I'll follow the crazy-trail to India where I've promised to write captions for a friend's coffee table book, but mostly I want to know why I keep dreaming of pyramids, crystals, Hindu Gods and cobras.

The pyramids rise into view on the horizon and the day takes on a dreamlike quality. It's like my subconscious is thrusting them forward and forcing my eyes to admit they exist — outside documentaries, dreams and DMT which, until now, is the only place I've seen them. The empty desert is actually full of sand. The world's greatest tourist attraction doesn't have tourists. Suddenly Moorlock's right in my face going, "Horse or camel? Horse or camel?" It seems we've arrived at the stables.

I grab Moorlock's collar. "I want a horse. A really fuckin' fast one."

We haggle the price down a hundred pounds and afterward giggle to ourselves about it being a buyer's market. Neither of us have ever ridden a serious horse before — let alone an Arabian stallion who's been cooped-up in a corral for two weeks because there aren't any people around to exercise him — but as soon as we see the sleek, chomping beasts, ready to sprint like the wind across the flood plain, I realize we've made a massive mistake and should have just gone with the camels.

The stableman, a short, leering Arab with a five-o'clock shadow and the squat, brutal thumbs of a dictator tells us to tip our guide if we like him and kill him if we don't. This causes the man who'd been saddling the horses — earlier introduced to us as Challied — to whip out a wicked-looking dagger from his saddle and taunt us to, "Go ahead and try it, fucking Yankees."

Moorlock crosses his arms and laughs. I reach to my belt, whip out a butterfly knife and deftly open the blade with one hand. Challied winks at me and puts his knife away. The stableman snorts, says, "Crazy Americans."

Impressed with myself for this act of bravado, I flip the knife around in an impressive display of manual dexterity then clip it back onto my belt like I've been practicing. I soon realize, however, that somewhere along the way I'd managed to lop off the tip of my middle finger. Like, there it is, lying in the dirt. Like, oh my god, I'm bleeding. Badly.

Moorlock takes off his sunglasses and says simply, "You are an idiot."

It takes three attempts at bandaging to staunch the flow of blood. The pain of humiliation is worse than the rubbing alcohol, especially when the stableman tells me, "Little boys shouldn't play with knives." When we finally mount up and trot toward the desert and the pyramids thrust themselves into the sky, I'm struck by the thought that it's somehow important for me to drop blood on Egyptian soil. In the streets, on my horse, in the sand. I won't be the first Jew to do so. Or the last.

We ride through a cemetery at the base of sandstone cliffs while desperate-looking vendors push sodas in our laps. One of them even goes so far as to open one. Annoyed, I give the cola back. Challied begins to lecture me in halting English that Egypt's economy is based eighty-percent on tourism, right now they're running at five percent of normal and people can't feed their families — or livestock — all because some fundamentalist...

"Alright, alright," I say, grabbing back the bottle. "Here, what the hell, I'm thirsty."

We loosen the reins and emerge from the cemetery, the pyramids loom and the sky is *so* blue. Challied cries, "Yallup!" and the horses take off. Mine is named Zabul which, in Arabic, means Really Fuckin' Fast but you can't complain when you get what you ask for. Today I'm yalluping a horse through Egypt on nothing more than a dream-whim from childhood. I take my switch to the horse's flank, he bucks a little like a car peeling out and races away from the echoes of a massacre that had him corralled for thirteen days.

There's sand in my eyes or maybe I'm crying. My hat

flies off but Challied will get it. Moorlock's not even trying to keep up and the desert ahead goes on for eternity. This horse, Za-*bul*, he wants to run so we charge to the top of the highest dune. I pull on the reins like I know what I'm doing. The stallion prances and comes to a halt. I pat his frothy hide, pull out my tobacco and roll up a cigarette. The blood has soaked through the bandages again and I get a spot of the stuff on the rolling paper. Adventure is sitting on an Arabian stallion, smoking your own blood on top of a sand dune, watching your friend and an Arab approach, the pyramids, mirage-like, shimmering behind them like something wet and newborn from a dream.

The day passes quickly. Photos, dismounts, blue-robed Bedouins begging us to ride camels. Entrance fees, smiles, and unanswered questions. The Sphinx: what's it mean? The Pyramids: why? The million-odd blocks each weighing three tons, ferried up the Nile during floods by slaves. The Jews, the pharaohs, the storied life of Moses... so easy to get lost amid all the speculation. What were the pyramids built for anyway? Were they tombs, temples, beacons to space aliens? Or were they initiation chambers designed to take young sorcerers into the fifth dimension where anything is possible, where an adept can manifest objects just by thinking them — where if you have a pang of fear then *whammo*, you die! Is that why they sealed off the down-sloping tunnel to the infamous Queen's Chamber in Chepren?

Sometimes when I dream, I see the astral pyramids upon whose geometry the Egyptian ones are based and they are the eyes of the mind of the Earth — and the Earth is a living, breathing, sentient being and her mind is not an idea but a *place* and you can get there by smoking DMT. Jung calls this place the "collective unconscious", the Hindus call it *brahma,* Rod Serling called it "The Twilight Zone" and my dad, the professor, just calls it "That Nonsense." All of them are right and all of them are wrong but there's something magical about the pyramids — they're not just a pile of rocks outside Giza — so it's *reverently* that Moorlock and I approach Chepren, the biggest one, while Challied hangs back and minds the horses.

The only other Western tourists in sight are two German couples on the backs of one-humped camels. The women wear *ankh* hats and Cleopatra t-shirts while the men, with sunburned necks and video cameras, shout at their Arab attendants in German while making quite possibly the world's worst home movies.

Let's assume that I *am* the Messiah and not just developing a Messiah complex.

Let's assume that some higher power has chosen me through the unfortunate device of a Messiah competition at the Burning Man Festival in Nevada. If that's the case, and I'm meant to learn my next lesson in Egypt — it's definitely the place for a Messiah-in-training — then I can't help but feel, and I know this sounds horrible, that the massacre somehow relates to my visit.

It doesn't make sense for six hired guns, four of whom weren't even Egyptian, to mow down fifty-eight tourists — including four honeymooning Japanese couples for crying out loud — all in the name of releasing a sheik who's been in a federal prison for *years*. Why not take hostages and make demands? Why just slaughter them all in an instant then claim responsibility a few days later by means of an anonymous letter? Yeah, people are assholes and kill the Yankees and all that but *none* of the dead were Americans.

The senselessness of it all reminds me of a story I heard about Adolph Hitler and how he was visited by an "angel" in his youth who told him that the Jews would be the ones to bring about Armageddon. Thus began an extermination campaign which wiped out most of the Jews in Europe but eventually led to the establishment of Israel as a Jewish nuclear power. Here at the pyramids, I can't help but wonder if the Forces of Evil know the Messiah is destined to come to Egypt in 1997 according to as-yet-unpublished Nostradamus. Unsure of his identity they set about trying to scare the guy off and while they succeed in ripping the heart out of the Egyptian economy and shooing the rich to Niagara Falls, they also make Egypt a lot more Messiah-friendly. Now he would have the whole place to himself without thousands upon thousands of loud-shirted honkeys filming stationary objects with video cameras.

I relate all this to Moorlock who rolls his eyes appropriately, his mohawk stripe blending into his sunburn. Suddenly, swarms of children are upon us and one boy shakes my hand so hard that blood from my wound drips onto the sandstone. That's the Egyptians — they love you 'til you bleed. A picnicking family offers us lunch. Soon we're eating *dolmas* and a bean paste called *fuul;* and even though it's North-Africa hot, the women are wearing so many clothes that undressing them with your eyes takes half an hour. Everyone wants Moorlock's picture cause he's a freakin' weirdo with his raspberry-swirl scalp, rhinestone granny sunglasses and holographic Norplant t-shirt. I let him have his moment. This is the most popular he's been since his *Arm the Homeless* campaign in Ventura.

That was the prank of the century, that one, performed in a country where gun control legislation as benign as "One gun, per month, per person" is handily defeated by right wing politicos under the argument, "What about Christmas?" Bang, here comes Moorlock on the eleven o'clock news in a white, collared shirt and black rayon tie. The worst of it is, he actually sounds reasonable when he leans his face into the microphone:

"You see, Tom, homeless people are disenfranchised citizens who are often the victims of assault and petty crime. Because of their lack of a permanent address, they cannot legally obtain a firearm permit. That's why my group here —" he points to the gaggle of respectably-dressed *other freaks* behind him shuffling papers — "have been soliciting applications from the local homeless community to ascertain which are deserving of firearms."

The camera cuts to the street where Stanos — attached by a chain to Clockwork the dog — is dressed like a troll in tattered Army surplus gear, wheeling a laundry-cart full of old guns.

"Keep that ****ing camera off my face," he snarls. "I don't do Ventura, dig?"

I'm secretly glad my finger's still bleeding. It keeps me grounded on the physical plane; keeps me from getting too out-there, too fearless. We buy passes to enter the Great Pyramid of Chepren — my teacher card scores zero by way of a discount — and enter the monument's singular opening, a rectangular hole in the sandstone. Three fawning, Egyptian high school boys, all wearing the same knock-off Reeboks and jeans, whisk Moorlock away in a whirlwind of camera fire but I am consumed by wonder. I saw *Raiders of the Lost Ark* seven times and I'm pushing on walls, looking for secret passages and widening cracks in the sandstone with my fingernails.

The others are waiting for me in the vault room, a wholly unspectacular arrangement. Square room, high ceiling, no hieroglyphics, some antique graffiti, a few slits for light and a granite sarcophagus lying open at one end that's way too big to fit through the door. As far as I know the Egyptians never built their tombs *around* their coffins so obviously it's some kind of teleportation or communication device. I lay down in the thing and concentrate on Sirius, the Dog Star, upon whose axis the pyramids are aligned. According to many occult books and stoners, aliens from Sirius report to our planet and sometimes incarnate the bodies of frogs. Only thing is, they can sense End Time coming so are purposely dying off — thus explaining our planet's catastrophic and mysterious loss of amphibians.

I go nowhere, hearing nothing.

The infamous fifth-dimensional passageway is boarded-up so I extend the pliers from my Leatherman. Just as I start on the lock, however, a guard with a machine gun doesn't have to say anything. Back on the outside we're handed more Cokes which we drink while circumambulating Chepren.

"So, what are you looking for exactly?" says Moorlock.

"Something magic."

"Could you be a little more vague?"

I tell him when I was twelve I used to play *Dungeons and Dragons,* like all nerds, until one day my Dad took me aside and said, "When are you going to stop with these role-playing fantasies? There's no such thing as magic."

"I cried myself to sleep that night but also had this crazy dream — the one the DMT reawakened. It was set —" I halt in my tracks and look around — "holy shit. The Yul Brynner robot from Westworld was *right there* and the only way to kill it — to stop the Machine — was to sell the family car, pawn my clothes, my toys, everything I had for this purple-black, opalescent crystal that was decidedly magic.

"Anyway, the next day I woke up and told my parents I wasn't having a Bar Mitzvah."

"So you never —"

"What? Became a man at thirteen? No, I did not — and neither did you. But I *did* have dream a few weeks ago where Irasha and I were climbing this very pyramid and found an amethyst crystal the size of an egg."

Moorlock furrows his brow. "Irasha. This is the chick with the dreads and the teepee?"

"Yes? And?"

"The same Irasha who claims she hatched a dragon under her kitchen table?"

"Yes, Moorlock, the one whose family was abducted by aliens, the one who watches Star Trek like it's the news, but may I remind you that *you're* the one who likes to steal boxes of rat poison and sneak them back into the store filled with candy, just for the thrill of wondering — never knowing — if some gray-haired cat-lady is leaving caramels around for the rats. So how 'bout we can the judgmental attitude?"

He blushes and scuffs his heel in the sand.

We decide not to enter the other main pyramids and instead bribe some guards to let us climb smaller ones. It's pretty much anything goes with the tourist cops because there aren't any crowds around to control. Nearby is a parking lot to the Wonders of the World with, like, three cars and a bus in it. Back at the stables, no treasures to speak of, we decide to tip Challied rather then kill him, seeing as I'm already missing some finger. After Moorlock changes my bandages, Mohammed leads us to a back-alley perfume shop to purchase essential oils.

A few months back I threw a rock at an attacking dog and cracked it on the rib. One week later, I had the exact same rib broken during a pick-up basketball game, call it karma. Irasha had applied the extract of cinnamon bark and, miraculously, the pain had dissipated — at least enough for me to teach kayaking. And maybe, okay, the placebo effect — ten days of echinacea and wow, no more cold — but I had experienced medicine working, tried some more oils, liked the results, so now I'm well and truly curious.

Moorlock's not so sure.

"Why not?" I demand. "We're already typhoid-vaccined up the yin yang, taking dreadful, dream-altering shit for malaria. Why not round out our immunological arsenal with something homeopathic?"

"I don't know, science?"

"Oh come on, man! You're telling me your sense of smell has *zero* effect on your state of mind, therefore *zero* effect on your state of health? I'm trying to locate a physical object with dream-travelling properties —

something transcendental. I don't want to be told, I want to find out. Forget about physics and genetics — this is *consciousness*."

Moolocks tilts his head to the side. "Good lord, are you saying you're not acting rational?"

Mohammed ushers us into a red velvet tent ringed with shelves full of glass-stoppered bottles. The shop belongs to a withered, old Arab. His eyes are dark, bewildered and sad, like the eyes of a man whose child died in front of him. He introduces himself as Mohammed — Moorlock and I exchange sidelong glances — then breaks out a finger-sized packet of weed, called *bhango,* and rolls our first Egyptian spliff. Meanwhile his wife, a black-robed mountain with eyes, slips wordlessly out to get us some dinner.

"These people who killed were not Egyptians," says Mohammed, his voice low and gravely from smog, sand and *sheesha*. "They were hired to cause trouble for all Muslims. I say, if they not like Egypt then come and kill us." He slaps his chest. "War is fine, but don't kill the tourists. Come and kill Egyptians. We are ready."

I'm never comfortable smoking weed in foreign countries, especially when I'm unclear on the penalties, but when the old man passes the spliff and says, "Get high before you die," I don't want to seem impolite.

Turns out the Egyptians pioneered oil extraction, teasing the essences out of the plants using heat and low pressure under the dunes. All the pharaohs were buried with alabaster casks filled with lotus, Melissa, helichrysum and others. Being the Messiah and all, I'm eager to pick up frankincense, sandalwood and myrrh — the oils brought by the three wise men to the baby Jesus — as well as pure Egyptian rose, rumored to be the best on earth, requiring some ten thousand petals to the ounce. Moorlock and I recline on plush couches while Mohammed and Mohammed clink out stoppers and daub our wrists. They assure us the essences are pure as righteous Muslims would never adulterate with alcohol. Every inch of our forearms is soon dotted with taster-whiffs of lotus, frankincense, neroli, geranium, myrrh, jasmine — until the smells become impossible to distinguish. By the time the submissive, black tent of a woman has brought our exotically-spiced macaroni, Moorlock is begging for me to finish my business so he can wash up and stop sneezing.

I blow the rest of my cash on oils. We exit the shop into Egyptian late dusk and, despite the fact we've been circling them all day, Moorlock and I, as if slapped by a doctor, stand and gape at the pyramids. I'm sad because our allotted day is up and we haven't had near enough time to explore. I'm also higher than I've ever felt off one joint as we head to the stables, climb a ladder to the roof and take in the Sound and Lights Spectacular.

Lasers, colored floodlights, canned orchestra, pure Disney — a voiced-over tour through Egyptian ancient history; Chepren lit up with flashing pink strobes. It's all so hokey, stupid and unnecessary but we lap it up anyway because it's spectacular. Plus the show is free from the roof of the stables. I learn the pyramids used to be encased in alabaster; smooth and not stair-stepped as they are today. Aside from the alabaster cap on Chepren the rest was hauled off for temples, tombs, mosques and other building projects over the millennia.

Then I notice something twinkling. Something in the middle of Chepren's northern flank where, by optical illusion, the illuminated rocks appear to bulge outward.

I ask Moorlock if he sees what I'm talking about.

"Yeah, it's probably a light fixture or something."

But while Moorlock is here for a week's vacation, blowing the bulk of his severance package, I saved for two years to make this trip possible. During that vagabond time I worked everything from teaching marine science to weaving dreamcatchers to walking an agoraphobic spinster's hybrid wolf to making waterproof fish ID cards for an LA scuba shop:

Widow rockfish have black intestinal linings to prevent their stomachs from glowing in the dark after a meal of bioluminescent plankton, thus avoiding predators.

The latter meant having to do desktop publishing — three solid weeks on a couch at the Moon, Moorlock's communal apartment — bartering weed and burritos for tech support while picking black ants off the back of my neck which had strayed from the condom that missed the trashcan. Two years of my life where I *didn't* have a car and I *didn't* have a phone and I *didn't* have an address — so this trip to Egypt, India and beyond? This *is* my life, not a break from it.

I light up a smoke, turn to Moorlock and tell him after we check out the bazaars and museums I'm coming back to the motherfucking pyramids and I'm going to find my crystal.

He nods blankly. "Yeah, it's good *bhango*."

The music reaches its epic crescendo, a megaton of electricity ignites the monuments — there can't be more than fifty people watching — the Sphinx yowls, the fireworks blast then suddenly, mercifully, the spectacular is over. The stars return to the sky in full force. Exhilarated, we gaze across the desert to the constellation of Perseus, low on the western horizon. He holds the head of the Gorgon Medusa who, according to Nubian legend, was not a snake-haired woman so ugly she turned those who gazed on her face to stone but a dreadlocked princess so beautiful that people who saw her fell instantly in love and died of unrequited passion.

December 2, Cairo

"Osteryonder hippie wakem?"

I groan and roll away from the voice. It's Moorlock speaking pig-Dutch again, a nasty habit we picked up in Amsterdam.

"Latem mornin, risenshinem. Nother day to seizenstein."

"Stupin' grotten!" I burrow back under the silky-soft cotton.

"Sleepem Egypt? Glockensploodle! Wander yonder guilders squander!"

There's no point trying to fall back asleep. The noise from the streets could be measured on a seismograph. Last night we stayed up late sipping *karkadeh*, smoking *sheesha* and listening to George rail on about the massacre.

"U.S. exports all the Arab oil then turns around and gives the profits to Netanyahu and Israel, Egypt's sworn enemies!"

As Jewish Americans, Moorlock and I can either go, "Ha-ha, motherfucker, we win!" which was his strategy or act sheepish and apologetic which was mine.

After breakfast we take to the streets on foot toward the Egyptian Antiquities Museum. Along the way we take off our shoes and enter an ancient, mosaic-floored mosque. Neither of us feel all that comfortable. On the way out, Moorlock buys a pack of *Man Woman Creme* from an old man on the pavement making willie-rubbing motions.

"Two hours," he says with a knowing smile.

We play Frogger with our lives every time we cross the street. The smog is so bad I can hardly keep smoking. At one point, a bus zips by me so damn close the driver reaches out and tousles my hair. Eventually, we enter the museum through a wireless, wooden doorframe built to look like a metal detector. Other than that, the security's pretty good — though dozens of Arabs with automatic weapons don't make me feel that secure. For the most part, Moorlock and I have the museum to ourselves. We spend the day staring at pyramidions, funerary barges and enormous stone statues of falcon-headed Osiris who flew the sun through the sky in his chariot ages before the Greeks had Apollo.

My head swims with mystery. In front of the golden headpiece of Tutankhamun I imagine spending the entirety of my life planning the minutiae of my funeral. A case of boomerangs hangs on one wall, purporting to be three thousand years old. When Australians and Egyptians invent boomerangs simultaneously, coincidence crumbles in the wake of shamanism.

As a writer, I decide that Thoth, ibis-headed God of Scriptures, is to be my patron Egyptian deity. For lack of better word I *pray* to him, to the idea of him, to what he represents. I imagine him floating over the astral pyramids inside a ring-shaped air bubble, like the one I'd seen on DMT. A host of unknown gods had been there, some had even answered questions — so why not ask them now? Why not ask them always? I pray to Thoth for help in loosening the precious ink, and also pray to Nephtys, winged Goddess of Magic, to help me find my dreamed-of crystal. When I open my eyes to imprint upon Isis — the ankh-wielding, snake-entwined Goddess of Beauty — I notice a stunning, young Egyptian woman sketching a statue of Anubis, the jackal-headed God of Embalming, in her notebook. She's slender, smiling, wearing trousers, naked from the collar up. I guess that she's a student.

While Moorlock gazes on bemused, I saunter up and ask about the long-lost eye of Horus, father of Osiris, and how it ended up on the US dollar bill. Her only Western tongue is French. I downshift into *français* like a Renault into third and tell her I'm happy to see such a beautiful Egyptian woman not behind a veil. She blushes and tells me I must be very brave to come to Egypt against the wishes of my government. While I don't succeed in getting her number she does accept a card from the Akbar. Heart in throat, I bid the girl *bientôt*, adding I will wait by the phone until she calls, thereby employing the dreaded subjunctive.

Crazy, jam-packed bus of Muslims doesn't stop but merely slows. Random helping hands of strangers pull us aboard: "*Salaam!* Hello!" The streets are full of people sweating, businessmen in polyester suits, beggars sleeping on the pavement, their scarred and broken hands outstretched. Muslim women hustle by all covered-up like private saunas, some with baskets full of laundry; the smell of diesel greets our noses, also garbage, heat and saffron, racks of fresh-baked puffy pitas breathing in the evening sun. Stepping off the moving bus into a crowd and falling down, Moorlock knocks a woman flat, hops up, extends his hand, his bald-faced smile, helps her to her feet then turns to me, explains that he was bowling.

Back at the hotel, George is determined to return us to America as ambassadors of Egyptian goodwill. When we tell him we need stylin', pimpin' Arab garb to wear, he snaps his fingers, gets a car and whisks us off to the bazaar. He leads us down a fetid alley to a shop where giggling crones in gold-embroidered veils pull robes called *galabeyas* off the shelves and shake them out for our inspection. At home I choose my clothes for versatility, sturdy things to wear outdoors in any type of weather but here with my Egyptian pounds I shop for style, *panache*, for things to wear on stage like I'm a rock star.

Moorlock nods approvingly at my gold-and-purple, maybe-woman's *galabeya*. "You look like King Mack Daddy Farouque," he says.

The pyramids have been around for four thousand years but when else in their history has such a lowly economic speck been able to chase a dream across oceans and continents and dress like he was king?

I select three *galabeyas* to send Irasha, two for my mother, one for myself and a neon-pink, wool robe for Mona, a red-headed, minxy philosophy grad student, bisexual stripper and one of my favorite people, bar none. When I wonder aloud if the robe will fit her, our happy-go-lucky glutton-shopping goes abruptly tense.

"Why are *you* buying something for Mona?"

"Come on, you and Greg brought her to the conference, she and I have always been friends and, you know... oh shit."

It's been over a year since Mona left Moorlock for another haircut-casualty computer programmer in his same apartment building — which, come to think of it, made him go postal, got him arrested, sent him to the clink and finally landed him in a psychiatric ward where he sat in a straight-jacket for three days spitting at nurses until the antidepressants he's still taking kicked in. However, because it's Egypt, because I'm feeling free and spendy, I lay my hand on Moorlock's shoulder and look deep into his baby-blues as they begin to twitch. I inform him that this past October, Mona had taken me out to lunch — to a deli inside a health-food store. There, while eating brown-rice noodles out of Styrofoam boxes with plastic forks and thirty napkins she'd told me I had always inspired her environmentally...

"...and, well, we spent the afternoon together, Moorlock. Karmically, sure, I know it was wrong because it turned out to be Yom Kippur and instead of fasting all day, repenting my sins, I boned and ate and drove and shopped — hell, maybe I'm not the Messiah, maybe I'm the Antichrist — but I haven't slept with Mona since because the *next* time I passed through town she had a boyfriend *and* a girlfriend and anyway, about this robe, I think she'd rather like it."

Ominous silence fills the cab. We pass a movie theater hosting an international film festival where the sex scenes haven't been edited out. Noting the queue is solely of men, I say, "Hey, George — do Muslim chicks not dig the movies?"

Freckled, orange Arab George turns around and tells

me — without the slightest hint of irony — that women who attend such films are regarded as no better than prostitutes.

"That's quite a double standard, isn't it?"

"Yes," says George. "It is."

I turn to Moorlock for his take. He clutches his bag of robes to his chest and mumbles how he needs to take his pills. Back at the room, he heads directly to the bathroom and locks the door. I sigh and slink upstairs to write — about my own heart being broken, though for a week there, I'd forgotten...

Jaime. Up 'til now my greatest love and, I'd thought, my soulmate. Six years we'd spent together, two weeks of which were in a tent we spread upon a field of yellow flowers while the greatest comet of our lives streaked through the skies each night. Huddled in that tent with maps and books we planned this trip together only I was like a tree and she was like a sapling in my shadow which is wrong, but hard to change. So I became a bird, a hawk, and perched among her sagging branches; begged for her to do the same — come fly away with me, my love — but when I flexed my wings and screeched, she became a dove, afraid of hawks and flew somewhere beyond my sight, a place where she felt safe. One day I'll cry because she left but not today because Osiris, hawk head, is the Sun God here in Egypt and I am following my dreams.

At three a.m. I eat the mint upon my pillow. Moorlock twitches underneath his single sheet. I know he's hurt because of me and even though he breaks down doors and beats up girls who steal his car, takes pills to make him less psychotic (and some to make him more), he's my friend — my friend for life — and wouldn't kill me while I sleep. Or, at least, I hope.

I hear voices as I'm fading out and realize that Moorlock is talking out loud. I turn to hear what he's saying — and tell him to fucking zip it already, neither of us have had enough sleep — but realize he isn't talking to me. He's talking to Mona.

She is kneeling on the carpet at his pad, the Moon.

"It's all very fascinating because a *meme*," says Moorlock, "is a tune, a story, a concept, a joke — any piece of information that can be replicated. In fact, *Mona*, most information is made up of *several* memes which spread on the level of the mind the way genes spread on the level of the flesh, mutating slightly with each transmission." His intensity escalates troublingly. "So you see, *Mona*, we're not all walking around collecting the information we find most useful. Instead, our minds are fertile agar plates for memes to grow and spread like *viruses*."

Mona looks terrified. Moorlock goes on to explain how in order to lend credence to his conviction that life isn't merely genetics alone, it's also about the creation of memes, he'd recently had a vasectomy.

It dawns on me: *What are we doing at the Moon when we went to bed in Egypt?* With this thought comes a tremendous wave of vulnerability, like finding oneself naked in the middle of Antarctica.

It appears I have entered Moorlock's mind.

Glancing behind me, I see my body asleep on the bed and — though I have a pang of fear — the part of me that plays with fire decides to press my luck. I stick my head back inside the Moon. It's amazing how well Moorlock's dream-mind has replicated the bongs, furniture, filthy carpet, sculptures made of empty nitrous oxide canisters, books of psychedelia and softcore Spanish porn. I've had out-of-body experiences before where my spirit gets up and flies around the room but this is something different, something I never even knew was possible.

I disregard the image and concentrate instead on the projector. Immediately, I feel Moorlock's ragged lungs exhale and that his throat is very dry; how the Effexor he's just taken creates a feedback loop which stops the hind-brain rage from boiling over to where he'd have to bunch his fists at lithe, unfaithful Mona and scream at her until she understands his pain. It's too much for him — or me — to bear alone. He should know that someone sees and cares and also that I've found this awesome power. I reach back to my body with an astral "toe" and touch it to my larynx.

"Moor-lock!" I hear myself croak. "Moor-lock!" My voice is weak and ineffectual. When it fails to rouse him I jump and wave my hands in front of Mona but I am like a snorkeller gulping air while they are quite at home and fish. Suddenly, I feel invasive like, *Who the hell am I to check out other people's dreams?* I snap back quickly to my body — pulled by an elastic type of love — and right before I force my eyes to open I have the thought: *Hearing other people's dreams is easy, all you have to do is listen...*

"Moorlock! Moorlock! Wake up!"

"Hmph-mmm — whazzat?"

I throw a pillow on the floor and kneel upon it.

"Moorlock, it's me. Wake up. I need to ask you something."

He smacks his lips and comes to rest upon his back.

I shake his sweaty, mosquito-bitten shoulder.

"What time is it?" he asks.

"Nighttime. Listen, man, I need to know what you were dreaming. Don't lose it — think back."

Moorlock opens his eyes, glances at the balcony, sees that it's still dark outside.

"Why are you...."

"*What were you dreaming?!*"

"Okay, okay." He sits up, rubs his eyes and frowns. "I was at the Moon and I was talking..." He glares at me. "Talking to Mona."

"About meme theory?"

"Yeah, yeah, that was it. I was really mad but didn't — wait a second, how do you know?"

"She was kneeling on the floor and you were sitting on the couch — is it true you really got a vasectomy?"

Moorlock switches on the reading light and sees my grinning face beside the bed. He palms his striped and sunburned scalp, throws down his hands and shouts, "What the fuck is going on?"

"Hold on, I'll get you a drink," I tell him. "You're really, really thirsty."

December 3, Cairo

The phone awakens us at half-past ten. Moorlock answers, says it's for me. I sandwich my head between receiver and pillow. A woman says, "*Allo monsieur. Comment ça va?*"

Somewhere in the mess that is my mind I realize I'm talking to the girl from the museum. I may be a lot of things, including the Messiah, but I'm not a suave, bilingual swinger first thing in the morning.

In halting French, I say I'm fine, still in bed and — long and awkward pause — what is an exam and are you eating dinner? This is followed by some idle chit-chat, half of which I understand, the other half is verbs. In the end, she decides I must be drunk, hangs up on me forever.

I groan and put the phone back down. Moorlock laughs at me from the bathroom. His mood is much improved since late last night when — in retaliation for dream-stealing news of his vasectomy — he informed me he had it on good authority that Jaime was having threesomes out in Utah where she was teaching children how to ski. Though Moorlock often pulls a hoax he's never known to outright lie and, after I threw up, he shook my hand, called a truce and grumbling, went back to bed. Minutes later came the call the prayer: five muezzins chanting in competing monotones from different mosques with separate loud-speakers. Stateside, they'd be fined or even jailed for noise pollution but here it's just another test to see what you can sleep through.

After breakfast, Mohammed spirits us to the Khan el Khalili bazaar in the Islamic section of Cairo. *The Stupid Tourist Handbook* informs me that this is the home of the Al Azhar Mosque, the world's oldest university, which currently houses over forty-thousand followers of Sheik Omar Abdel-Rahman. I read this passage aloud to Moorlock who bobs excitedly next to the driver like a Hun child eager to enter his first battle.

The bazaar is festooned with hand-painted banners: *Luxor: Never Again; Egyptian People Sorry, Love Tourist;* and, my personal favorite, *Egyptians Fight Terrorism to Death!* We exit the cab and follow whim down twisting alleys full of rotting garbage, barnyard animals and urine. We buy pearl-inlaid jewelry boxes from a pearl-inlaid jewelry box maker, drink Turkish coffee in a crowded café and learn from a Canadian expat that we've wandered into the local side of the bazaar as opposed to the tourist section across the bridge. He says it's a dangerous place to be white.

A pudgy, teenage student named — what else? — Mohammed, offers to be our guide and help us hunt for bargains. This is total bullshit because our bargain is his cut but what the hell? We let him lead us through the maze and even borrow my expensive Ray Ban sunglasses. I have no fear of theft because he who jacks a tourist after Luxor will be hung and beaten by the crowd. In reality, I feel safer buying saffron, scarves and incense in Islamic Cairo then I do, say, buying electronics at the swap meet in LA.

We buy presents for our friends — goods so fine they're better than money — and every purchase is a haggle, an act, a deal, a scam. It's not a UPC code being waved over an infrared scanner by a bored, impatient checker, it's an *interaction*. For myself, I buy a vest of emerald, hand-embroidered silk woven by the half-blind man who sells it. I tell him it's the finest garment I have ever owned and when Mohammed translates this, the tailor's jaundiced eyes grow moist and he wishes me good luck for a hundred-fifty years...

Laden, sweaty, needing showers, Mohammed, Moorlock and I slip sideways through the crowd, past ice-carts drawn by donkeys and vendors who thrust their scarves so close we smell the wool. When we reach the road dividing the bazaar Mohammed hails a cab. When I ask for my sunglasses back he frowns with chubby cheeks and puppy eyes and says he'd rather hoped they were a gift. I laugh and give him fifteen pounds *baksheesh*, which the handbook says means *tipping* but better translates to *the cost of doing business*.

After loading our bags into the cab, Doughboy Mohammed makes us promise to meet him here tonight to see the whirling dervish dancers. It isn't until we're seated and belted that we notice the cab has a red, white and blue striped interior with gaudy, green prints of the Statue of Liberty on the seats. A postcard-sized Old Glory flaps from the antennae, over a screaming American Eagle air-brushed on the hood. The driver smiles a gap-toothed grin and pops a trance-techno tape into the stereo. It blares full-blast through quadraphonic speakers as we pull into the bustling Cairo traffic at a crawl.

Rising to our right in ancient, fundamental glory stand the minarets of Al Azaar, home to forty-thousand would-be terrorists — or so *The Stupid Book* implies. We're sitting ducks but fuck it, here we are. I unbuckle my seatbelt, roll down the window and start to dance. Children on the street look up and point, buses lean as people rush to check us out, hang out of windows, welcome us to Cairo. Moorlock laughs and does the robot; we're bobbing heads and waving hands and waggling our pussy-eating tongues in view Muslim women while the driver of the taxi next to us starts dancing techno-boogie too.

Horns start honking to the rhythm and soon there are a hundred people staring, some in laughter, some disgust, some in "what-the-hell-is-that?" *A-ooooooooooo!* I howl like a coyote from the hills of

Hollywood where I was born. I'm an American Jew in post-massacre Cairo, shaking it up in a Fourth-of-July taxi cab. Everyone around me is my sibling here on planet Earth and I am free and following my destiny. I have been in love and I have left my body with my spirit and I am *not* afraid, so Egypt? If you choose to kill me do it now or forever hold your peace.

"It's an excellent day to die," shouts Moorlock. "An excellent, excellent day."

Dinner atop the Akbar again. For me, the vegetarian: *falafel*, *fuul* and *baba ganouj* — fried garbanzo spice mash, Egyptian refried beans and puréed eggplant yogurt mix respectively. Moorlock gets a steak. In a sudden fit of recklessness we also gobble down an uncooked tomato-onion salad. After *karkadeh* and *sheesha*, Mohammed drives us back to the bazaar where we meet up with Mohammed who introduces us to his friend Mohammed and these two Mohammeds — who we nickname One and Two to keep things sane — lead us through the bazaar to Two's house. One, our chubby friend from earlier, is fifteen, restless and wears a dirty t-shirt with a soft drink advertisement while Two is eighteen, the eldest of nine and sports a wicked, curving scar across his forehead. He's also freshly shaved and wears a collared shirt so clean and white it couldn't have come from inside his own building.

The pad is a tiny, half-built, brick construction filled with dust, loose boards and scrawny, laughing children gnawing pitas. Eleven people live here supported by one myopic shoemaker and one teenage Mohammed hustling tourists. We scramble to the roof under the dim pinpricks of stars and look out over the City of the

Dead, Cairo's cemetery slum. Number One produces a newspaper bindle of schwaggy, Egyptian *bhango* which Two proceeds to roll with expert care.

They have us read a letter from a German travel agent informing them there will be no tours this year. Five joints are rolled and slowly smoked and soon I'm feeling Amsterdamaged, buying handmade women's shoes from Two's tobacco-chewing father. Once upon a time in ancient Egypt, an ibis stole a woman's sandal and dropped it by a pharaoh. He searched the land until he found the sandal's owner, who he made his bride. Sure, the Reeboks might be fake but Cinderella is a knock-off fairy tale in these parts and just to let my people know I'm sending these bright red shoes to the Moon with a note reading *If the shoe fits, woman, wear it*.

"We miss the whirling Dervish by an hour," says Number One while Number Two arranges bikes for us to hire. Nothing keeps you wholly present like speeding stoned through dirty streets on brakeless bikes, your balls in mortal danger. As we ride, Number One chants, "Grass! Grass! Grass!" just to prove that no one knows the meaning. We stop at a café where men in flowing robes and linen hats play *baccarat* while smoking *sheesha,* mouthpieces never dropping from their lips. The waiter brings us each a Stella beer except for Number One who gets a diet Fanta.

"So, Mohammed," says Moorlock. "How'd you get the scar across your forehead?"

Two snorts. "Egyptian mothers."

One afternoon when he was six, his mother caught him selling hash and flung a saucer at him, bam!

Number One shows-off an ugly triangular welt on his hand from when he'd been caught with a stolen five-pound note. His mother had made him sit and watch while she held the knife above the candle.

"Yeah, hurt." He shrugs. "But now I never steal."

"When I was boy," says Number Two, loosened by another beer, "I live with my family in Cairo. I go to school like good little boy but I get into trouble with teachers. They want to throw me out of the school. I was buying tobacco and mixing with henna, selling as hash to tourists. My father says to me, 'Okay, you work or you go out on the streets' and me? I don't want to make fucking shoes. I leave home at age of six, gone five years from Cairo."

Our *sheesha* pipes stop bubbling.

"Let me get this straight," says Moorlock. "You got kicked out of school for selling fake hash and left home when you were six? No fucking way."

Mohammed bugs his eyes and slams his beer down hard. "Yes fucking way! Ask Mohammed, ask my family, they tell you. I leave and travel Egypt five years. Aswan, Luxor, Sinai, Hurghada. I not go to school but I learn." He taps his temple. "I learn how to be myself, to be Egyptian. Sometimes I work in café, make two pounds. Sometimes I not eat twenty-four hours. I sleep in streets and policeman wake me, say, 'Sleep somewhere else or we take you to the jail.' In jail is safer, get bed, eat. 'Take me,' I say." He laughs.

"When I am eleven after five years travelling Egypt I come back to my father in Cairo and say, 'Here I am. Want to study, work with tourists.' I start school again and now have two more years before university."

I'm humbled by his broken words, embarrassed by

my middle class. This scar right here I got from woodshop at a Jewish summer camp when I was ten...

Moorlock pays for everything. While pedaling back we race into a dirty cloud where it becomes impossible to see. I dismount, run the bike to a halt then grope along an earthen wall. A bomb? A collapsed building? A camel's dirt bath — what? I hold my breath while inching forward, at the mercy of the bazaar, blinded by its fetid spirit. For a moment, before I stumble from the cloud to find the two Mohammeds smiling and Moorlock coughing violently, for a moment I am not invincible and feel a pang of fear. As we walk our rented bikes into the night and toward the sound of Sufi women chanting, Number Two grabs my arm, slows my gait to his and says, "Now you walk like Egyptian."

Back at the hotel, I change my bandages while Moorlock crumbles *bhango* bought from Number Two. He asks if I might roll us a joint.

"Very funny." I roll up a beaut despite my wound. We adjourn to plastic chairs on the balcony. The noise from the train station greets our ears like a symphony of faulty hydraulics.

"Do you realize that it's *never* quiet?" I ask. At that precise moment the loudest car horn I have ever heard blasts so loud and long that Moorlock has to take three breaths before replying, "No, it never is."

We spark up and discuss Mohammeds, what we bought for whom and how we haven't seen a gorgeous tourist woman yet. Moorlock lets his guard down, starts to gush about his past, his lovers men and women and how not long ago he was making fifty K a year designing software, putting mirrors on his ceiling —

"Fuck the goddamn earthquakes" — so he could better see the freckled haunches of his stripper girlfriend. Those were the glory days of the Moon — when homeless kids came off the street to surf the web and broadcast pirate radio; where bongs were bought and spilled each week, stray cats ate forty-dollar duck pate from off the low-shag carpet and every Wednesday was your birthday, just bring the mushrooms, nitrous, E, lay down on the floor and laugh while Moorlock, in his leisure suit, fixed fearless drinks with pink umbrellas and no-one ever really knew who put the headless rabbit in the freezer…

Moorlock had it made back then but never knocked on wood so when the stripper went legit, turned in her whip and beeper, left him for the guy downstairs, he'd tried to win her back by pounding, screaming at her door. For that, he'd been arrested and sedated, came out and tried to save the world by telling kids to do what's right: burn down their useless schools and educate themselves. Once again he'd been arrested only this time lost his job, perhaps his way, so when the crackhead stole his car he couldn't wait to beat her.

"It was pathetic." He lolls his head. "She was lying there whimpering with her stupid broken arm and I was just kicking her 'cause she was lower than me. That's why I had them snip me, man. I'm just not father material."

He licks his lips and takes a complicated swallow. "This is some really strong weed, huh?"

I assess the damage and find that yes, again, I am more stoned off one joint than I have ever been in my life. All my muscles are pleasantly tingling. It feels like the first time I've sat down in a week. I start to roll another *bhango*-booyah but my tongue is so dry I can't even moisten the edge of the rolling paper.

"Dude, what's your problem?" says Moorlock.

"Same as you, man. The she-left-me blues."

I take a sip of water and run my tongue across the glue. The taste transports me direct to Bang Ben, a rocky beach in southwest Thailand. Four years ago, out of cash and far from banks, I'd stumbled onto a primitive guesthouse that, incredibly, accepted credit cards. The next day the manager offered me heroin, said I could pay for the stuff on my plastic. He produced a bag of what he called "white mountain" — as opposed to the "black tar" they sell in New York. I'd licked my pinkie and tasted it like a pro. The exact same taste is on the rolling paper now.

"Uh, Moorlock, we got a problem here."

I grab the *bhango* and switch on the light. Sure enough, the crumbly, brown weed has been salted with something tan and granular. I lick my finger and taste it again.

"Guess what? This shit's laced with heroin."

Moorlock leans back and smacks his lips again. "Yeah, it's really nice, huh?"

"You mean you knew? And didn't tell me?"

"Relax, man. I was just thinking how this feels a lot like shooting morphine."

"I'm tossing it."

When he doesn't complain I fling the packet off the balcony and watch it flutter to the trash piles below.

"Bad *bhango*," says Moorlock, like he's scolding a dog. "Bad, bad *bhango*."

December 4, Cairo

Sleep comes easy. Humid winds. I dream or maybe travel on a carpet made of silk to where Ramses the Great — the Peaceful Pharaoh, whose statues guard the freeways — kicks his way through modern Cairo like Godzilla. Challied greets me at the stables, tells me that Zabul is sick but says he has a faster horse and asks me where we're going. I look up at Chepren and again see something purple glitter deep within the stones. Behind me, Ramses laughs like thunder and destroys the Hilton.

I rise and stand on shaky legs; shuffle to the toilet for a stinging, dehydrated piss. Thoughtlessly, I drink from the tap — another risk to life and limb — then apply a mix of frankincense, sandalwood and myrrh to my third eye, temples and earlobes. In the dark I put on Army shorts, butterfly knife, clean socks, leather boots, Ganesha t-shirt, canvas river hat and a belt-bag I generally wear over one shoulder — full of pens, oils, smokes, plastic octopus, Leatherman, guidebook, journal, first aid kit, water bottle, energy bar, headlamp, tampons (sometimes you gotta light a fire, sometimes put one out) and the rubber, squeak-Buddha prize from the Burning Man messiah contest.

I leave a note informing Moorlock I'm off to find a magic rock and where and when to meet at the bazaar. Then I kiss his peeling head goodbye.

Within an hour, I'm at the stables asking Challied to bring Zabul only to learn the horse is sick and would I like another? It's an easy walk to Chepren but the part of me that's not concerned with paper money — the part that dreamed Zabul was sick, the part that smoked the DMT, the part that bought the plane ticket — knows the harmonious path is aesthetic and thus to approach the pyramids on horseback. I buy an apple from a nearby stall and quarter it while the grizzled stableman looks on and urges me to cut another finger. Challied brings out Black Star, an immense Arabian mare, two hands taller than Zabul, black as night, with a striking diamond of white between her eyes. I bribe the horse with half the apple then treat a cut on her nose with a single drop of lavender.

The stableman bums a cigarette and asks where I'd like to ride today. I tell him I'm headed to the solar cross which lies at the center of a nautilus-like Fibonacci spiral upon whose third whorl the pyramids are built.

"Beneath the cross lies a spaceship," I tell him, "designed to take a forty-four chromosome human being into Christ-consciousness and stabilize him — or so I read in a New Age book somewhere."

The stableman frowns and takes a thoughtful drag.

"You take horse for four hours. You look around, find what you're looking for, great. You not find, not my fucking problem, okay?"

We haggle terms then Challied and I head off at a canter. Dawn kisses the tips of the pyramids.

When we reach the dunes beyond the cemetery we turn our horses east and watch the sun rise over the Nile. It's a solemn, timeless moment, no soda-wielding beggars, only a Bedouin in a sky blue robe carrying an urn to his tiny hovel. When the sunbeams reach the Sphinx we race one another across the desert, kicking up sand, clinging for dear life, but taking papyrus switches to flanks, urging the horses faster. We ride until the pyramids are lost from view then stop at a roped-off archaeological dig abandoned for lack of funding.

For twenty pounds *baksheesh* I'm allowed to thrust my hands into the rubble while Challied nervously chats with the guards — soldiers from a nearby military base. I wonder what the structure might have been: a tomb, a prison, a kitchen, a temple? To the untrained eye it's just a crumbled-sandstone mesa but to a grown-up twelve-year-old it's a doorway to a magic realm, something the modern world has never seen. Under Egypt there is death, Anubis, mystery, statues worth a million English pounds and all it takes is a good guess or a lucky shovel to unearth the next Tutankhamen.

I find what I believe to be camel teeth.

Before the heat becomes too strong, we mount up and begin a slow, deliberate trot toward Chepren. I scratch the diamond of white on Black Star's forehead. We crest a small dune and the pyramids reappear, a sight that inspires awe even on the second day of viewing. My ancestors may have built this place as slaves before the Exodus, walked around the Sinai forty years without a home, despised by all, but I was drawn here. Three times now I have found a jewel inside a dream of Egypt — once when I was twelve, once before I left the States and once in thirty seconds late last night when something purple glittered on Chepren's northern flank. We ride for half an hour until we reach that middle pyramid, topped by alabaster, flanked by Menkaure and Cheops, guarded by the Sphinx.

I tell Challied I plan to climb, halfway to the top or more. He scowls and tells me not to do it as I'll surely be arrested. I dismount, ask him why he thinks I came to Egypt after dozens died in Luxor. He shrugs and takes my reins and switch.

"Because I don't answer to my government. I answer to my heart."

No one looks twice or tries to stop me as I approach the mighty Chepren and begin to climb. The best way to steal something is to walk right up and take it like it's yours and in this way I climb and climb and slip and climb again.

"Come down! Not safe!" someone shouts from below.

I turn and squint into the sunlight. It's an Egyptian man not wanting me to set a bad example for his prepubescent son who also wants to climb. I laugh, climb higher, hoisting myself then standing up, fourteen, fifteen, sixteen levels. My finger starts to bleed again. Far above a falcon cries and now the shouting starts in earnest. Two tourist cops with holstered pistols are urging me to stop but they won't shoot because of Luxor and now I'm halfway to the top. The falcon circles closer, closer and as the cops begin to climb I peer inside a crack between the stones…

Inside is something dark and round but out of reach, just beyond my probing fingers. I spin my belt-bag to my stomach, find my head lamp, turn it on and see a piece of ordinary rock but green and out of place between the yellow two-ton blocks. I find a pen, glance behind me over Cairo and spot the stable's rooftop far below. A crowd of Arab picnickers have gathered to watch the cops draw close enough for me to hear their boots upon the sandstone. I touch the object with my pen. It moves. I remind myself that this is real and not a dream as I unclip my knife and move the object toward the opening, using blade and pen like chopsticks, policemen shouting, drawing closer, and it's just a piece of dark green stone until it tumbles forth into the sun...

Deep in the labyrinth of Khan el Khalili, I find Moorlock smoking *sheesha* outside last night's café. Surrounded by Arabs, he wears a white, Muslim skull cap and brand-new, white sweatsuit that says *Brave Mofo* across the chest and *Batman-Rambo* down the sleeves. Next to him sits Number Two and above them hangs a banner reading, *In Egypt, you will never be stranger*.

"You'll never guess what happened." I take the proffered stem of Moorlock's pipe.

"Let me guess, you woke up with the worst hangover of your life and your head still feels like a chloroformed cotton ball?"

"Have you seen Mohammed?" Mohammed cuts in. "He said he meet us here five, now six." He looks distressed and not as impressively clean as before. A number of pimples have appeared on his face.

"I have no idea," I say. "I've been at the pyramids all day. Thanks, by the way, for the heroin."

"Sorry, dude." He shrugs sheepishly. "I never buy from those motherfuckers again."

I turn to Moorlock. "You taught him to say *dude*?"

"And motherfucker. How'd it go at the pyramids?"

I produce the egg-sized stone from my pack and lay it on the table, green side up. Moorlock turns it over to reveal a field of jagged purple — the highest wavelength color we can see. And while ruby is a low-vibration red, appealing to the flesh and blood, amethyst's a purple stone, a calling to the spirit.

"Hot damn," says Moorlock. He examines the crystal. "I knew you wouldn't come back empty-handed."

"I had to bribe two cops. Fifty pounds apiece."

"You fool!" Number Two explodes from his chair. "For one hundred pounds you buy purple rock the size of this table. They bring from mines, near in the desert. This purple rock is everywhere."

I tap the amethyst. "Yes, but *this* purple rock was wedged inside a crack halfway up Chepren — I had a dream it would be there."

Number Two shakes his head in disbelief. "Maybe some old woman put there for luck. Husband die, she tries to make magic."

"Maybe, but if all I wanted was a purple rock I never would have left the states."

The amethyst story takes a back seat as I learn that Moorlock has bought a case of duty-free Heineken as a present for the Mohammeds. He'd stored the beer at One's house but now Two is panicking because One is nowhere to be seen. Moorlock heaves a sigh and says he understands why someone's mother might burn her own child's hand for stealing.

At sunset we walk through the City of the Dead, where half a million destitutes scavenge an existence amongst the graves of untold millions more. The air is pierced with ululations of grief and the croaking laugh of African ravens. Anubis meanwhile lurks in the shadows while Nut, the Sky Goddess, swallows the sun with a diesel-fume, afterglow chaser.

I don't want to be an American anymore. I want to be a global citizen. I want to spread my tentacles over the earth and know this place as a planet, without nations. In two weeks I'll have to answer the question, "What are you doing in India?" If I tell the truth — that I'd dreamed, hallucinated and found a crystal inside an Egyptian pyramid and now was following a calling toward the Hindu Destroyer God, Shiva, plus a four-armed Vedic serpent I'd embodied once on DMT — I will be roundly dismissed as a hippie, and possibly deemed insane. Those who are close enough to know me however, know that I'm a terrible liar, that I make up in experience for what I lack in imagination. Or so I like to think.

As we stand upon the ramparts of the City of the Dead, Moorlock turns to me and asks, in a sombre tone, "Do you think it's a dragon egg?"

"I hope so. That's what Irasha would probably think."

"And what will you do if it hatches?"

I smile and take the amethyst from my bag.

"If it's a dragon, I'ma ride it."

We find Mohammed Number One, all nervous smiles and sweaty handshakes, at his father's children's-clothing stall. Moorlock smolders. Number Two looks fit to kill. Weary from surfing psychedelic tsunamis all the way from California, I assume the role of mediator with the last of my emotional energy. Turns out that Number One had quote-unquote misplaced the gift and that, above all, Moorlock is a dipshit for buying Muslim teenagers a case of goddamn beer. While the argument drags on, I buy a gaudy fez from a woman with no teeth while an actual mummy — a burn-victim swaddled in gauze — shuffles between the shouting Mohammeds, pushing a portable IV. No one bats an eye.

Then I spot a Heineken label tucked behind a box of dresses.

Chuckling, I scurry behind the stall and heave the case upon my shoulder. The Mohammedan argument halts for but a second.

"So you try to take our gift from me, you motherfucker," says Number Two.

"I was... I was... to give..."

"Why'd you bring it here?" snaps Moorlock. "Why didn't you leave it at your house?"

"He wants to sell it," Two hisses. "He does not care about friends. Only money."

One and Two begin to shout in Arabic. One's father goes back to hawking clothes. Moorlock asks if we should spilt the case between them as originally intended. I tell him I have a better idea.

"My Arab brothers," I yell. "Stop fighting, stop lying, stop everything!"

The bustling crowd turns toward me momentarily. I hoist the case of beer above my head.

"We live on the same planet! We breathe the same oxygen! The sun shines on Luxor, Europe, America — *we are all one people!*"

I set the box on the ground with a thud, tear it open and pass out beers with wild abandon. They say that Muslims don't drink alcohol, that fundamentalists want to kill Yankees but tonight in the Khan El Khalili bazaar, under the shadow of the Al Azar Mosque, Egyptians surge forward to drink German beer opened by a Jewish American's Swiss Army knife. Both Mohammeds take a bottle, a white couple from Australia joins the party, Moorlock clinks a toast with Number One's father and, while sadly no local women step forward, my heart beats proud and full of human joy. Aside from water into wine I don't know if Jesus or Buddha or the original Mohammed ever said, *This one's on me!* but it's the best I can do to promote world peace in a crowded bazaar with a case of warm beer.

We return to the Akbar to pack our things and say goodbye. I give George my butterfly knife, which he'd been eyeing, feeling it has served its purpose. After a last meal of *falafel*, *fuul*, *karkadeh* and *sheesha* we retire to our room, content and exhausted, where I fall to a deep and much-needed slumber. As I drift toward the thousand-petalled lotus of light, each petal of which is a separate dimension, I'm tapped on the shoulder and turn to find Thoth, my patron deity, the ibis-headed scribe of the ancients.

"Come on, I want to show you something," he says, his voice more understood than heard. I notice he's dressed as a Zoot-suited gangster. He spirals me into a dream of his own making where the pyramid of Chepren is newly-built but still without its final coat of alabaster. It looks nearly identical to what it does today with its stair-stepped design and haunting majesty only this time, instead of picnickers, tourists and camel-ride vendors, the foreground is filled with brown, sweaty laborers unloading oxcarts of semi-precious stones.

Thoth and I watch as turquoise, moonstone, lapis and amethyst are piled into baskets and hiked up the pyramid. The stones are stuffed into each and every crack, perhaps to give the monument more power. These people are my ancestors, I realize, with dark, frizzy hair, burdened backs and bent noses. I turn to Thoth and bow my head in thanks. He smiles as best he

can with his curving, ibis beak, opens up a perfect palm
and says to me, "*Baksheesh*?"

METALOGUE

Now, DMT breaks down with monoamine oxidase
A common enzyme in your bloodstream there, ace
And my trip only lasted five minutes, that's true
But watch DMT, man, that shit *changes* you...
Within fifteen minutes I was back in my car
No fuzzy head, no hangover, no scars
And the astral plane is not very far
Even though the word astral implies the word *star*...
Without further ado, I went back to my life
Went back to the woman who would be my wife
But the seeds of destiny had already been sown
And you know what they say, you can never go home...
Started hangin' with friends from the Novelty conference
Reading unscientific but maybe-true nonsense
Becoming more certain I'd seen the Lord Shiva
In that UFO floating over the pyramids
But while I prepared to chase the Godhead
My girlfriend was battling with demons instead
Depression, anxiety, pink pills in her head
"Help me, no, leave me — I love you," she said
And when I said, "Darlin', you think I should go?"
She said, "Baby, I left you a long time ago…"

"Well, fuck that," said my friends. "Hell, come with us!
Jump on our Technicolor schoolbus
Beelzebus, man, it's the bus from hell

And here, take a hit of this dope that you smell
You'll have the best time that you ever had-a
We're off to the Burning Man Festival in Nevada!
Six thousand motorheads, artists and fools
No water, no roads, no regard for the rules —
The most dangerous art festival in the world
Blow your mind, man, meet some new girls
So get outta your funk, say goodbye to your lethargy
Come burn a four-story neon man in effigy!"

So I put on my purple velour octopus suit
Loaded up my bag with drugs, sushi and fruit
Drove to the desert and just blew my mind
Saw crazy art projects I can barely describe:
A mountain of pianos, flaming TVs
An ice sculpture built in a hundred degrees
Learned the word Techno-Pagan while I was there
Sort of hippie-meets-cyberspace, devil-may-care
Got high from the chaos, smoked grass and got higher
Filled out an application to be the next Messiah!
And I've no fuggin' clue what I put on that form
But it must have been somethin' good that's for damn sure
'Cause after the neon-green man burned down
(electricity's nothing when fire's around)
The Messiah judges came up and said, "Cousin,
Your application was chosen out of more than a dozen
So bring the world peace, prosperity and joy."
And they handed me a rubber squeak-Buddha toy...
Little toy hands holding coffee and phone
Wide awake and spreading enlightenment from home
And that night I ended up just outside Reno
Playing slots at Sierra Sid's gas station casino

Using quarters that an old woman had given me
("It's easier to win with other people's money," she told me)
And I pulled the steel arm while squeaking my Buddha
Until my friend Crash came up and said, "Dude, uh,
There's a guy in the parking lot, wants to score green
And he's willing to trade for... dimethyl tryptamine?"
Now, I don't believe in coincidence, friend
'Cause these things are means and coincidence an end
I said, "Grab him and hold him– I'll go get my pot."
Then I played my last quarter? And hit the jackpot!

Back in California, not sure where to begin
I knew it was time to break up with my girlfriend
But before I could speak of our love dissipatin'
(the polygamous nature of octopus matin')
She turned my head to one side and said, "Oh my god"
The earring she'd given me six years ago was gone…
We said our goodbyes that same afternoon
Then I went to a friend's place we all called the Moon
Where bongs, computers and freaks offered healing
Under naked, black-lit body prints on the ceiling
And I bartered some sushi for a massage
Stretched in the parking lot, under the stars
And then I lay down in an empty bathtub
Gave praises to Gaia, the heavens above
Turned out the lights, got ready to soar
Blocked off the light leaking under the door
And my friends, my ground crew, around me they huddled
The veritable mission control for my space shuttle
And I embraced the base pipe just as before
Broke through the membrane on hit number four

And the Powers That Be said, "It's cool that you scored
But you *die* if you take DMT anymore..."

In no place to argue I said, "Fine by me"
And astrally incarnated as the muse, Poetry
A four-armed cobra, a mountainous snake
With a mouthful of venom just ready to make
The almighty Word bend to my will
Tail coiled beneath me to spring for the kill
A serpent decidedly Hindu by nature
But older than that — it defied nomenclature
And I stayed there for seconds, for lifetimes, for hours
Until I thought, *Hey, I should test my new powers!*
So I invoked them by speaking aloud the word, "*Love*"
And began to descend tail-first to the bathtub
Re-entered my body and opened my eyes
(the third one is *massive*, as wide as the skies)
And I was reborn, so to no-one's surprise
I pissed myself and started to cry...
But now I had words, flesh and fire, believe
That humans have rarefied powers indeed
And I turned in the darkness and said to my friends,
"*Water!*"
And it was the voice of the Serpent...

Well they brought that water and I took a sip
And then I let them in on my trip saying,
"*I am not Brahma or Vishnu or Shiva*
I'm the psychedelic rebirth of my namesake John Muir
and
The mortal incarnation of the Divine Serpent, Poetry
My word is my will and I hereby decree
That Poetry, I am your master and slave

And if you'll but love me I'll be your gentle knave..."

After that, I worked my last season
To write it down proper, a good enough reason
Had a dream that an African sorceress friend
Found a crystal with me at the Egyptian pyramids
Amethyst, which she tied-up in my dreads
And said it would hatch, for it was an egg
Of a dragon or an ethereal being
Woke up and cancelled my job teaching skiing
Cashed in all my savings, got jabbed, a new pack
An around the world ticket I couldn't take back
But two weeks before I landed in Cairo
Blood spattered from fifty-eight tourists on heiro-
Glyphics, horrific how those people died
Gunned down in Luxor with no place to hide
And the terrorists' note which appeared in the news
Said they're sorry they killed no Americans or Jews...
Well that's me, Baba-G, but I ain't afraid, see
To die on the way to fulfilling my destiny
And my fourth night in Egypt I dreamed it again
Climbing the pyramids, finding a gem
Only *this* time I knew exactly the place
Got out of bed with a smile on my face
Chartered a horse and enacted that dream
Rode out to Chepren with a full head of steam
The centerpiece of the grouping of three
The one that's always been calling to me
And while the police shouted, "*Stop!*" from below
I climbed where no rational person should go
And suddenly I was a twelve-year-old boy
My life an *adventure*, the world to enjoy
Halfway to the top, I stopped and looked down

Between ancient stones, I saw something round
But deep, out of reach, so I pulled out my pen
A nudge made it budge so I prodded again
And while the cops mounted the pyramid's stairs
I birthed that object out of its lair
And it's purple and clear, half the size of my fist
A glittering chunk of pure amethyst...

II. INDIA

December 14, Bombay

Mother of Gods, mother of nations, what brings me into this madness called India? There are those who say Christ wandered these lands for twenty years before returning, enlightened, to Bethlehem. I wonder if he had stomach trouble too. Have I been chosen or have I been forsaken, because right now it's feeling a lot like the latter, curled on the floor of the Bombay train station with a trio of Greeks I met back in Cairo, staring at the rafters trying to spot the biggest rat while around us a chattering tide of brown bodies flows over the dirtiest floor in the world.

I'm approached by two barefoot, determined child-beggars, smiling through crusts of dried saliva. I wave them away but the boy grabs my hand. He kisses it, quickly, leaves it wet. Alexi the Greek, who's been here before, tells the kids to get lost, "*Tello!*" As they trot away on malnourished limbs I wipe the back of my hand on my jeans.

It's a hot, humid midnight in the city of Bombay and our train doesn't leave until four in the morning. I ask the Greeks to guard my pack as the Imodium has loosened its grip on my bowels.

In a slippery, broken-tile cell with no door I squat over a blasphemous hole in the floor. Big questions arise: Why have I been eating raw, uncooked vegetables as if I had a titanium immune system? Why am I not doing this in a hotel? Why didn't I cash-in my flight voucher to New Delhi? And, most importantly, given the season, why am I here so early? The latter is easy: Because my college friend Barry invited me to write for *The International Silly Straw Experience.*

I like to think I can sniff a good story and here's one about the world's greatest drinking-straw sculptor on a mission to photograph as many different people, in as many different parts of the world, sucking as big a variety of tubular sculpture as he can create in three years time. A bestselling book would certainly follow: a huge, coffee-tabler needing captions, a cover blurb. The *Experience* is sponsored by *Silly Straws Inc.* — meaning unlimited straws and supplies — but the project's real backer is Barry's billionaire uncle. I was in the lobby. Barry held the elevator.

It had seemed like a brilliant idea at the Moon, smoking bongs on ripped couches while listening to Portishead. Barry suggested we synchronize travels, meet on the Ganges somewhere around Christmas. He'd cover expenses. I'd lay the groundwork, plot an itinerary and learn a bit of Hindi. Soon, same as him, I'd be known for my work: Barry was already showing in galleries. After print would come television, film, an art movement — *International Silly Straw* world domination. Right now, however, crouched over a burbling nadir while a wizened old man inspects my package while he pisses, right now I'm wishing I'd never left Egypt. That I'd stayed to free-dive for lobster in Hurghada. That I'd never given ol' Barry *my word...*

I return from the bathroom a half-hour later, shivering, pale and drained from my efforts. I'm pleased to find Alexi still guarding my pack and more pleased when he palms me another Imodium.

Yesterday in the Cairo airport, I noticed a long-haired, biker-type ruffian — handlebar mustache, black leather jeans and a screaming-eagle tattoo on either forearm — smoking the same brand of roll-em-ups as I did. I recognized him from the massacre-memorial at Hatshepsut's Splendor of Splendors. There, we'd been herded with twenty other white people — good for the cameras — behind President Mubarak and Omar Sharif and watched the unveiling of a quartz-colored, upraised Fist of Defiance to the sound of a thousand Muslim men banging tambourines.

The biker introduced himself as Alexi. We got to talking about the kind of weaponry we'd seen in Luxor, my favorite being the combination machine-gun/grenade-launchers carried by Mubarak's presidential guard while he'd been impressed by the F-14 fighters patrolling the Aswan dam. Next thing you know, I'm downing duty-free whiskey with Alexi, his sunshine-blonde, biker-chick girlfriend, Alaf, and Alaf's brooding, brunette sister, Vera, who speaks no English. The Greeks have travelled extensively in India and know how to get by, high and on the cheap. They invited me to accompany them to the Taj Mahal by rail — just to get it over with, been there, done that — and yesterday I could trust my gut so figured my flight to New Delhi be damned, the Greeks can show me the ropes so ride with them.

My troubles began on arrival in Bombay: chills, cramps, scrambling out of the customs line to the thankfully Western toilets. The Greeks had waited in baggage claim for almost an hour while I wrestled with my intestinal demons. I saw their patience as an act of good faith. Truth is, I'm nervous about being on my own in India and nothing can tell you what to expect. That reminds me: I've switched from *The Stupid Tourist Handbook* to the staid, more conservative *Stupid Tourist Guide* series.

The cab ride alone blew my tiny, monkey mind. This is a town where businessmen on mobile phones step over near-naked double amputees, never breaking stride. Where skyscraper-billboards reading *Intel Inside* seemingly grow out of corrugated slums. Barefoot children kick oily rag-balls through traffic while their parents boil rice on the side of the road. The heat and the crowds, the smog and my cramps, the five-year-old kid with no ears, only scabs. He clung to the door so I gave him some change. He nodded and faded back into the horror.

"If they have two eyes, two legs and two hands, no *baksheesh*," said Alexi. "Even still, you don't have enough rupees."

We had fifteen hours to kill before our train — not enough, said the Greeks, to warrant a hotel — so we stowed our bags in the station cloak room and set about walking the streets. Our first stop was for greasy, vegetarian *thalis* — whole meals served on compartmentalized metal trays. Afterward we wandered to a meager stretch of beach where the locals squat down on the tideline to defecate. At least five Indians approached every minute, selling pencils, yo-yo's, sweet-masala chai. They grabbed our necks and began to massage them and if we refused they just flat-out begged.

To their credit, the Greeks appeared to enjoy themselves, laughing like it was all some big joke. They parried back offers of peanuts, ear cleaning (the guy had a cotton ball stuck to a wire), nail-polish, foot rubs, coconuts, whistles, peanuts again and *chai, chai, chai.* Surrounded by skinny, needy brown people with callused feet and ragged clothes I realized I'd be in this country for months and *me*? America — been here six hours. *Excuse me?* No thank you, don't need my boots polished and *what*? How is it different from America? You can't possibly be asking me that after six hours and — *huh?* What's the best thing about Bombay? I'd have to say *leaving* but I haven't had the pleasure yet — *goddamnit, no!* I *don't* want to shake your hand again because last time it turned into a two rupee hand massage, and just when I was at the point of screaming — "Fuck off and leave me alone!" — Alaf took me under her arm and spoke to me like an angel.

"Never lose your sense of humor," she said. "Once you lose your sense of humor, it's over."

Which is why, laying back on a Hindi newspaper, spread on the floor of the Bombay rail station, when Alexi points out a rat in the rafters at least as big as a possum, I laugh.

Man, do I want to love India. Her people, her temples, her curries, her chaos. Her potential to stimulate spiritual growth. An hour before our departure however, railway security gleefully informs us we're camped at the wrong bloody station. It's three a.m. and all the cab drivers know we're desperate. When they triple their tourist-rate prices with a smile, a crack appears in Alexi's collected cool. He reddens and shouts at one of the drivers but the crazy thing is, the angrier he gets, the more the Indians seem to enjoy it.

At first glance it's like they're delighting in his misery which, on a surface level, they probably are. Luckily when you're nauseous, sleep-deprived, jet-lagged, with the runs and having a nic-fit at three in the morning you reach a kind of transcendental hysteria which allows you to take the perspective of God. From this vantage point, I'm able to see that what the Indians are doing is *balancing* Alexi's anger with amusement. *And* they're ripping us off.

It costs two hundred rupees to get the four of us to the proper station which, in my mind, is just over five bucks but to the Greeks — who bought Hindi newspapers to sleep on because they cost half a rupe less than the English papers — two hundred is a crime against the Socratic Method and occasion for them to seethe. All I want to do is lie down on the train, wake up in Agra feeling well-rested and eat a bunch bananas. However, all fifteen million residents of Bombay know *that's* not going to happen because that would fall under the category of an expectation, India eats expectations for breakfast and it's just about breakfast time when we finally board our train.

It is two hours delayed.

My boxer shorts are drenched with sweat. The specter of crotch-rot rapidly approaching, I slather my nuts with tea tree oil which gets them stinging refreshingly. Afterward, I padlock my pack to the wall and stretch out on a bunk to sleep. Only my new companions won't stop talking, all three of them chattering away in Greek. They're not even having the same conversation, there's all these other Greek people around, Vera's stabbing some guy on the beach and Alexi's a little boy wearing red overalls, kicking a ball across the yard to his father. I realize, with a touch of annoyance, I'm astral-projecting myself into dreams again. Too tired to care, I force my eyes open, consider the visions I've seen for a moment, then free-fall into unmemorable slumber.

December 15, Pujab Mail

"Chai, chai, chai!"

The sing-song chant of platform vendors rousts me into the noonday sun. Alaf rolls and hands me a cigarette. As I lay there, come to my senses and cough, I become aware of a developing chest cold. I haven't changed socks since Luxor and — having slept in my boots at the recommendation of theft-conscious Alexi — my feet are itching like crazy. Groggily, I rise, buy tea through the window and, as we creakily resume heading north, fold down my seat and admire the scenery.

Rice paddies, zebu, swaths of yellow dirt, women relieving themselves in plain view; young boys playing cricket, a flock of ring-necked parrots — all whiz by in an Impressionistic blur.

Alexi offers his flask of whiskey. I'm glad to have a nip but not in the mood for light conversation: How long are you travelling? What brought you to India? What do you do for a living? It bothers me that despite — or thanks to — my astral incarnation as some kind of Vedic serpent, I'm just another hippie on the tourist trail. This partly explains why I'd jumped at the *Silly Straws:* to rise above the find-yourself fray and be in India on business.

"Where do you live in America?" asks Alexi. He replaces the flask in his black, denim vest.

"All over." I say. *And so it begins.*

"Everywhere? Even Texas?"

"No, not Texas. Just the west coast."

He joins me in staring out the window. I already know he repairs cars in Athens and that he and Alaf have been together five years.

"Do you work?"

"Sometimes."

"Where?"

"California."

"Hey, doing what?"

I look into his eyes and sigh. His features are pointy and sharp, like a hawk's.

"I teach kids about wilderness and do a bit of writing. Some people think I'm a marine biologist."

Alexi frowns but doesn't press. Instead he breaks out pictures of his Harley. Meanwhile, Alaf braids her hair and Vera, grimacing in her black leather jacket, exacts sweet revenge on an apple with her pocket knife. It's hard to believe she and Alaf are sisters. I ask Alexi what Vera's deal is and suddenly he too becomes vague: "Ah, she works nights in the Greek tourist industry."

My stomach twitches like a bear in hibernation. *What am I doing with these people?* I had a voucher to fly to New Delhi and instead I'm taking the slow train to Agra? Sure, Alaf — *cough-cough* — I'd love another *bidi*, which is basically a rolled-up tobacco leaf that does to the lungs what the space shuttle does to the outer atmosphere during lift-off. Ooh, and — *grumble-grumble* — a spicy, breakfast egg-thing wrapped in newspaper followed by some milk masala chai? Why not! Nevermind the only cow I've seen so far was eating garbage behind a Bombay curry house. Have I learned nothing — *sudden cramp, more whiskey*? Has India robbed me of my will to live after less than a single day? At the next stop I buy an English language newspaper and learn, to my great surprise, that yesterday a plane broke down on the runway in Bombay and all the afternoon flights had been cancelled.

The difference between a twenty-two and a twenty-four-hour train ride is, of course, the last two hours. Rolling into Agra before dawn, I am one sick little cephalopod. I'm also ravenous. Atop my upside-down volcano I've added veggie *samosas* wrapped in banana leaves — communally dunked in hot, lentil curry — bananas, tangerines, chai after chai after chai after chai and all of it handed through the train windows. I took an Imodium after that but my body was all, *Yeah whatever, dude*, so I spent those last two hours in a shifting toilet painting a stripe down the tracks with my *thali*.

In Agra, we learn that the Taj Mahal is closed on Mondays — which seems just random enough to be true — but I could give a fuck less about reflecting pools and marble inlay. All I want at this point is a place in which to heal.

Everywhere around me is death. Flocks of vultures, postcards of the Destroyer's wife Kali with her bloody scimitar and necklace of human skulls. We hire an auto-rickshaw for the day — a yellow, three-wheeled, motorized death trap. Somehow, the four of us squeeze onto one of them — damn the Greeks and their frugal insanity — and cross a river that smells of petrochemicals and death, death, death. At home you never see it but here it's all around you. It's in the bloated cow floating down the river, ferrying a flock of feeding crows. It's in the three-legged, one-eyed dog. It's in the eyes of broken beggars lying on the street, no chance to live. Trash and death walk hand in hand through the crowded streets of Agra, not hiding in the graveyard or the landfill but in the air and by the road and there for all to smell and see. When Alaf finishes her box of cigarettes and throws it from the rickshaw, no one says a word — because the problem is the box and not the place she puts it.

The weather is frigid this far north. Bundled-up in sweaters, hats and new-bought gloves we huddle together and plot our next move. Nobody fights the corner for Agra. Faced with the choice of spending the night to check out the Taj when it opens tomorrow or continuing three hours north to New Delhi we unanimously decide to get the fuck out of Dodge.

This decision is reinforced when, after breakfast, we head to the Mughal Red Fort, Agra's tourist attraction number two. "No, I don't want a bullwhip, thank you. Please get out of my face with the postcards. Yeah, those are some handsome toilet brushes but, see, I'm living out of a backpack. Nope, gotta rickshaw, just had breakfast, just changed money, don't need film — can I have another quick look at that bullwhip? — and this is my impression of a chicken: Buc-buc-buc...*bu-caw!*"

Touts aside, the Red Fort is impressive. Meandering

courtyards, geodesic gardens and walls upon walls of blood-red stone. Standing on the ramparts overlooking rice fields, I'm entranced by the rhythmic chisels of stone-cutters continuing their endless cycle of repairs. Alaf motions me to a balcony out of view of the patrolling guards where I find Alexi crumbling hash. I tear into a pomegranate and toss a good-sized chunk to the monkeys. The back of my throat tastes like diesel. I wish Jaime were here. She'd rub my head and keep me from smoking. Alaf asks me what's wrong 'cause I'm crying. I tell her I just want to take a fucking shower.

Even Vera has to laugh. The hash goes down hard and little too hot but my perspective begins to change for the better. Soon, instead of cursing my being here, I'm smoking a joint on top of a fort with three biker Greek friends I made back in Cairo. Not homeless but travelling, not jobless but bossless — and when I lay back to look at the sky? I realize that some of the vultures are *eagles*.

"You want winter, go north," says Alexi, twisting his mustache. "You want summer, go south. You want desert, go to Rajasthan."

Alaf wraps her arm around my shoulder. "You can have anything you want here. The Indians say anything is possible."

"You want surf, go to Kerala. You want yoga, go to Rishikesh. You want gems, go to Jaipur. You want sex, go to Pune."

Vera says something to Alaf in Greek.

"Possible and cheap," Alaf translates.

Alexi takes the last drag off the joint and throws the roach over the railing. It fizzles into the moat far below.

"I feel like I'm in the middle of a bicycle wheel," I

say. "Where all the spokes are equidistant. When you're in a land where anything is possible and you can have anything you want, it all boils down to one simple question."

"What do you want?" says Alexi.

"I already told you," I say with a sniffle. "I want a fucking shower."

It's nine p.m. and I'm watching a prepubescent boy grind and place malachite into a mosaic end-table by candlelight. We got hustled into a craft shop somehow. I'm trying to summon the energy to care how this poor kid's been making this table for months — and it's certainly not a labor of love — but I haven't had a decent night's sleep in three days and now there's a headache on top of my cold, my diarrhea, my cough, my cut and my fungus.

After the Mughal Fort today, we hiked over some rice paddies to get as close as we could to the Taj Majal, arguably the most elegant building in history, rising from the mist like a fairytale castle, and the four of us were standing in a muddy field watching women make cooking fuel out of cow dung *barehanded*. Duality comes fast and furious in India: skyscrapers and slums, *thalis* and diarrhea and, most immediately, gorgeous end tables being made by small children hunched over grinding wheels after dark.

By the time we get to the train station I am beyond caring, beyond exhausted and steadily approaching whimpering hysteria.

"Ten minutes? The train won't be here for another *ten minutes*? Well then! Let the monkeys have the bananas! Hey Alexi? You know what happened to me today? I left half a bottle of water in the back of the rickshaw and when I went back to get it was *gone*. That's how bad things are, man — half a bottle! What's my story? My *real* story? You want the one about the girl who left me? The one about my octopus, Clyde? Or do you want the one about you playing soccer with your father the day after your mother died?"

Alexi pales and gawks at me, the look on his face one of alienated awe. Fascinate and repulse — the octopus' curse. It's a look I've seen many times before.

Thankfully, the train arrives before I'm forced to explain myself. Only it's not a sleeper train. It's packed with commuters. A teenage boy asks if he can sit next to me and when I say sure, he motions down the carriage to the *ten other members of his cricket team*. Despite Alaf and Vera's faces of fury, the teenagers whoop and cram into our berth. Before replying to their What-name-what-country-how-long-Indias, Alexi turns to me and growls, "If you don't stop them, these people will climb into bed with you."

The cricketers stick with us all the way to Delhi. In my delirium I turn the ride into a three-hour Hindi lesson, tearing the last pages of my journal into flash cards. The youths are more than happy to oblige. By the time we roll into the station, I may be a member of the living dead but at least I can ask "Why are you staring?" in Hindi.

The taxi queue is a mass of barking confusion. Alexi nobly enters the fray. While he haggles prices, the sisters and I stand and shiver, our packs growing heavier by the second. I think of all the unnecessary shit I'm lugging around: mask and snorkel, hardback books.

Suddenly Alexi, shouts, "One hundred fifty rupees?

You are a *criminal*, man!" He returns to the group, hoists his duffel to his shoulder and demands a bespectacled Indian student-type the fastest way to the bus station.

"What's going on?" I ask the mad biker.

Alexi finishes getting directions — which appear to involve not one but two buses — then explains it's only five kilometers to the budget hotel area, no way a taxi's worth more than a hundred.

It's after midnight, eight degrees Celsius, I'm wearing all the clothes I have, suffering enough minor ailments to send a wiser man to the hospital, so if Alexi the Greek thinks I'm hiking four blocks to take two buses right now, all over a bunch of Monopoly money, then dude must have eaten some bad *spanikopita*. As he marches indignantly in the direction of the bus station I turn to the throng of drivers and yell:

"Taxi!"

Inside the curvaceous, Indian-built Suzuki, Alaf and Vera keep whispering thanks. I just kind of nod and squeeze my ass cheeks tighter together. Alexi gets into the passenger seat and immediately starts in on the white-turbaned driver.

"We give you one-twenty," he says to the Sikh. "One-fifty is too much. The Indian price is sixty."

The cab driver frowns, turns off the ignition. Explains that there's four of us, plus all our luggage. Before the conversation gets any further, I lean forward and say, "How 'bout I give you two hundred?"

The ride passes in silence. Alexi sulks in wounded pride. Frankly, I'm impressed he can summon the energy. When we reach the Paharganj bazaar — empty of life, save some wandering cows — I pay the driver, gather the Greeks and lead them along, like a hamstrung Tantalus, from hotel to hotel to hotel. Some are full, others closed, still others don't have either hot or running water and just when I feel like Varuda, the Dwarf of Ignorance upon whose back will be danced the last dance, I notice a waist-high, brass statue of Shiva seemingly guarding one of the guesthouses. He's in *Nataraj* form: one hand holds a drum to shake it all down, one cups a flame to burn it away, one is drawn back to sweep away the rubble and the fourth is palm up, tattooed with an *om* symbol to tell us don't worry, it's just End of Days.

The guesthouse is called the Hare Hare Krishna which is fine because I'm fully willing to shave my head and start the incense ball swinging at the airport in exchange for a private toilet and place to lie down. Lucky for me, membership's not required. The price, however, is outside the Greeks' range. I bluntly inform them that, "Hey it's been great" take the keys and head to my room up the staircase.

And oh, what a room: mildewed carpets, flaking paint, no heat, no windows, ratty sheets, two cockroaches — and if this is what you get for five bucks a night, I'd hate to think what the Greeks are getting for three. I drop my pack, leap onto the toilet, rest my forehead against the tile wall and after a messy but quick evisceration, I tiptoe to the communal shower across the hall.

The hot water lasts a merciful minute before the showerhead begins spitting snowmelt. Shivering, coughing, I dry off, order tea, make the bed with my own sheet and blanket, disinfect and re-bandage my finger, drink the tea, apply tea tree oil, roll and decide not to smoke a cigarette, pound a full bottle of water, shit twice more... when I finally lay my head on the pillow it's three o'clock in the New Delhi a.m., the hour of the Hindu creator god, Brahma...

I stand at the back of a fancy restaurant. In front of me, under a huge chandelier, little boys in tuxedos and little girls in evening gowns are sitting around a malachite table. The tablecloth is stained with food. The kitchen doors open and an army of Indian waiters appear, each with a domed, silver platter. The waiters wear rags and many are disabled — missing eyes, missing fingers, some of them even on crutches — yet still they bring the platters forward and graciously set them in front of each child.

The domes are lifted to reveal chocolate truffles, cheesecakes, ice-cream sundaes but the children turn up their noses in disgust. Unfazed, the waiters return with more platters — candy, pastries, root beer floats. This time the kids respond with harsh words and some of them push their desserts to the floor.

From the base of my spine, a boiling rage. It creeps to my belly, enters my heart then shoots down my arm like a burning ejaculate. A melon of flame appears in my hand. I draw my arm back to burn away the table, destroy the ugliness of a rich child's ennui, at which point I notice, up in the rafters, the chandelier is smiling at me...

I'm reminded of a time, back in California, when Jaime and I were falling apart. We were having dinner at a friend's house when someone in the street shouted, "Hey everybody, come look at the rainbow!"

It was the best rainbow I'd ever seen, a one-hundred-eighty degree double-wonder. We watched it for an hour while dinner grew cold. As soon as we turned to re-enter the house however, the porch-light in front of us suddenly exploded.

Everyone froze as the broken glass tinkled onto the driveway, the empty socket fizzling. I remember saying, half-seriously to Jaime, "Was that electricity expressing indignation *at the scene of natural beauty we just witnessed?"*

The light from the chandelier is like a gas, but coalesced into a cloud-like entity. To pin a word on this being is difficult, but I'm inclined to call it a genie. An *evil* genie with hundreds of hands, each of them holding a gaseous paintbrush. These paintbrush-bulbs are responsible for the restaurant: they are somehow creating the scene by illuminating it.

When I realize my anger has been misdirected, the ball of flame turns to smoke in my hand. A head-sized, stone idol appears in its place, floats to my shoulder and hovers cross-legged. The genie's smile turns into a scowl, its eyes into psychotic mirrors of mercury. Its ten hundred hands begin painting more furiously, making the beggars more grotesque, the actions of the children more unconscionable.

I'm suddenly consumed with a messianic *knowing* — as sure as the idol is perched on my shoulder — that when Biblical God said "Let there be light" he was talking about the sun, the star, the campfire, the candle. No mention was made of the electric light that man creates by burning coal, damming rivers and splitting atoms, and that at some point in recent history, humanity said let there be *my* light, motherfucker, who needs you? But something went hideously wrong when we rubbed the magic lamp of Thomas Edison to conjure the genie electricity — because instead of us controlling him, he's controlling us! Within a few decades we're spending ninety percent of our time inside, under fluorescent bulbs, staring at screens while the destruction of our Earth becomes like dawn: we know it happens every day but rarely see it because if you're rich and live inside, the lights stay on 'til half-past twelve and the cream-puffs keep on coming.

When a white puppet boy goes so far as to kick a brown puppet waiter for daring to eat a fallen truffle, the idol on my shoulder whispers in my ear and I begin to sing. *In Sanskrit*. The song is a battle song and though I've never heard it sung I know the words by heart. The people in the restaurant freeze and disappear as the genie pulls up all its hands to cover up its thousand ears as I fly toward it singing. We grapple in the space above the great, round table, fighting like a yin-yang rolling down a mountain. The genie's strong but no match for the idol's song. Its eyes begin to freeze and pop — short circuit in electric agony — but just before the final verse we're surrounded by a dozen roaring chainsaws.

My song has no effect on them. The genie draws up laughing. To save my life I'm forced to stop, release my foe and just like that, the idol's gone, its words somehow forgotten. As the chainsaws fly straight toward me, pulsing, revving, screaming for my blood, I jerk awake in my hotel room to the blare of my alarm clock.

I'd set the thing the night before to wake me for the train. Its glowing face reads four a.m.

Brahma's hour is over.

December 16, New Delhi

I sleep well past the twelve o'clock check-out — looks like another fine night at the Hare Hare. After several bloody mucous squirts I order "jam tost" and "boil eg" from room-service. While I'm eating, three Indian men enter my room without knocking, just curious to see who's staying down the hall. They stand at the foot of my bed, bobbing heads. "What name?" they ask. "What country? How long India?" Remembering my dream last night, I don't get angry, rush to judge or act like an ungrateful child. I am new to India and do not understand the rules. Instead, I answer all their questions, walk them out, smile goodbye and lock the door behind them.

It's four p.m. by the time I step outside to greet my first day in the Indian capital. Instantly, I'm besieged by merchants selling jewelry boxes, hookahs, garments made of homespun wool. My stomach fills with guilt and sinks. One out of every ten faces is white while the other nine are Indians, begging, asking, tugging at our sleeves. Above us, the air is lousy with wires — so many they halfway darken the sky. Most of them are garlanded with tinsel for Christmas, a tourist holiday at best in India. Literally, metaphorically and undeniably, electricity holds us under its power. I walk down the street shrugging off hands, more horrified by the state of the world then ever before in my life.

I spot a sign reading *Net Services* and sure enough find a dingy room with a computer where I can check my e-mail. Though it seems like sacrilege against the sun, I buy the ticket, take the ride and find I only have one message. It's from Jaime. She is well and likes her job in Utah. She asks me how I am, and to please say hi to Barry. It strikes me she and I are only friends now. Strikes me where it hurts.

I find the Greeks haggling in a clothing stall for goods they'll sell in Athens at ten times the price. Alexi buys a gauzy shirt to keep the sun off his tattoos. Noticing the Indian men wearing shawls against the chill, I buy a handsome olive number for less than two dollars. To assuage my guilt about the human cost of all these crafts, I give the toothless, shopfront beggar — like a karmic parking meter — two rupees *baksheesh*.

I join the Greeks for *thalis* but am weary of their company, of reigning in my mother tongue to accommodate their high-school English. They ask what my plan is. I tell them about the drinking-straw sculptor and his photographer, how I'd arranged to meet them in Rishikesh. This is the site of this year's Kumbh Mela — where Shaivite holy men come out of the mountains to bathe in the Ganges, often for the first time since the last Mela twelve years prior. That, and a lesbian painter I'd failed to turn once told me it was beautiful.

After dinner, Alexi shows me how to haggle. He tells me the trick is to never have your heart set on anything. You go in, look around, counter at one-third the offered price and when the seller acts insulted, you shrug and walk away. He demonstrates the technique on a *chillum* — a straight, stone pipe you hold between the knuckles of your fist. After a minute of good-natured argument, followed by Alexi's dramatic walk away, the shopkeeper beckons us back like old friends and sells it for half his original price. While the sisters continue to stock up on *saris*, Alexi and I go back to their hotel room where he teaches me to load and smoke a proper *chillum*.

Afterward, we exchange addresses and shake hands with the soul-brothers' grip. I thank him for organizing train tickets, rickshaws, food, etc. and tell him one day we'll go back to the Taj — if they ever move it out of Agra. We have a good laugh, he sells me some hash, but as I'm turning to go, he stops me.

"How do you know my mother died? Not Alaf or Vera say they told you."

"I heard you while you were dreaming," I say. "I didn't mean to pry."

III. THE YOGA OF RISHIKESH

December 17, New Delhi

Barry arrives in ten days time. I need a place to heal, Delhi is decidedly *not it* so I rise, pack, suffer in the john, eat a few "banana creeps", find the nearest travel agency/batik emporium and buy a one way-ticket to Rishikesh. Once my bags are safely stowed underneath a bolt of cloth, I hire a Sikh auto-rickshaw driver to commandeer my day. Sikhs are forbidden to drink, often carry daggers and are known throughout history as proficient warriors. All, to my mind, necessary traits for negotiating New Delhi traffic.

The day becomes a blur of sight-seeing, shops and errands. At a relatively modern Hindu temple — my first in India — I remove my shoes and lay orange marigolds before the *murti* of Ganesh. An avatar is the physical embodiment of a principle and elephant-headed Ganesh embodies the principle of *You can be a god too, even with the head of an elephant*. I respect the Hindu gods and goddesses because, in the same way an airplane looks purpose-built to fly and a submarine looks purpose-built to dive beneath the sea, a four-armed elephant riding a rat while holding an axe, quill and magic seashell looks purpose-built for astral realms where anything is possible. However, when I shared this with my father the professor, he said, "Astral?

Temporal? What are you talking about?" Then he said he was worried about all the drugs I'd been taking.

Back at the travel agency, I'm shouted at for being late, stuffed in the back of a bicycle rickshaw and pedaled across town to catch my bus which is, of course, delayed. When I ask the rickshaw driver *how* delayed — before he pedals off and strands me on some random, unlit corner — he says, "No worries, mate," and wobbles his head in a loose, figure eight. It's a gesture halfway between yes and no, with a smile both sympathetic and condescending. Already I've seen it more times than I have fingers. I'm calling it the Hindu headshake.

I sit on my pack and roll a cigarette but it doesn't make the bus come any faster. Today, my Sikh driver tricked me into his uncle's carpet shop on the pretense of using the toilet. When I saw the demo loom I burst out laughing. One thing I don't have in my life is a *floor* but in a land where anything is possible, the crazy dysenteric white boy with the credit card just might blow ten grand on a carpet. *Never lose your sense of humor* has become my mantra.

A bus arrives with one empty seat, all the way at the back. When I discover the bearded gentleman next to me is the son of the high priest of the Golden Temple in Varanasi — possibly the holiest temple in all of India — I ask him what's the deal with Hindu End Time.

The man's name is Manoj. In lilting, Brahmin-Indian English he tells me that soon the Muslims and Christians will start to fight again and wipe out seventy percent of the world's population.

"There are four great Hindu ages," he says. "The

Satayuga, where the character is harmony; the *Tretayuga* where a note of discord can be heard; the *Dvaparayuga,* where the character is fifty-fifty, good and evil; and the *Kaliyuga*, where we are presently meeting, where the character is even the prophets cannot be heard above the fray."

I tell him that sounds like my problem exactly.

Manoj introduces me to Lakshmi, his new bride sitting next to him. She's the most striking Indian woman I've seen yet, with a braided rope of jet black hair and dark, wet-driftwood eyes. She wears a silver *salwar kameez* and a twinkling, ruby *bindi* on her forehead. She touches her fingertips together and says "Pleasure to meet you" — but does so with an English accent. Turns out she's a second generation Brit named Patty who fell in love and went native on her third pass though India. She cheerily informs me it took two girls three hours to paint her feet with henna before the wedding and that she and her new husband are travelling to Rishikesh on honeymoon. Meanwhile, Manoj, wearing a handsome, creme-colored suit, smiles a Hindu statue's smile of wistfulness blended with perfect contentment.

The ride is your typical third-world overnighter: screaming children, windows that won't shut, previous wrecks at the side of the highway and road-works pitching the bus like a gondola during the storm of the century. It's impossible to sleep and after six hours I stop trying. When our driver lights his cigarette with *matches* while playing chicken with an oncoming ammonia tanker, instead of freaking out or getting carsick, I continue to pester Manoj about the Kaliyuga.

As I understand it, according to scriptures, Vishnu

the Preserver will incarnate on Earth ten times before the Shiva performs his grand dance of destruction. The tortoise was number one, Buddha was number nine and ol' Vishnu could bust into double digits any day now. They say the last thing we'll see is a horseman named Kalki — descending from the heavens, astride a white horse, wielding a sword of flame.

"It seems to me," I say, "that the tenth avatar arrives to teach humanity the next lesson after compassion only to find it's *way* more fucked-up down here than can be solved by a mere incarnation. So Kalki goes back to Vishnu and says, 'Listen Dad — or sorry, boss — they're cutting down rainforests to sell cheap, holy cow burgers at the drive-thru' to which *actual* Vishnu replies, 'Bring me my horse!' and becomes the heralding horseman himself. Which, to my eyes, would make the next incarnation after Buddha essentially a stable boy."

Manoj nods thoughtfully — or maybe it's the bus bumping into and over an ox-cart — then tells me to be a good person and not concern myself with esoteric nonsense.

We arrive in Rishikesh on a frozen, gray dawn. I see the Ganges for the very first time, snaking its way through the tree-covered hills. While Lakshmi and I sip chai, Manoj scares up a man with a wheelbarrow to transport our luggage across the Lakshman-jhula footbridge. Here, according to the *Ramayana*, Lakshman, brother of Rama, Vishnu's seventh incarnation, crossed the Ganges on a bridge made of jute while pursuing the demon who'd captured his sister-in-law. Soon, I'm standing where myth and geography converge, on a miniature, steel-colored Golden Gate suspension bridge a hundred feet over the swirling, green rapids of India's most-revered river: the Ganga.

Prayer bells resound from a pair of white towers. Far below, men in loincloths bathe upon the *ghats* — stone stairs leading into and under the river. Manoj informs me no cars are allowed on the opposite bank where, unlike most of the country, it's quiet. After crossing, we push past some wandering cows then stop to light candles at a shrine to Ganesh, Remover of Obstacles. God of, among many other things, starting journeys.

Manoj and Lakshmi are staying at a Hindus-only ashram but drop me at a little, green gem called the Shanti. The newlyweds bow "*Namaste*" and depart and while *namaste*'s literal translation from the Sanskrit is simply — "not me, you" — in practice it's come to mean "the seed of the divine in me recognizes the seed of the divine in you." This seed is your *atman*, your soul, your life-force which connects us all to the oversoul, *brahma*. So when my first Indian friends tell me "*namaste*," it means so much more than, "Dude, catch ya later."

For twice the shared-bath rate, I take an ensuite double.

"Does the room have hot water?" I ask the receptionist.

"Yes, yes." He Hindu headshakes.

I neglect to ask him if there's any cold.

After dancing around in scalding hot water and drying myself with a threadbare towel, I rub essence of peppermint, lavender and ginger on my stomach then lay down to catch what I missed on the bus. As soon as my head hits the pillow, however, a thundering series of knocks hit the door. Annoyed, I climb out of bed, fling the door open and find a six-foot black man in a polyester shirt holding an armload of brightly-wrapped presents.

"Hey, man, what's happening?" He brushes past me. "Crazy getting up here with that detour, huh?"

"What's going on? I've never seen you before in my life."

"Oh, you know, just bringing you some presents." He drops the packages onto the bed. "I know you don't buy into Christmas and all, but anyway, man, welcome to India."

Actually, maybe I do *know this guy. Maybe we used to play basketball or something.* Once more I feel a tremendous sense of vulnerability. *I'm dreaming again — lucid dreaming.* My visitor takes a chair and smiles knowingly.

My first instinct is to wake myself up but curiosity gets the better of me. I notice the oils on the bedside table, my pack spilling clothes, puddles of water on the bathroom floor. The room is exactly as I'd left it. Gleeful, I leap to the bed and begin to rip opent the packages. Underneath the fancy bows and wrapping paper however, the boxes are empty. They're *decoys,* I realize. Still, I make it a point to open every single one. The man in the polyester shirt starts to laugh.

"Are you laughing at me because I'm *thorough*?"

"No, I'm laughing at you because you're pregnant."

Confusion washes over me. *Mona? Dysentery? Pregnant how?*

He points at my journal. Pregnant with *words* is what the man means.

I extend my hand and step toward him.

"My name's Ian — but you probably know that

already. What's *your* name?"

His smile fades. "Neves," he says, taking my hand.

"And where do you live, *Neves*?"

His face starts to bubble and melt like hot wax.

"*In your head!*" he roars.

I wake up screaming.

December 18, Rishikesh

I rise at noon to the bidding of dysentery, an ailment which scoffs at topical homeopathy. Finding myself so ugly on the inside I'm possessed by an urge to dress/smell my best. I shower again, carve steps in my sideburns, mix sandalwood oil with the essence of rose, put on clean shorts and my silk vest from Cairo then head to the little café on the roof.

I have arrived.

After enduring the world's longest train ride, the world's deadest cow and the world's cheapest Greeks, I'm standing refreshed in a marmalade sunbeam, next to a river, surrounded by mango trees.

Even better: a pout-lipped, young woman in black is sitting alone at one of three tables. Her black, coiling hair is black, coiling beautiful, her figure is dreamy, her sweater is tight and, when I ask to join her for tea, she dips her sunglasses down on her nose and inspects me with eyes as green as the Ganges.

Her accent is French. "How are you feeling about the swastikas?"

The railings are practically made of the things — always disconcerting for a travelling Jew. They're dotted on the walls inside the hotel. There's even red swastika stickers on the windows.

"Well, seeing as they pre-date the Nazis by millennia and derive from a naturally-occurring rock formation on the southern face of Mount Kailash in Tibet — the source of five rivers including that one there — I'm feeling pretty darn good. How 'bout you?"

"Mmmm, and they also represent the great wheel of karma, the arms of the galaxy and the geometry of seashells."

I make a show of uncurling my finger. "You mean the Fibonacci sequence?"

She tries not to smile. "Bien. Asseyez-vous."

I ease into French and a swastika-covered chair, the scent of pure rose wafting up off my skin. Her name is Marie-Claire, she's been here two months. A computer programmer from Paris — another Jew. I find myself filled with impossible lust. We both order pancakes, papaya and...

...next thing you know, the two of us plus one guide are clinging to a rickety, Indian river-raft, hurtling through Class V rapids of snowmelt because Marie-Claire didn't want to go rafting alone. After ten minutes we're soaked to the skin, the Imodium wears off and the amoebas want out. I'm forced to dig a hasty cat hole in the riverbank. When the sun disappears, the wind blows my hat off. Why spend my first peaceful day resting up when I can follow my dick toward an adolescent notion that the unshaven French are the world's greatest lovers? When we finally float back to town, hours later, I've usurped the oars in an effort to keep warm; more miserable than I'd ever been on the train but baptized by the holy Ganges to be sure.

Rishikesh: self-proclaimed Yoga Capital of the World,

a string of temples, ashrams, restaurants and shops put on the map by a visit from the Beatles. The place reeks of incense, cow dung, and wool — like most of Uttar Pradesh, I'm guessing— but it's the footbridges that make the place special. That, and being mobbed by Hindu holy men called *saddhus*. The Kumbh Mela, said to attract ten million of them, is billed as the largest religious pilgrimage on earth. It officially starts next month in the nearby town of Hardiwar but already every dreadlocked, trident-wielding, forehead-painted unwashed mountain Shaivite who's anyone seems to be milling around. Downstream, the riverbanks buzz with construction: bridges, power stations, new *ghats* and other infrastructure. The equation appears to be two-hundred bare-chested laborers plus two hundred plastic baskets equals one bulldozer.

There are no bulldozers.

After the day's third shower, I rendezvous with Marie-Claire. As we thread past the yoga-heads and knick-knack peddlers, I ask her to imagine an ash-covered *saddhu* drinking cherry Kool-Aid through a nine-colored Silly Straw roughly resembling a ruptured intestine. Marie-Claire has the typical, bleeding-heart reaction: "How can you put such cheap, Western trash between the lips of these proud, ancient people?" My stock response, carefully rehearsed, is that the straws, as art, are beyond reproach and the photos, like Andy Warhol's soup cans, are meant to be provocative.

The Stupid Guide recommends the Draupadi Restaurant or, as it turns out, the twin Draupadis. Back when the guidebook was printed six months ago there was only one Draup, owned by two brothers who, after falling out over women or money, split the place straight down the middle. Now there's two Draups, next door to each other, with identical menus, identical signs and two near-identical, blue-painted clowns standing outside hustling foot-traffic. I say *near*-identical because one of them is actually bald while the other is wearing a blue, rubber skullcap. The decision is made on the hinge of this detail, for herein lies the true Draup's authenticity.

Poor Marie-Claire. She looks ravishing in her tight, black sweater, red lipstick and *trousers* which proves she has *legs* — not merely two feet sticking out of a *sari*. The Indian men can't seem to help themselves. What amazes me is their lack of subtlety — they openly gawk in the same manner as they sidle up to piss on the sides of buildings. Marie-Claire bares her teeth and snaps, "Why are you staring?" — one of three phrases I can translate to Hindi. When I do, an old man seated near us replies, "Because she is beautiful." And more so when she blushes.

Feeling bold, I order the *Royal Rajasthani Thali* — a meal and a half for a buck and a quarter. Marie-Claire orders "please not spicy spaghetti". While we eat she laments we're two Jews on Shabbat and there's not a glass of red wine to be had. Both meat and alcohol are forbidden in Rishikesh — holy writ that's enforced with more oomph than US drug laws.

"Yes, yes indeed, it's a pity," I say, but inside I'm pumping my fist going, *Fuck yeah! I've done the whole Westerner trip, bring the mirror worlds. Novelty, good, weird and evil — just show me. I'm not yet suffused with spaghetti ennui. I still get a rush getting onto an airplane. So what if you can't drink red wine in this cow-town? A sin and a crime and a fine if you drink it?*

You can sit in the dirt and whuff chillums *with the* saddhus *on the steps of the Rishikesh police station.*

We finish, we leave, we stroll down the river, sitar music playing somewhere in the background. Soon we're cross-legged on top of my bed, passing a joint back and forth until, *en français, nous sommes cassés.* Literally, until we're broken. I confess to freebasing DMT, seeing Shiva and afterward gobbling books on Hindu mysticism; to astrally incarnating as the Serpent Muse of Poetry and how, "There is no drug trip better than that and, if there is, you can keep it, bartender."

Her laugh makes me realize how lonely I am, how I want her to like and accept me *so badly* — for someone as beautiful, bold and affectionate to do what Jaime couldn't and join me in travelling. However, instead of asking for the hug I sorely need, or admitting that, "Hey, I not feeling so well — maybe you could come with me to the hospital?" instead of being real, or asking about her, I switch topics to *The International Silly Straw Experience.*

"I'm thinking a spiritual pilgrimage," I say, spreading promotional stills on the bedspread. "I see *saddhu*s breaking coconuts in front of Silly Straw Shivas, farmers drinking milk through Silly Straw zebu. Profane and sacred, following the Ganges. Rishikesh to Calcutta by way of Varanasi."

Marie-Claire picks up my favorite Polaroid: a licorice-black Masai warrior drinking cow's blood through a Silly Straw vampire. "You make these things in Calcutta?" she asks.

"Scavenging beggars drinking Kool-Aid through sculptures? It's toys in hell, giving art to the hungry. Think of the juxtaposition."

Marie Claire's face darkens. "This word I don't know. But how can you give... *toys* to these people? Toys to people who have no food?"

"Well, from what I understand, Barry makes a bunch of straws, people are generally excited to drink through them but if they're not, they're offered some money. What are you getting so excited about?"

Marie-Claire tosses the Polaroid on the bed, stands and wipes the creases from her trousers. "You will *pay* these people? You will pay some man with *leprosy* to suck stupid straw and smile for your camera?" She clenches her fists, turns red and blurts out, "You make *mickeys* of these people!"

Assuming she means Mickey Mouse I start laughing. This, it turns out, is the wrong reaction. Red-eyed, she paces and rants in French, comparing our creation of a coffee-table book to turning a profit off Roman gladiators. If there's any chance of me getting laid tonight, it's time for some Olympic-calibre backstroke.

"Come on, Marie, I'm just a writer — shit, I've never even *met* the photographer. Anyway, maybe you're right about Calcutta. Trust me, the last thing I want to do with a Silly Straw is make a mickey out of a leper."

"I will go back to my room now. Thank you for nice day and dinner." She forces a smile and moves toward the door, her face so snow-white-with-red-lips it looks porcelain. "You think of what I tell you here tonight. You think of how you try to make money off these people."

"Oh, for crying out loud," I exclaim, spreading my wings and flying off the handle. "People *like* Silly Straws, Marie-Claire. They make children smile. This has nothing to do with Roman fucking gladiators!"

She unbolts the door and steps into the hallway. "You sell your spirit for business, *mon ami*." She walks away, turns and adds icily, "*Bon rêves*."

Anger, toothbrush, toilet, pillow. A vertiginous plunge down the steps of a catacomb. I'm wandering underneath Chepren again, only this time it's crowded with loud-shirted tourists. Cameras are flashing, tour-guides are blethering and Neves — white pants, green shirt and a red bandanna tied over his afro — is threading his way toward me down the stairs. He grabs my arm, pulls me though the crowd and flings me into an empty, stone antechamber.

"You just don't get it, do you?" he says. "Tell me why I'm wasting my time here?" His face is a caricature of barely-controlled fury, hardly the jive-talkin', high fivin' *brotha* who brought me an armload of presents this morning.

"But what did I —"

"That French bitch, man! You lost your composure. She started gettin' all bent out of shape — prob'ly 'cause she got her *own* shit to deal with — and what do you do? *Namaste* and be chill? Naw, you lash out, get all worked up. That shit's gotta roll off your back like water — like *water* muthafucka!"

I turns up my palms. "Neves, ease up. I'm learning, I'm *becoming*. Have a little patience."

"Patience?" he thunders. "Do you think this world's got *time* for patience? You ain't the Messiah, man, you ain't shit."

At this point another Neves walks into the room — identically dressed and built like the first — only this Neves is all smiles, punches my fist and says, "Sorry

I'm late, man. I *love* this here pyramid."

Stunned, I look from one Neves to the other. The new Neves turns and notices his twin. But instead of fist-bumping and asking what's up, he cups the man's head in his oversized palm and dashes it violently into the sandstone. The first Neves falls, dripping brains, to his knees then pitches forward in rapid convulsions. The new Neves covers his mouth with his hand like he'd accidentally spilled wine on the carpet.

I pound on the pink, curving doors of my eyelids, desperately trying to wake myself up.

"Neves, what the fuck? You just killed yourself, man!"

Before spiraling out of the underground dreamworld to stare at the swastika bars on my window, I hear Neves laugh and say reassuringly, "Naw, I just killed the angry me."

December 19, Rishikesh

Bitterness after breakfast in a hole-in-the-wall café where Marie-Claire has left me to buy herself a bus ticket. A few minutes earlier, while crunching our muesli — no mention made of Silly Straws or gladiators — I informed her I'd self-diagnosed with dysentery but couldn't decide between amoebic and bacillary. Maybe breakfast wasn't the time and maybe I was doing more talking than listening but the upshot is *Find your own way to the hospital, Hollywood* which I plan to do at the end of this cigarette.

Behind me, a chubby, old Indian baker serves fresh-baked brown bread to the tourists and yogis. There's a *saddhu* outside. I buy him a scone. Now he has something to eat while he begs. I'm sensing the chaos begin to calm down, the eye of the hurricane starting to widen. It's a chance to reflect on the curse of the Greeks: "What do you want where anything is possible?"

My mind wanders back to the last I saw Barry: months ago, at a gallery in West LA. He'd just sold a print for three hundred dollars of an aboriginal grandmother, naked as a jay-bird, sucking Kool-Aid through some kind of couch spring on steroids. I remember a pear-shaped, middle-aged woman storming out citing popular MTV-culture run amok. Her offense had amused us both at the time.

"Happens everywhere we go," he'd said, clinking my Sauvignon.

No, the *Experience* isn't what brought me here. Barry hadn't even agreed to a contract. Just travel expenses — "We'll just see what happens." A chance for the struggling writer. A favor. He knows full-well I'd written a novel and had it rejected by two-hundred agents. But now there was something even greater to aspire to: for the first time in India I feel Shiva's presence...

He's watching the Mela take shape all around us, looking down from his DMT air-bubble spaceship. His disciples, the *saddhus,* are gathering by the Ganges, the watery road to his home in the Himalayas. I'm tempted follow the river — drop everything — get swallowed by India, hook, line and sinker but I've seen the flyers posted around town by white, Western mothers bereft of their children saying, *Have you seen my little boy, aged 27, who never came down from that mountain?*

I wince when the cigarette burns my fingers. The

body is the temple to the soul and mine's crumbling. It's time to get up and head over to Hardiwar — to prove to myself and some nurse that I give a shit. I throw an American-sized tip on the table but as I'm collecting the rest of my belongings, a tall, thirty-something Australian bloke enters, sits down at my table and eyes my Dutch tobacco. I recognize him from the swastika-infested Shanti, a resident of one of the eighty-rupe dorm rooms. When I offer my smokes, he orders us coffee. It seems my intestines will *never* get sorted.

Paul — that's his name, with his Nepalese skull cap, dirty wool shawl, shaved head and bead necklaces — tells me I must be quite the rich man with my two-hundred-fifty rupe ensuite double. A six-dollar room makes me out as king pimp while stateside I don't have a phone six years running?

"No, I'm afraid I'm not rich, just ill — and can't be caught running down halls for the bathroom." I reach to ignite his cigarette with my lighter.

"Illness?" he says. "What kind? I'm a doctor."

Standing atop the Lakshman-jhula footbridge, tossing a handful of pellets to the catfish, I reflect on my barter of smokes for medical advice — quite pleased by the life/death duality of it. After describing my symptoms to Paul, a Samaritan working for Doctors Without Borders, he immediately identified my parasites as amoebas and took me around the corner to a back-alley pharmacy. There, I purchased a course of Tinidazole — over-the-counter from a bored-looking nine-year-old. Kid said he was working the register for his uncle. Sixty-five rupes. Paul said he overcharged me.

I've still got some time before Barry and his

photographer, Lars arrive, long enough to practice what I'm calling the Gospel of Paul, his advice not to plan but be present and react.

"Yeah, but I already *made* plans," I told him.

"There's no sense in agonizing over where you're going until you learn to embrace where you're at. Part of where you're at is having made plans. You're in Rishikesh, mate. What are you going to do about it?"

This is when the little voice inside my head — the one installed by and belonging to my mother, a woman who's been practicing Hatha yoga twenty years — says, *You'll try DMT but not a little yoga?*

To go by the flyers and early morning chanting, not to mention three pages of advice in *The Stupid Guide,* this is a town for serious yogis. Since I've never done more than stretch before basketball — and never understood the allure for my mom — I track down the honeymooners at their Hindus-only ashram. Manoj directs me to the nearby Ved Niketan.

"Is it nice?"

He Hindu headshakes. "It's good for beginners."

Leaving them to get back to the *Kama Sutra* lying open on the coffee table, I adjourn upriver to the statue-festooned ashram. It's a Soviet-style horseshoe of blocky, concrete longhouses arranged around a red-terraced Vishnu temple. Taking in the rusty fences, chipped stairs and yellow-grass courtyard, I'm unable to spot a singular frill. For a hundred rupes a night you get your own cell, two *thalis* and a mandatory five-hours per day of yoga instruction. The receptionist directs me to an Indian man under a tree bending far enough forward to touch his neck to his scrotum. As I approach he goes into a handstand, somehow interlacing his ankles and forearms.

"Please, you can call me G," he says softly, decontorting. Middle-aged. Long, salt-and-pepper hair hanging loose. He tells me the next course starts in two days.

"Do I need to sign some kind of release form?"

He Hindu headshakes. "You need only showing up."

Back at the Shanti I pack my things and prepare for an overnight at some nearby cave-temples. Marie-Claire wanders by, says she's headed to Dharamsala, hoping for an audience with the Dali Lama. She invites me downstairs for *bon voyage* tea at the Shanti's puke green, always-empty lobby/restaurant. While we order, the TV blares a Bollywood action movie for the sole benefit of the hotel staff, all men. When I ask where the women are, the manager says they aren't permitted to socialize with tourists.

Marie-Claire breaks out some Indian chocolate which tastes equal parts cocoa, sugar and candle. She tells me my room number, 133, is magic, blah-blah, numerology, the Kaballah.

"The real magic number is seven," she says, stirring my loins again with her accent. "This is the most powerful number of all. Your room 1-3-3 adds up to seven."

For the sake of conversation I tell her 133 was also my college dorm room number, as well as the address of the last place I rented. The phone number there, by random assignment, had configured to IANS-133.

"What's so special about seven anyway? Aside from creating the earth in seven days."

"Ah!" she says, brightly. "There are seven continents, seven days of the week, seven planets we can see, four mothers and three fathers in the bible, Joseph dreamed of seven fat cows, seven skinny cows which brought to Egypt seven years plenty, seven years famine and red Indians, from your own America, planning ahead to seven generations."

"I have to admit, that's a whole lot —"

"Rainbows *also* have seven colors. They say seven chakras, seven notes on a scale — oh! And Shiva is not only Hindu god in India. *Shiva* is the seven-day Jewish mourning period. It comes from the Hebrew *si-ba* or seven."

Pleased as punch, she pours us tea. I add how seven squared equals forty-nine, the number of days in the Tibetan Bardos, which is also how long it takes for the sex organs and the pineal gland to appear in a developing fetus. As we sit there nodding, stirring our tea, contemplating *what the fuck it all means*, a shabby, English hippie I'd seen around town who smells like he's been here since hey-day '63, strides into the restaurant, flops at our table and flashes a bottle of contraband whiskey. Marie-Claire excuses herself to the bathroom. I tell him no thanks, I'll stick to legal weed.

"Look at you miserable wankers," he growls. "Eating second-rate chocolate, watching Hindi TV. I overheard you checking out of here. You moving into an ashram or something?"

"Day after tomorrow. Yoga starts every morning at *seven*." I toss him the rest of my Maruti wax bar. He catches it grumbling. Unwraps, eats a piece.

"Yoga." He snorts. "Stretch yourself out so you can sit still — for Westerners with bad backs and heart disease."

"*Duuuude*," I drawl, giving him the full Malibu. "It's the yoga capital of the world, Baba G."

Crooked, yellow teeth cut a smile through his beard and after he takes a long nip of his whiskey he tells me he's been coming to Rishikesh since before the Beatles met the Maharishi. He's seen it all, this wilted flower child, this embittered, Grateful-Dead-parking-lot casualty. Long ago he left the path, preferring to sit back and snipe from the shrubbery; to give every seeker behind him a bad name; to remind us they did it all first in the Sixties. I find myself beginning to anger, an unwelcome emotion given recent dreams. The misdirection of fireballs toward children. How Neves had dashed out his twin's angry brains.

The waiter returns to refill our teapot, sets down a bill for two-times-seven rupees and it strikes simultaneously that dreams are like mirrors, the hippie beside me is just another traveller and Neves, spelled backward, is seven.

LISTEN, JACK

Made four new friends on the bus to Nowgoan
A hill-station town spelled nothing like it sounds
Couple South African blokes, Steve and Paul
Melissa and Katie, just back from Nepal
The latter, American sisters from Boulder
With first degree sunburns and bare, freckled shoulders
Making us laugh when they tag-team chastise
The Indian men for the grabbing of thighs
"You cannot relax with these people," they grouse
"Without getting ten wayward hands up your blouse!"
And the five of us end up at the same hotel
Cohesive caravan starting to gel
The showers are cold, the rooms got some roaches
No one cries or complains; we make the most of it
Head out to dinner, long walk across town
To a candlelit, thatch, two-bit place to eat chow
Order rice, curry, greasy fried things, roti
Wash it down with Thumbs Up, a cheap knock-off of Pepsi
And Paul from Johannesburg can't understand
Why he meets so few third-world-travelling Americans
And Katie, god bless her, tries to explain
How our friends are tied down to their jobs, corporate chains
Don't even really explore their own country
Go home every night to a bar, watch TV —

"Four-point-five hours a day," I chip in
"The average American watches television
Ninety percent of our time inside
Homes, cars, computers, TV and phone wires."
And Paul's forehead bunches up and his upper lip curls
"Then how come you think you're the best in the world?
If you don't even take the time to explore
Even the things right outside your front door
If you have no sense of international scenery
How can you claim that you're the best country?"
And I smile while Melissa tries to explain
That only maybe half of our nation's insane
And a small but good part of America's masses
Don't see the world through red, white and blue glasses...
But I take one look in the South African's eyes
And can tell right away the man still isn't satisfied
"Uh, may I explain?" They say, "Go ahead, please"
So I clear my throat and roll up my sleeves and say,
"Listen Jack,
No other nation plays NFL football
If they did, we'd whip the stretch pants off them all
We got the best defense, we throw the best passes
We got the fastest and best-paid fat asses
And football? Well, they say it's like war
What do you think we like it so much for?
Expensive equipment and ligaments tore
Pigskin in the end-zone, baby, that's how you score
And the Superbowl might not be much of a game
But we love a good blowout; watch the shit anyway
So what if the underdog happens to lose
You go give your wife one hell of a bruise
'Cause football reminds us we're the only and best

Better than Africa, Europe, the rest —
Fuck with us, man, we'll beat you down quick
Give you a taste of that Tomahawk stick
USA, we're the best! We're number one!
And you can't say shit because we got the guns
We drive the biggest cars, fill 'em full of cheap gas
Try to change that and we'll blow up Iraq
And we know these oil wars are not about people
It's about keepin' the dollar the root of all evil
So go ahead and whine about American pride
About how we're spendin' all our time inside
About all the third world laborers who died…
'Cause we got the best football players world-wide."

A MESSIAH'S LAMENT

Christmas morning, waking up
With sinking feelings in my gut
Lack of path or love — who knows?
Why every day this feeling grows…
Far from home and losing touch
Chasing women as a crutch
And Buddhists tell me not to cling
To terror, beauty, anything
While men with guns guard Buddha's statue
Can there be Buddhist killers, Siddhartha, I ask you?
Nostalgia be the death of me
Of lovers past and DMT
Wonder, can I find the key
Unblock the veins of destiny
Stop my species 'fore we summon
Something wicked this way comin'
Hatch the Chepren dragon stone
To figure out the great unknown
And break the curse of every Jew
Who asks, "If not Jesus then who?"

IV. NAGA BABA

December 28, Rishikesh

The last several days have been uneventful, spent practicing Hindi, patience and yoga. I've also been walking the river with Manoj and learning as much as I can about his hometown, Varanasi. It feels good to have a simple routine, less like a tourist and more like a resident. My evenings involve either reading in my room or getting to know other students by the campfire. There's only fifteen of us staying at Ved Niketan, though the compound has room for more than two hundred. Their peak yoga season begins in the spring when the warm weather draws famous teachers to the valley but for now I'm under the tutelage of G whose credentials boil down to "coming from the mountains."

    The classes are taught in the carpeted temple, surrounded by posters of Vishnu's many incarnations. The room is pale blue, dimly lit by candles and might be the only place in town without incense. Every foggy, freezing morning we arrive in loose clothes and thin woolen shawls, begin breathing exercises, nostril by nostril, before limbering up with sun salutations. As the pace and postures become more intense, we shed the shawls and start to sweat. Then we do headstands, cross legs and do twists, at which point G walks around chanting at us. This is the crazy part. This is where the bass-like vibrations of his voice penetrate into the cartilage of my joints, as if he were singing me into position:

"Relax your whooooooooooooole bo-dy."

"Caaaaaaaaaaaaaaaaaalves!"

Thing is, it works. I'm able to go deeper — yet I can't help but feel like it's cheating. As an Aussie guy put it: "How my s'posed to do back in Sydney the bastardry done to us under that temple?" After a particularly grueling session, followed by more of G's good-good-vibrations we approached him during his evening *thali* and asked him what style we were actually learning.

"Eez eet Hatha?" asked one of the Spanish girls. "Veenyasa?"

"Your life is as long as your spine is flexible That is the kind of yoga we are doing." He picked up his fork then put it back down. Thought for a moment. "We are also doing breathing."

Other than that, eating simple, feeling healthy, I've come a long way from the train station in Bombay. My only slip-up was a hot, German truck-driver I watched getting robbed on the bridge by the monkeys. Ten of them. Slid down the wires like ninjas, clawed open her blue, plastic baggie of oranges, half of which spilled off the bridge into the river. I helped her see the funny side. Her breasts were enormous. We got to talking and, same as Marie Claire, she told me she was frustrated wandering around on her own. She wanted help navigating the Indian grope-fest and, as a throwaway, expressed some misgivings about her boyfriend back in Dusseldorf. I recall how when Gandhi got an erection he referred to the moment as his "darkest hour" and in that same spirit I blew off the day's lessons to accompany her to a "legendary" palm-reader.

Next thing I knew, a man with goggles of muscles surrounding his eyes from a lifetime of squinting told me straight-up that I was an only child with a "much-thinking father" who disapproved of my "methods".

"You are seeing things in dreams or meditation you are not being ready for, no?"

When he looked up I did my best not to react but he rubbed a bit of oil on my palm, got his glasses: "You have respect for all Gods but only believe in the One."

Was that true?

"Your fate line comes out of your moon," he continued. "Always are having the life of a traveller."

This is easy to say to a white, western tourist washed up in the shop of a Rishikesh astrologer but then he said, "Only are loving one woman. Your dream, making writing your living this lifetime."

I misted up instantly. The truck driver scowled, obviously never having met a Californian. Lastly, the palm reader dealt me a blow: "one of your friends is backstabbing you."

Of course, I could make all my dreams come true if I purchased the palm reader's *stones of prosperity*: an oval, yellow sapphire that looked like clear gold and an emerald the color of dew on a grass blade. He'd hit me so close to the nerve, I was tempted.

"Twenty-thousand rupees — very good Walmart price. Your ego is troublesome but your third eye, very deep." He left the two stones on the counter under a spotlight, took the German girl's hand. "You are having two sisters."

This complete one-eighty from spirit to business,

then back again, broke me out of his trance. And though I'd been hoping to purchase some gems — and also find out how such things are done — I pretended I needed to go for a cigarette, hailed an auto-rickshaw and slipped, like an octopus, back to Ved Niketan.

This morning begins much the same as the others. After yoga and *dhal* I report to the Shanti only this time the clerk says, "Your friends are here!" and cheerily directs me to room 123. Excited to put all my plans into motion, I open the door to their room without knocking, showing all the privacy consideration of a native.

A friendly American face I can talk to!

I find my compatriots crashed-out on their beds, dead to the world and listening to Walkmans. I shake Barry's leg and he pops one eye open.

"Oh my god," he says. "You have dreadlocks."

Barry and I went to college together at the University of California at Santa Cruz. We lived in the Turner House residence hall, birthplace of the *Fish Rap Live!* student newspaper. I'd written a marijuana grow-tips column, under the pseudonym Dr. Harry Buds. This helped a few people grow dope in their rooms and gave me a taste for writing for the common good. Turner was out of control even by Santa Cruz standards: campus dealer in the TV lounge, homeless shelter in the basement, our preceptor — our only adult supervision — a predatory, pill-popping Marxist bisexual. The Santa Cruz Sentinel even ran a story on us, under the headline *Dormitory Free For All*. Barry had been pictured half-naked on the cover: saucer eyed and sucking a Silly Straw banana slug.

Barry is a Methodist kid from Orange County, grew

up in a mansion out of Architectural Digest. His father's a dentist but his uncle's a computer tycoon. "He makes money," says Barry if anyone asks him.

The summer before Barry's junior year, his girlfriend left him and went back to her ex. He went off the rails on nitrous oxide for a bit then picked-up some hobbies on the advice of his psychiatrist: a clarinet, a surfcasting reel, a Silly Straw making kit, a full-immersion course in conversational Italian. He even tried growing marijuana hydroponically — before I had met him, before I could help. In less than two months, he'd flunked out of summer school, caught his first tomcod, ate it, got food poisoning, torched all his clones with a sodium bulb and had his clarinet seized and pawned by his housemates.

"Practice on your own time," they'd said.

When his ex called to tell him she'd gotten engaged, he opened the only box he had left; something he'd bought as a goof at a novelty shop. I picture him stoned, by himself, in his underpants. He's sitting in a fleabag apartment in Watsonville — Barry never did have a taste for the finer things. It's Friday night and he's thinking of her as he picks up and plugs in his first set of heat-tongs. The straws go from noodles to spirals to daisies to broken red hearts with blue sidecar apes. Next thing you know he's doing bachelorette parties and being featured in novelty trade magazines. His work was amazing: some straws were like whales with the draw at the tails. Others, Kool-Aid samurais committing *hare kare*. His room was always littered with crumpled ones and fives but Barry had never been in it for the money.

By graduation he'd sculpted at Hollywood parties,

variety shows and benefits at the governor's mansion. How far could he take this whole Silly Straw business being maybe *the greatest drinking-straw sculptor in the world?* When his uncle gave him twenty-odd grand to find out, and *Silly Straws Inc.* pledged unlimited supplies, *The International Silly Straw Experience* was born and Barry, a big fan of Dr. Buds, had invited me to write.

Barry sits up looking jet-lagged, disheveled. The lint in his five-o'clock shadow makes me smile. He runs a hand through his thinning, blonde hair. It's like waking him up before class to get high. After explaining my dreadlocks aren't dirty — "I wash them but that's about it, go fuck yourself" — he introduces me to his photographer Lars, a six-foot-three, chisel-jawed kid out of Rochester with a crew-cut. Barry tells me they met in New York at a Fotomat where Lars was complaining about the quality of his prints.

"His attention to detail, that's what impressed me," says Barry. "I showed him my photos. He said he could do better. Three years later we've been from Australia to China."

Lars' accent is thick as a bookie from Queens. "I thought I'd be stuck doing weddings my whole life. Then this guy shows up talking all about Silly Straws — I thought he was makin' a porno or something."

It doesn't escape me they're both wearing khakis, t-shirts, plaid flannel and Vans —nouveau grunge— while I'm rocking fisherman pants from South Thailand, a *kurta*, a shawl and Velcro river sandals.

"How long have you two been in town?" I ask. "I left a message for you at the desk."

Barry rubs sleep from his owlish, blue eyes. "Got here yesterday, late afternoon. Your temple was locked by the time we went by."

"What is that place anyway?" Lars wants to know. "Those statues outside are *freaky*, man. Looks like a commune, Chuck Manson style."

"It's a *yoga* ashram," I say with a wink. "Come down tomorrow and give it a try."

Barry slaps my leg. "We're leaving tomorrow. Get in three shoots, then bail tomorrow night."

"Don't... don't you want to see this place first?"

"Nah, we already walked around this morning. Nice bridges, but there's no way Lars can work with this light."

"But I thought we — anyway, leaving for where?"

"That's up to you, yoga boy. You're the guide."

Lars stands up and points out the window. "The sun doesn't clear that ridge 'til eleven and by then the straws are way too bright. Don't worry about it. You couldn't have known."

He opens the bathroom door then wrenches his head back.

"Jesus, Barry, what did you do? You gotta pour *water* down that hole, man."

"Can't help it," says Barry. He grins at me impishly. "I've always loved Indian food, all those spices."

I glance at the mess spilling out of their backpacks: CD cases, camera equipment, some clothes. Most of it though remains in their packs. They're ready to leave at a moment's notice.

"You know, the Kumbh Mela starts next week," I say. "It's the biggest religious festival on earth. The holy men come out of the mountains to bathe. I figured you might want to check that scene out."

Barry scratches a bug-bite on his cheek. "Sounds crowded."

"Ten million pilgrims, that's what they say." I flop in a chair at the foot of his bed.

"Crowds are *bad*," says Barry.

We fall into silence.

Lars reappears from the bathroom and gasps. Tries to pull open the window. It's jammed.

Barry says, "How 'bout you give him the speech?"

"Yeah," says Lars, "it's about that time — but I'm lighting some incense, don't care if you hate it." He lights a stick of complimentary Nag Champa. "We are image gatherers — that's the first thing you gotta understand. We're not tourists, we're not on vacation. We have no interest in seeing the countryside. We're here to gather as many images, in as much diversity, in the shortest amount of time that we can."

"We got a system," Barry chimes in. "The Arrival, the Sculpt, the Shoot and the Get Away. We do it at sunrise, in the late afternoon or whenever the light's not too harsh, like when it's cloudy. The people are dark here so we don't want night shots — basically, we're slaves to the light. The rest of the time you can have to yourself. We're here to shoot two hundred rolls of film."

"In three weeks? That's almost... ten rolls a day."

"I only use twenty-four exposure film," says Lars.

"And the straws?"

"Picked up our resupply shipment in Delhi," says Barry. He unzips a compartment inside his backpack, starts pulling out bag after bag of colored straws. Two hundred per bag, nine colors in all. "Check this out. They just came out with a new color: *amethyst*."

He passes me a foot-long straw, hard as fingernails and almost the same color as my crystal. Which is weird.

"And where do I fit in?" I shift in my seat. "I mean, you know, when I'm not writing captions."

Lars looks at Barry. "He could pass out some drinks or something?"

"Maybe," says Barry. "But not right away. For the moment I want him to watch how we operate. To write a good story, he's gotta have space."

I try to bend the straw into a horseshoe but being room-temperature, it splinters and breaks.

"Forget about it," says Lars. "Those things are impossible. Only Barry knows how to make 'em."

Ping-ponging back and forth they tell me about their trip: three months, one to go, and the last of their project. They'd started in South Korea, went up to Vietnam, Hong Kong, Beijing, Japan, Siberia, then caught a few day's R&R in Malaysia.

"Siberia in *winter*," Barry clarifies.

As they rarely spend more than three days in one place — they're exhausted, they admit, and can't wait to go home — they're curious as to why I've spent so long in "Yoga Town." When Lars asks what originally brought me to India, it all comes out in a rush: total meltdown. McKenna, DMT, the UFO air-bubble, the Serpent Muse of Poetry, the Burning Man messiah contest, Neves, dream stealing, climbing up Chepren — how the whole thing came out of a dream I had in childhood.

"But when I saw Shiva? Like, up on the astral plane? The pyramids up there were just like in Egypt — so what if he's taken a physical form." I heave a big sigh.

"Which is why I came India."

Silence follows this burst of glossolalia. It's the first time I've laid it all out on the table — a convoluted mess and yet I feel purged. Outside, the spider monkeys cackle from the mangoes.

Barry stands abruptly.

"Why don't we go on a shoot?" he says. "It's mid-afternoon but the light's pretty good."

"Great idea," says Lars, spinning toward his pack. "Hey buddy, what did you do with those batteries?"

They rush around the room preparing their kit, mixing up Kool-Aid and snapping on lenses. I've made them uncomfortable, I realize, ashamed. I promise myself to make up for it by being helpful.

"Hey, you guys mind if I smoke?" I hold up the last of my Dutch duty-free.

Barry's jaw drops. "You're fucking kidding me. Since when did Harry Buds start smoking legal weed?"

I lead them along a dirt road through the forest. The afternoon light creates photogenic sunbeams. The weather has warmed considerably since this morning and we're walking the best way to walk, which is aimlessly. After some chit-chat regarding our favorite knock-off gear — Barry currently sports a Los Angeles Bulls baseball hat — Barry tells me the first shoot in a new country usually indicates how the *Experience* will fare there.

"Our first shoot in Africa?" says Lars. "Capital of Tan-zany-a? Barry gets mobbed by at least fifty kids — totally normal, happens every time — but this time they cut through his shorts with a razor blade. Made off with two hundred bucks and his passport. We're a wet dream for pickpockets, man. We create a crowd then give 'em a distraction."

"Africa was a catastrophe," says Barry. "You can't help those people. No food, voodoo medicine. The worst three weeks of my life were in Africa. Except for maybe China. And, oh my God: Paris."

He narrows his eyes at a group by the roadway, some farmer-types loading a donkey with hay.

"Them?" says Lars.

"Nah," says Barry. "They're wearing Western clothes. First shoot should say *India*."

The road meanders away from the Ganges, past primitive huts and into a clearing. We decide to fork back toward the river on a footpath searching for unsupervised children like pedophiles. Passing some old folks breaking up wood, I exchange a few words of greeting in Hindi. I tell the boys I've been taking lessons and have built up a decent, straw-friendly vocabulary. We get to talking about my role in the project — not only captions but intros and segues. Lars asks me the kind of thing I enjoy writing.

"Pretty much all the wild shit that's been happening. My journal is starting to feel like a novel and I'm kind of excited about what happens next. This month's been like a DMT trip come to life."

"How many times have you smoked it?" asks Lars.

I count it out on my fingers. "Just four."

"Was the pyramid-UFO-Shiva the best?"

"I don't know about best. It was certainly the most vivid."

"Are you going to do it again?" asks Barry, suspicious like maybe I'll bust out and blaze.

"Not after the Serpent." I shudder involuntarily.

"That was the end of my DMT days." I explain how when Moorlock's college friend, Greg — another guy I'd met at the novelty conference — while working the base pipe after I disassociated, accidentally poured molten DMT on my tongue, it had either informed or *become* the cobra's venom.

"I couldn't taste anything for a week. It was horrible."

Barry snorts, tries to stop himself then busts up laughing.

"Am I being mocked by a *Silly Straw sculptor*? I think we're both equally ridiculous, no?"

"The serpent of poetry at the center of the universe? That's the most pretentious thing I've ever heard in my life."

"Yeah, well, that's what happened. If it makes you feel better, after I was reborn — into the body you see before you today — I pissed myself on my friend Kevin's futon, opened my third eye and cried like a baby."

"You've fucking lost your mind," says Barry, leaning against a nearby tree.

"Anything is possible in India." I Hindu headshake.

Lars says, "I will *never* smoke DMT."

The path peters out in a copse of young teaks, a picturesque tableau overlooking the Ganges. As this marks the end of inhabited Rishikesh, Barry suggests we return to the Shanti. Lars however spots a plume of smoke wafting over a nearby hill. It smells like a mixture of marijuana and woodsmoke and indeed its source is an orange-robed *saddhu*. He's sitting crosslegged under a banyan tree puffing a *chillum* next to a small fire. When he sees us, he touches his fingertips together and motions us over to join him with his trident.

Bulletheaded Lars pulls us into a huddle. "I like this light. What do you guys think?"

"I'd rather do kids," says Barry, apprehensively. "I can't just walk up, make a straw for this guy."

The great banyan creaks in a gust from the river, its great mass of aerial roots dripping vines. Everything about the scene says Holy India.

"Don't worry, Barry. I'll introduce you."

"It's just one guy," reckons Lars. "And he's mellow. Besides, I could sure use a hit off that pipe."

"Alright, let's do it," says Barry. "The Arrival."

The *saddhu* hasn't moved since waving us over, his trident outstretched as if he'd turned to stone. There's a bright crimson *tika* mark dotted on his forehead, flanked by three, broken horizontal white lines. His hair is a thick, knotted hammock of dreadlocks which puts my own wispy linguinis to shame. He's barefoot, his dark skin smeared grayish with ash. In contrast, his bright orange robe is immaculate.

"*Namaste, baba.*" I bow, my eyes level. The *saddhu* nods back, motions us to the ground. He asks us in Hindi to take off our shoes. I remove my sandals. My friends unlace their Vans.

"*You speak Hindi?*" the saddhu asks.

"*Hindi tora-tora* —I speak little," I reply.

The *saddhu* winks and tugs at his hair.

"*You have Shiva bhakti*," he says.

"*Thank you.* Uh, right: *these are my friends from America, baba. They have a present for you. This is Plastic Baba. He's crazy. He wants to make a...*Silly

Straw *for you*."

The *saddhu* throws his head back to laugh —then eerily freezes and no sound comes out. He faces me again, this time deadly serious, points at my forehead, then taps his red *tika*.

"*You have Shiva bhakti.*"

I struggle to find a fitting response, a reason for why he's ignoring my friends. "*You... know?*" I manage.

"*Acha, I know.*"

He nods and goes back to tending the fire.

Barry fidgets, crosslegged in the Indian dirt. There's cow dung and stray bits of trash at our feet. Both he and Lars are wearing white socks.

"What did he say about the straws?" asks Barry.

"Uh, well, he didn't say anything. He told me I had *Shiva bhakti*."

"What the hell is that?"

"Devotion to Shiva? People tend to go either Vishnu or Shiva in this country."

The *saddhu* picks us his clay *chillum* and ashes it, tapping the wide part against a rock. From a pouch at his waist, he produces a square of newspaper. He unfolds it to reveal some greenish-brown powder.

"Ground marijuana," I whisper. "It's called *bhang*."

Lars sits up straighter. "Now we're talking."

The *saddhu* taps his lips with two fingers. I hand him my Amsterdam rolling tobacco. He unceremoniously dumps it into the *bhang*, making me wince — the local brands are *awful*. The saddhu pours the mixture into his hands and rolls it together between palms. He places the bolus on a pebble in the *chillum* before wrapping the mouthpiece with a shred of dirty cloth. Finally, he wedges it between his knuckles and picks up a flaming twig from the fire.

Whuff, whuff, whuff, the *saddhu* fistipuffs. He passes the smoking device to Lars. The New Yorker takes a few solid lungfuls but Barry can't seem to keep the thing airtight. In the end he leans back and sucks it straight: "It's like getting high with chopsticks," he coughs.

When it's my turn I take a few hits, pass it on. The bowl goes around and around and around.

"Beautiful color, that robe," says Barry. "Would it be over-the-top to put orange in the straw?"

"I don't know, but that *bhang* knocked me out," says Lars. He nudges my elbow. "Who *is* this guy?"

The *saddhu* hums softly, adds sticks to the fire. He looks anywhere between thirty and sixty.

"He's a holy man come for the festival downriver — *Excuse me, baba, what is your name?*" — which in Hindi back translates to "Me excuse, your name what is?"

"*Naga Baba.*" He fixes my gaze. The whites of his eyes are like wine-soaked boiled eggs.

"*Baba* means holy man, *naga* is snake. *Where are you from Naga Baba, G?*"

"*Kailasa,*" he hisses.

A chill goes down my spine. "He says he's from Mount Kailash, Shiva's mountain in Tibet. It must be at least a thousand miles away..."

Barry whips off his Los Angeles Bulls hat. "We're losing daylight, man. Ask about the straws."

"Naga Baba," I say gently, "*this is Plastic Baba. He wants to —*"

"*Fir!*" he shouts. Birds scatter from the banyan. He tugs at his robe then points at my clothes, the gist being,

You should be wearing *this*.

"Look, this is taking too long," says Barry.

"So make him a straw, already — sweet Jesus!"

Barry rolls his eyes, goes into his daypack and pulls out a handful of different colored straws. Next, he unravels a set of heat tongs — like needle-nosed pliers attached to a cord. He plugs them into a battery pack on his belt. They hum into life and begin to glow orange. The tip of an amethyst straw is soon melted and fused, end-to-end with a white one: the Sculpt. The fused straws are softened, carefully twisted and gradually, the sculpture begins to take form. Periodically, he blows through it, testing for leaks. The smell of burnt plastic enters my nostrils.

I feel someone tug at my pant leg. It's Naga Baba, holding a hazelnut-sized seed on a string.

"*Rudraksha*," he says, tapping his larynx where he wears a necklace of similar beads. He ties it around my neck then points at my belt-bag.

"Looks like he wants to trade," says Lars.

A bit overwhelmed by the whole situation, I pull things at random out of my bag. Rubber squeak Buddha toy, bottles of oil, my Leatherman tool, a wallet-sized photo album. Naga Baba snatches the album from my hand. When he opens it, a spare passport photo falls out. He studies it a moment then tucks it in his pouch.

"Gone," says Lars, chuckling.

"Hey photo guy," says Barry, "how 'bout you get your camera out?"

The *saddhu* flips through my pictures at speed, unfazed by them all, nevermind how outrageous: Moorlock's pink mohawk, the Burning Man burning, Beelzebus, Clyde, Jaime swimming naked. When he gets to a shot of the pyramids, however, he excitedly jabs his finger at Chepren. Points at my belt-bag then back at the pyramid.

"No fucking way. You have *got* to be —"

"Alright, lets get him to drink," says Barry. "Lars, you got your Kool-Aid bottle ready? I think we should go with Caribbean lime."

I wrest my attention from Naga Baba's finger and focus instead on Barry's creation — a tinker-toy, alien leg bone abstraction.

"*Show me*," says Naga Baba tugging my pant leg.

"You drink through here." Barry rises to his knees. He places the straw in a cup of green liquid. Pantomimes sucking. "First we take photo then —"

"*Fir*!" snaps Naga Baba.

"Oh, right, sorry," I say. "That means later."

Fumbling, baked, I produce the balled handkerchief and untie it, exposing the amethyst crystal. It's the first time I've taken it out since Egypt. I don't remember it being quite so purple. Lightning quick, Naga Baba snatches it, presses it up to his forehead and — "*Ommmmmmm....*" I'm reminded of G and his powerful chanting, only this chant goes straight to the base of my skull.

I hear what sounds like a bumblebee trapped beneath a piece of cellophane. It gets louder, but also higher in pitch. My eyelids fall irresistibly closed. "There's something…"

The first thing I said when I smoked DMT, according to people who'd been in the room, was simply "Oh, this" like I'd seen something familiar — like of course *I had left my keys on the dresser. Coming to, on the couch, I'd felt reassured — the place I had gone, above all, had been fascinating. Not only that I'd be back, many times. Not as faith or belief or as fact but experience.*

For a moment I see all: the jungle, the river, every tree, every house, every bird, every stone and I am a meaningless particle of everything. The Serpent, the Word, all That Nonsense, the om...

The vision fades out of my mind like a firework. The *saddhu* stops chanting. I open my eyes. Barry and Lars are putting their shoes back on.

"Hey guys, where's my crystal?"

"In his bag," Lars replies.

After a strenuous wrestling match with Naga Baba — who giggles the whole time like a devious child — I manage to wrest the amethyst from his pouch and pantomime it's not a good trade for the *rudraksha*. He Hindu headshakes and offers me his trident: a meter-long pole with three flattened steel prongs.

Barry snorts impatiently.

Lars says, "Break that motherfucker."

I take the trident, set the crystal on the ground.

"Can't believe I'm doing this..."

Whack! Whack! Whack!

Sparks fly from the stone when it finally cracks but thankfully, the main body of the crystal remains whole. This, I tuck carefully back in the handkerchief. I give Naga Baba the pinkie-sized cutoff. In return, he rummages through his pouch and hands me a golfball-sized gray, granite *lingam*. It's a representation of Shiva's phallus although, to my mind, it looks like a gravy boat.

"*Go to Neel Kanth*," he tells me in Hindi. "*Take this lingam to Neel Kanth Temple.*"

"*Neel Kanth?*" I repeat. He nods the affirmative.

"*Can Plastic Baba give you a* Silly Straw *now*?" I motion toward the alien leg bone which Barry holds limply down by his knees.

"*Acha.*" Naga Baba sticks out his palm. "Donation, one hundred rupees only."

There's something disconcerting about the sight of a *saddhu* sucking a Silly Straw. Something on the darker side of ridiculous. A banana-peel pratfall that breaks someone's arm. Once the straw and cup are in place, the Shoot begins, meaning Lars takes pictures. He uses two top-of-the-line SLR's with motor drives, filters and multiple lenses. I'm impressed by the way he rolls in the dirt with disregard for everything except his equipment. Checking his light-meter as if it had a pulse. Referring to colors in terms of their texture: "That green's kind of fuzzy — I need to crisp it out."

While he stalks around Naga Baba — who blows bubbles through his Silly Straw and thus isn't *technically* drinking the Kool-Aid — I apologize to Barry for monopolizing the light. He tells me he needs time to process then get back to me.

When the Shoot is over, before making the Get Away, Lars hands Naga Baba a hundred rupee note. The *saddhu* accepts it, bowing in thanks and offers Lars a small chip of bark.

"*Go here*," he instructs him in Hindi, which I translate.

Lars stares down at the bark. "To the tree?"

"Probably the one where Buddha was enlightened. In Bohd Gaya — I'm actually planning for us to go there."

Barry shakes his head and gathers his things, "You got the raw end of that deal, Lars. As for you, Serpent

Muse, you might want to wrap your twenty arms around getting us into the light where it's warm."

Sprawled in a hammock, surrounded by fog, deliciously sore in the aftermath of yoga, wrapped head-to-toe in a rough-spun blanket, I observe the comings and goings of Ved Niketan. Orange-robed *saddhu*s gather on the *ghats*. My classmates collect steaming buckets for showers. A muddy-legged cow hoofs it through the front gate and begins chomping newspapers left in the courtyard. *What makes you so holy, you lumbering beef bag? You just took a crap on the steps of the temple.*
    "The great cosmic dumbness of God," said Gandhi.
    "Provider of mulch for the mushroom," said McKenna.
    I reflect on him now, the leprechaunic alchemist whose book *Food of the Gods* proposed how our ancestors climbed down from the trees and encountered psilocybin mushrooms sprouting from dung on the African savannah. Eating those mushrooms improved the apes' vision but also increased their capacity for language. Consequently the human brain in the last million years has evolved more than any other organ in any other animal. McKenna's appeal to my scientific curiosity tempted me outside the boundaries of science but now that I'm out here, where anything is possible — how far am I willing to grow out this hairstyle?
    During my Hindi lesson the other day, I learned "*gu*" means light and "*ru*" means darkness, and a *guru* is one who brings light into darkness. The light that McKenna brought blazed like a stadium during halftime at Monday Night Football, the Superbowl, and it might be a cop-out, a shortcut, a joy ride — the so-called

"businessman's lunch" of the spirit — but I never felt my divine spark in synagogue like I did when I smoked DMT to the pyramids. How can we reconcile wilderness with technology? The UFO Oracle's answer was beauty so if the harmonious path is aesthetic and I want to shine my own light into the darkness, the plan is to climb to that same sacred realm only *this* time bearing the light of a candle.

I hot-bucket shower, put on sandalwood and myrrh then cruise to pick up the *Experience* at the Shanti. Barry appears in a much better mood, having taken a two-hour nap and drunk real Darjeeling. While we walk through the main shop and restaurant area, brushing back menus and crafts with our forearms, Barry and I catch up on the good-ol'-boys network, starting with David Holthouse, the Fish Rap's founding flounder. His crystal-meth story just got nominated for a Pulitzer. Crazy Q-ball's at large, on the run and still dealing. Former anti-smoking activist Leo Kozar's in Viet Nam doing market research for Philip Morris.

"Which makes him a drop-out *and* a sell-out."

Barry's smirk turns into a frown. "Where's Jaime, by the way? Did you guys —"

"In Utah." My heart cramps. "She's a ski instructor now. We're still friends, she says hi."

"Sorry, man. Though to be honest, I'm glad she's not here. No woman could have handled what we dealt with in Africa."

"She was a Women's Studies major. I'll be sure to tell her."

"I don't care if it's chauvinistic, it's true. Besides, we don't need any more distractions."

Lars sets his jaw. "No women 'til the book tour."

We head to the roof of true-bald *Draupadi* and order a ludicrous spread of cuisine — four kinds of curry, *briyani*, *chapatis*, greasy fried things, six Cokes and three coconut-rice puddings. It all ends up costing four dollars apiece, the most I've spent yet on a meal in India. Afterwards, almost too bloated to breathe, I wish I'd just gone for my usual *thali*.

Over tea, we go back to complaining about women. I blame the Experience for the scene with Marie-Claire.

"I had her in my room, getting stoned on my bed. You guys owe me, big time — and I want a French girl."

"Fuck le French." Barry stifles a belch, his face beading sweat from all the hot chilies. "That French chick can eat my American hot dog."

Lars laughs. "We didn't go down too well in Paris."

The photographer has the best heartbreak story by far, involving a parasite he picked up in Madagascar:

"Everyone thought I was just being moody —" his accent alone could have driven a yellow cab — "Crying in bed, being fed by my mom. But then I got this e-mail from a guy in the Peace Corps. Said everyone in the village had gone crazy from this parasite. I took antibiotics for three days and then it was like I walked out of a cloud. Then I was all, 'Where's my girlfriend? What day is it? Oh my God, she took my fuckin' car!'"

"Africa." Barry slouches deeper in his chair. "Don't send them more food, just leave it. Abandon it. I'm telling you, man, that place robs you of hope. If India's like Africa, I'm going home."

"Come on, man, stop being such an asshole — you guys only went to Tanzania and Madagascar."

"Like I'm going to change my mind in Rwanda?

When this project's done I'm never leaving America."

I ask if there's anyplace they had enjoyed. In stereo, they come back with Australia. That was their first international trip. The Aussies were friendly, even the aborigines. Scandinavia came a close second, the children were polite and they never got hassled. Russia was brutal but the Silly Straws went down well — made them feel like goodwill ambassadors. The French, however, were "too repressed" to pose with Silly Straws and the Germans had "photographed like depressed Pennsylvanians." After Poland and an ill-advised shoot in Sobibor — "The kids? They loved us. The parents not so much" — they went back to the States with some two thousand images: Lars to the darkroom and Barry to his uncle.

"He made me fill out a proposal, mission statements," says Barry. "That's when I realized it wasn't just about the straws. We'd spent so much time in America and Europe, trying to please little kids on the ground, that we still didn't have what the public was looking for." He circles his finger around the Draupadi. "People who don't look like us. The third world."

With the help of an advertising consultant he targeted places he felt contained the most saleable images: China, Africa, Siberia, Southeast Asia, India — South America probably wouldn't be necessary if they captured "the Mayan look" in Honduras. Impressed, Barry's uncle had talked to a friend who arranged them some kind of a tax-free grant.

"That's when it started to feel like work," says Barry. "Right about the time we flew into Tanzania."

I ask the *Experience* what they thought of China because, in the back of my mind is Tibet. They look at each other and shake their heads knowingly. The best advice they can offer is: "Don't do it." Coal-burning plants upriver from cities, unreadable signs, inhospitable villages, being openly sneered at by people in the street and called, *la wai* — derogatory slang for "old foreigner".

Lars signals the waiter to bring our check. "We met this American guy in Beijing? Owned a toy factory, took us in? He told us it was cheaper for him to hire someone to block the sun from his desk then it was to buy a *windowshade*, man. That's the value of human life in China."

"There's so many people," says Barry. "Such cheap labor. It's a fact: the Chinese will take over the world. You know, I never thought I'd say this about anyone but I hope those people have a nuclear civil war."

Dozens of *saddhus* clog the main footpath along Rishikesh's car-free eastern bank. They're huddled in groups around open fires, begging alms, smoking *chillums,* chanting *om-namah-shivaya*. Their robes only cover-up half of their bodies, yet so far I've not observed any to shiver — and here I am wearing both fleece and a shawl, wishing I'd thought to put on an extra sweater. Barry seems uncomfortable with so many of them around — he was clearly unnerved by this afternoon's encounter.

"You're saying ten million are coming to town? What I wanna know is the fastest way out of here."

To that end, we stop to buy train tickets to Varanasi. I tell them if they want diversity of images we're not going to do better than Shiva's holy city.

"The Hindus have been burning their dead there for

millennia — plus I'm friends with the son of a high-ranking priest. He put me in touch with this guide who's got it dialed."

"What's the light like?" says Lars

"Well, it's on a floodplain..."

It's usually hard to book sleepers on short notice but not when they're headed away from the Kumbh Mela. I've decided not to push my objections on leaving. My only stipulation is to visit Neel Kanth temple. *The Stupid Guide* places it thirty kilometers north — and the train to Varanasi departs tomorrow evening. Barry and Lars say they're fine with this plan as long as we're able to get two more shoots in.

Back at the Shanti, Barry pulls me aside. He's apparently processed and wants to talk. I suggest we go sit along one of the *ghats* while Lars goes upstairs to zone-out and write postcards. We find a quiet spot overlooking the river at the foot of a dilapidated statue of Hanuman, The Monkey God.

"Avatar of friendship," I explain to Barry, "who, if you want to believe the Ramayana, did Lord Ram — Vishu's seventh incarnation — a solid by taking a monkey and bear army to Sri Lanka."

"Okay." Barry peers up at the statue which, it turns out, is missing half its face. "I'm not feeling happy at the way things are going. There's a few things I need to express about today."

"I figured as much — shoot."

"Basically, when we talked in California, I thought I'd be working with you as a writer. I never signed on to be with *The Serpent* and frankly I'm beginning to worry about you. These dreams you keep talking about are probably from Mefloquin and you're so self-absorbed it's almost arrogant. A drug turned you into the Serpent of Poetry? You're acting like you're twenty-three or something."

I accept his critique surprisingly well — five hours of yoga a day will make you circumspect. "Alright, I admit I've been self-absorbed but... Barry, I found a crystal I dreamed of in childhood —"

"There you go, talking about yourself again. Your ego is practically screaming 'Look at me!'"

"This from a guy who makes Day-Glo Silly Straws and wants all the villager kids —" I catch myself. "No, no, go on. You're right. I was being defensive."

Behind us a group of yogis walks by. I recognize a few from the ashram and wave. They remind me that lockdown starts in an hour. I bum a couple *bidis*, exchange *namastes*.

"Listen," says Barry, as the group moves away, following paper prayer boats bearing candles downriver. "I want this to work, and it will if we try, but there's three things you did today that we're just totally... *wrong*."

"That's a strong word."

"Wrong in terms of what Lars and I are trying to accomplish." He stands up and paces below me on the stairs. "Okay, three things: number one, I don't want to hear about the *Serpent* anymore — or anything else having to do with DMT. Be humble, man. Have some people skills. People don't want to hear about these things."

I cross my arms. "Fine. Number two?"

"Number two is: *keep your head together, man!*" He opens his hands and shakes them at the sky. "You *knew* I was nervous about the first shoot and nothing would

have gone wrong if it was just Lars and me. We'd make the guy a straw and be on our way. But suddenly he's vibing your Shiva energy —"

"There's nothing I could have done about that!"

" — and we end up sitting there, trading bullshit and crystals and you end up believing what he said! Ian, that guy was a *bum* on the side of the road who spends his day covered with dirt, smoking weed. His only saving grace is he doesn't drink alcohol. All these guys want is your money, believe me."

He's so goddamn sure of himself, I start laughing. "Barry, that guy saw through us like glasses of water. Why do you think he demanded *baksheesh*? He knew you were rich and using him for something — and don't be so quick to judge *what* I believe."

"Sorry, man, but I saw the same thing in Africa. The more these people renounce their materialism the more they're after your money. You gotta be careful, you can't lose your head. This is a third world country."

I open my arms, let them fall to my sides. "Listen, Barry, your straws are incredible — no-one is denying what you do is unique. Hell, anyone can write or hold a camera. It's just, well… I'm writing a true-life adventure here, man. Real time. Present tense. I *need* to walk on the spiritual side and part of that *is* being out of my head."

"Which brings me," he says, "to point number three. Lars and I don't want to be in your book. If you do put us in there, you have to change our identities and you can't use Silly Straws. Otherwise…" He lets it hang.

Everything up to this point has been banter — predictable territorial pissings between the *International Silly Straw Experience* and the *Techno-*

Pagan Octopus Messiah. But point number three freezes me in my tracks. I blink at him uncomprehending.

"You... you can't tell me what to write any more than I can tell you how to make straws."

"Lars and I are doing a family-friendly project. How's it going to look if you write about our drug use?" He zips his windbreaker up to his chin, sits down and adopts a conciliatory tone.

"Ian, I'm your friend. I've known you since college. *Ask Harry Buds* was some funny-ass shit, man. We want you to write about how kids love Silly Straws. People's reactions. You know, funny captions."

"Dude, I already said I would do that. But as far as my own book? I mean, after Naga Baba?" I suck at my teeth, searching for compromise, a way to appeal to the crumbling blue Hanuman. "I could maybe — *maybe* — take you guys out right at the point of this conversation."

Barry clutches his head and leaps to his feet again. "You don't understand what I'm talking about — we don't want to be in your novel *at all!* Lars and I are private people. We never imagined we'd be characters in a book that frankly, man, gives us the creeps."

"What about the people you put in *your* book — it's not like they have any choice in the matter. And why are you always speaking for Lars?"

"He didn't feel comfortable telling you himself."

We squint at each other, him standing, me sitting. His fists are clenched, he's red in the face. I feel myself starting to backslide toward anger, precisely the plane where he wants to engage.

I take two deep breaths.

"Well?" he demands.

"Well, I don't know. As the mortal incarnation of what I'm not supposed to talk about, I have an obligation to my version of the truth. You're asking me to censor my journal, Barry, and honestly, I don't think I can do that." I light up a *bidi* and stare at the Monkey God.

"Are you going to give me an advance?" I ask.

"Ian, your last two books haven't published. If we like what you give us, we'll give you a cut."

"If, Barry. Always the if — how 'bout a contract?"

He rubs his bald patch, says he'll pay for expenses, no strings attached, tickets, hotel, food but none of it seems to be worth three weeks time, let alone censorship — I snap my fingers.

"How 'bout I change up your names and identities unless you decide not to pay me for my time. You can't leave me holding the bag here with nothing."

"No Silly Straws either?"

"No Silly Straws."

We shake on it.

India suddenly intrudes on our meeting in the form of three *saddhus* approaching the shrine. They seem more like partying teenagers than holy men, rattling begging buckets and making too much noise. Barry and I go back to the Shanti. There's still some hostility but I'm glad we've talked. Up in their room, we find Lars cleaning lenses, pass around the peace pipe and laugh at the swastikas. As the hash molecules filter into my bloodstream, I accept I probably *could* be more humble. Tone the whole DMT Serpent noise down. Focus on Silly Straws. Practical matters.

Lars seems genuinely grateful for the hash. At length

he asks us, "How did it go?"

"We're good," says Barry, shooting into the bathroom. "I actually got him to admit being human."

"I'm going to be more businesslike," I assure him. "Keep my journal and visions to myself. In return, you guys can be a little less cynical — make the most out of India, you know?"

"Phew." Lars exhales a huge cloud of smoke. "I thought you were going to make us do yoga."

"That'd be a start," I say, standing to go. "We are in the self-proclaimed yoga capital of the world."

"Oh yeah?" Barry pokes his head out of the bathroom. "And we were in the dog-eating capital of the world back in Nam but we didn't eat any dog."

Back in my candlelit cell at the ashram, on a lumpy, cloth mattress, incense smoke all around, I pick up my journal to make the day's entry. Dizziness overtakes me. I let the pen drop. Warm waves of energy pulse up my spine. It feels like I'm floating on top of the bed, like I could just drift away over the mountains, my body the only thing holding me back.

To some people, Naga Baba might be a guru, to Barry he's a greedy, stoned beggar in the streets — what was that old Buddhist proverb again? The madman drowns in the sea the mystic swims...

There's a tug at my waist. Then again, more insistent. Like a disembodied arm pulling me toward the sky.

Come on, says a voice, without words, *it'll be fine. You're in a safe place — there's a temple outside.*

Now I *am* drifting over the bed, looking down at myself. My hands clench in panic. I grab hold of my real hands — my physical hands. The arm tugs my waist again, jerking me backward.

No, I'm not ready, I try and express, but can't reach my voice. All I have are my hands. The arm at my waist tugs again at my belt, hitching my body ass-first across the mattress. Now, I'm half-hovering over Ved Niketan, saddhus on the *ghats*, white cows in the courtyard, desperate to keep my head above water — or at least below the ceiling, where I can see my body.

The entity — whatever it is — gives up. My body falls bruisingly onto the floor. Rubbing my ass I return to full consciousness.

"I said I wasn't ready!" I shout at the darkness.

All of the candles have burned themselves out. I fling open the door and wait for my heart to slow. *Maybe I am getting carried away.*

"They play, but play rough," McKenna had said about the machine-elves.

These were the beings he met on DMT, which he alternately described as self-dribbling jeweled basketballs. He also called them Tykes, in reference to Heraclites: "The Aeon is a child at play with colored balls." *Maybe Barry's right and I should keep my head together. Concentrate on writing, getting paid for my work. That's what I wanted to do anyway, before I started chasing dreams to where anything is possible.* And here I remember the voice of the palm reader: "You are seeing things in dreams or meditation you are not being ready for, no?" and "One of your friends is not your friend. One of your friends is backstabbing you."

V. THE INTERNATIONAL SILLY STRAW EXPERIENCE

December 29, Rishikesh

"Random, third-world chewing barbiturate?" I offer the packet of *paan* to Lars.

"No way, man," he says, behind mirrored sunglasses. "On the road I gotta look out for my safety."

I offer the *paan* to Barry up front.

"My lips," he says. "I gotta test straws. What could you *possibly* be thinking?"

"I don't know. Gotta try everything once."

I pinch a fat lump of the tobacco/betel nut mixture and tuck it between my lower lip and teeth. The Jeep lurches along a thin, jungle road. Soon my head is pleasantly tingling. When I try to spit the red juice out the window I only succeed in projectile drooling. Chuckling, our driver, Prasad, slaps in a cassette; the whiny nasal soundtrack to a Bollywood movie.

None of us got enough sleep last night. Lars had nightmares, Barry diarrhea and I found myself wide-awake at four, afraid to close my eyes and drawing spirals in my journal. At sunrise I packed, went to my last yoga class, did my first eagle without falling over, promised G to start doing my own "daily practice," tipped him fifty bucks and checked out of the ashram. It's time to leave Rishikesh. I've lost some ten pounds here and I was already pretty skinny to begin with. The only thing left is saying goodbye to the honeymooners and taking Naga Baba's lingam to Neel Kanth temple. Barry wants to do a couple kid-shoots along the way — it was too foggy to go out this morning — but so far we've only seen *saddhus* and road-repairmen. The mood in the Jeep is already getting testy.

Rounding a curve though, we spot a group of children playing ball and stick at the side of the road. They get covered with dust as the Jeep skitters past them. Lars says he's happy with the light under the mangoes. He asks Prasad to pull to the shoulder and, once the dust clears, starts slapping on lenses. Meanwhile Barry switches on his tongs, straps his Silly Straw holsters to his belt, steps out of the Jeep and proceeds toward children, twirling his electrified pliers like a gunslinger.

There's six kids of varying ages and dress, from *saris* and *lungis* to trousers and sweaters. When Barry reaches them, he quick-draws a Silly Straw and deftly tongs it into a corkscrew. Two children take off at top-speed toward their village; the other four shriek with delight at Barry's knees. Smiling benignly, he beckons a girl-child. Four straws later, she's holding a straw ballerina. Lars slips out of the Jeep like a panther, whispers to me not to get in the background, approaches the little girl, offers her a metal cup and fills it with cherry Kool-Aid from his water bottle. She sips through the straw and what do you know? The liquid swirls up the swathes of her dress. Barry makes a dragon and tests it for leaks. Lars darts around taking readings with his light-meter.

Within view is a tributary to the holy river Ganges,

rice-fields farmed on the hillsides for centuries, a ramshackle cluster of mud and thatch houses — and a Jeep where the stasis dissolves into novelty. Some villagers approach like a spaceship has landed: farmers climb out of their fields to the road, betel-chewing matriarchs talk in hushed tones. Every few minutes a new sculpture appears and before long the crowd has grown to several dozen. The straws become abstract and the Shoot begins. Lars directs children this way and that, coaxing them to drink, face the sun or toward his camera.

A stern-looking woman comes out of the trees, shouting in Hindi and waving a rake, but fifty rupees and she gets with the program. For a hundred, she sucks through a Salvador Dali hippo.

This is my punishment for getting too "out there." This is the butterfly knife at the pyramids — a self-inflicted injury to keep me in my body.

I will get swallowed by this project, I realize.

Red-gummed and woozy, crouching behind a tree, indulging myself in a dark ho-ho-ho, I'm approached by an Indian man in a *lungi* holding a Silly Straw mantis with three antennae. He asks if I speak Hindi and if so, Namaste: what in Great Glorious Fuck is going on?

"*This is Plastic Baba. He's crazy. Children love* Silly Straws *around the world.*"

I shout to Barry and ask for some Polaroids but he's mobbed with children and calls back, "Not now!"

"*What is your religion?*" the farmer asks, frowning.

"*I believe in brahma,*" I reply. The oversoul.

He frowns and waggles his straw like, "What's this?" I shrug 'cause I really don't know. "*A job?*"

Back in the Jeep, making the Get Away, the children

all running behind us, eating dust, Barry says, "See? They never knew what hit 'em. *That's* the way it's gotta be done."

We lumber along the road toward Neel Kanth, the gravy-boat burning a hole in my pocket. Lars frets about dust getting into his lenses. Prasad shakes his head at Barry in bewilderment. I'm nervous about going up to the temple, about Naga meaning snake, about what we'll find — I just want to drop the thing off and be done with it. What I wouldn't do for a glass of red wine…

As we climb higher, the valley narrows, plunging the Jeep into deepening shadows. Deprived of the sun, Lars looks suddenly anxious. He asks Prasad, "How far to the temple, G?"

I like how he uses the respectful, "G". Lars, at least, appears to be trying but when Prasad says, "Forest temple, one hour," Lars thumps the seatback and asks him to pull over.

"This temple, is it big, much sunlight?" he asks.

"No, very small. Much darkness," says Prasad.

Lars turns to me and shrugs apologetically then pushes through the seats to consult with Barry. They learn from Prasad there are no more villages between the place we just left and Neel Kanth.

"We gotta turn it around," says Lars. "Get in an afternoon shoot on the footbridge."

"If you want," offers Barry, "you can get out and hitchhike. We can meet at the train-station later tonight."

It's three o'clock now and we haven't seen another car.

"Please don't ask me not to do this," I say. I'm suddenly angry but more at myself for lacking the balls to get out of the Jeep. I take the gray granite lingam from my pocket. "He told me I had to take this to the temple."

Barry puffs his cheeks out. "And after the temple, you gotta climb the mountain. And after the mountain, you gotta find the gnomes —"

"It's *my* fault, I didn't bring the flash," cuts in Lars. "Anyway, it's India, mon. Go with the flow."

Prasad says, "Neel Kanth, very beautiful. We go?"

"Nah, we turn it around," says Barry. The Jeep executes a seven-point u-turn and soon we're rumbling back toward the Ganges.

A few minutes later Barry turns around with *maybe* a flicker of guilt in his eyes, assures me we're going to start fresh in Varanasi: "I really appreciate you making this sacrifice." I pocket the *lingam* and gaze out the window, spit out the rest of the horrid betel. My whole face is tingling and numb, like from Novocain.

When we pass the site of our last sculpt and shoot, we find the road littered with shards of broken plastic. The kids are playing ball and stick like before. The farmers are back in the fields, as per normal.

"There's not a Silly Straw in sight," I say, dumbfounded. "Jesus, we've barely been gone fifteen minutes."

The Experience grins, waving back at the children. Lars says, "Yeah, sometimes it works out like that."

December 30, Varanasi

The Stupid Tourist Guide does little to explain

Varanasi. I'm not even sure the writers have been here. The place is like Disneyland, sex, or hot chilies: no string of words can supplant the experience. We arrive after dark to the usual chaos, drivers and commission men grabbing our arms. The sky is brown with diesel and spiderwebbed wires. Beggar kids crab upon snowdrifts of garbage. The first thing that doesn't sit right is the smell. We get in a taxi and haggle over a dollar. Can't see the river because of the buildings — until we're on top of it. A glimpse of the *ghats*.

The bodies burn twenty-four-seven in Varanasi, fifty-two, three-sixty-five-point-two-five. Manoj said they've burned, unbroken, for four millennia. "The world's oldest city, still going," he told me. "You will go there and not believe your eyes." Right now there's no time to believe it or not — too many touts waiting inside the roundabout. The cab driver drops us, unable to get closer, meaning we're going to have to walk to the guesthouse.

"Come stay my hotel! Good-day, river tour? Bhang lassi! Best Benares boat tour! One pen!"

"Hey writer guy," says Lars, "get us the fuck out of here!"

"Chapati, chapati! What country? How long India?"

Tearing my eyes away from the river, the dull glow of funeral pyres on the *ghats* — which appear through the smog like small, burning islands — I take out two bills and accost a small child.

"*You know Moksha Guest House?*" I ask him in Hindi.

"*Moksha!*" He excitedly bobs his head yes.

I give him the first bill, ten rupes, twenty cents, holding the other one back. "*Take us there.*"

The kid grabs my hand and pulls me down an alley. He wears underwear, a ratty brown sweatshirt and flip-flops. Barry and Lars follow blindly at my heels. Lars swings his daypack onto his stomach. Glimpsing the Ganges to our right at every crossroad, we move through an irregular canyon of buildings, the crowd getting thinner, the alley getting narrower. Now it's the sounds *and* the smells that don't sit right. Wails of grief among the generators — or am I imagining? Stereos playing BBC World Service, *Dil to Pagle Hai*, a cricket game —

"*Moksha*."

The beggar child points at a concrete doorway. No signs, just some flickering fluorescents with bulbs that needed to be changed during the Reagan era. The kid snaps the note from my hand and runs off. The three of us peek our heads over the threshold. Inside is a room full of shriveled, old people. No beds, just some benches built into the walls which people either lay on or slump alongside.

"What kind of guesthouse is this?" says Barry. "It's like a hospital without any equipment."

"This isn't a guesthouse. *Moksha* means release."

Lars says. "Fuck me. These people are *over*."

A crone, her bald head poking out of a headscarf, extends me a skeletal hand with a figurine, croaks something in Hindi I don't understand then draws back her lips: all gums and black teeth. I've seen a few corpses before — one fresh, after a freakish bus accident in Thailand — but I've never seen anyone *decelerate* before, hours from the end, and look me in the eye.

A harried-looking woman comes out of the back,

hustles over, grabs hold of my arm and leads us out.

"What does she want?" I gesture toward the crone.

The woman Hindu headshakes. "Not having any mind."

Barry and Lars look exactly how I feel: ashen, confronted, unable to process. We stand in the squelch of the cobblestone alley, above us a lattice of wires hung with laundry. I gather my wits and ask the hospice keeper which way to the Moksha Guest House — not *moksha* itself. Luckily, we appear to be on the right street, just keep going straight for another half-kilometer.

"Easy mistake," I say with fake confidence, the old woman's death mask still burning in my psyche. Teeth grit, I usher the Experience downriver. "Good place for a shoot?"

"Just keep going," says Barry.

At one of the crossroads we find a hand-crank well, surrounded by stalwart stone buildings carved with gods — the Varanasi equivalent of New York brownstones, only with gargoyles a thousand years older. Our way is blocked by cows: enormous white bulls eating hay from a trough, red and gold fabric around their horns. Nandi, the white Brahmin bull, Shiva's mount. Four of them.

"Shit," says Lars. "What do we do now?"

There aren't any people around besides us. I don't want to backtrack, get lost in the dark but I also don't want to sit twiddling our thumbs, exposed, with all our gear. I'm left with one option.

"Huh-huh-huh!"

I reach out and slap the nearest bull on the flank, pushing it gently but firmly to the side — just like I'd done several times back in Rishikesh, imitating the locals. It had worked like a charm. Only these four bulls aren't emaciated garbage eaters, allowed to roam free by virtue of being cows, these bulls are healthy, well-nourished, *venerated* — and have right of way, as I quickly find out. As casually as someone might pick up a milk crate, the bull swings its head, jabs its horns under my arms, forklifts me up off the ground — pack and all — and deposits me a few feet away on a doorstep.

Then it goes back to eating hay.

The sound of Barry and Lars shouting "Jesus!" produces a light inside one of the brownstones. A series of locks are thrown and two Medieval doors, at least ten feet tall, swing into the courtyard. An old man in a dhoti appears, rubbing his eyes. White lines on his forehead. I'm guessing a priest. He sees me and wobbles an amused Hindu headshake.

"Huh-huh-huh!" he commands. Obediently the cows file past him through the doorway.

"I thought cows couldn't climb stairs," whispers Lars.

"Try telling that to them." I bow to the priest.

Barry shakes his head. "So you're telling me the nicest house in town is for animals that do nothing but shit and block the streets?"

New Year's Eve, 1997, Varanasi

I have no dreams. Not sure if I sleep. We roll out of bed at five and get our gear together. I try to do yoga but get in the way — turns out my own room isn't part of expenses. The Moksha Guest House provides us with tea then dispatches us outside with Manoj's friend, Sammy: Tamil-brown, early-thirties, big smile, long black ponytail, white kurta hung over a pair of black Levis. Within fifteen seconds we see our first body, wrapped in white fabric embroidered with silver, being bourne on a raft of bamboo toward the Ganges. It's trailed by a good hundred arm-waving mourners.

"Very important man dying," says Sammy, indicating the huge, creaking ox-carts behind them. "Not mango wood. Very good wood, maybe teak. Three hundred kilos for burning one body."

We give the procession a respectful distance then fall in behind them, merging into foot traffic. Glancing over my shoulder, past Barry and Lars, I glimpse another litter a few blocks behind us. Upon reaching the river we find open sky, something we haven't seen since our arrival. The Ganges is wide as a lake here, dirt brown, lined with women scrubbing clothes, soapy kids and wet garbage.

I ask about the longboats bobbing at the water's edge. Sammy tells me they're mostly for transport, not fishing. I get hung up on "mostly." Barry and Lars get ready for their shoot.

"I'm just going to watch. Get a feel for how you operate."

I find a quiet spot near an overturned dingy, sit down crosslegged and soak in the scene. There's a funeral pyre twenty yards to my left, beyond that another one. Plumes of smoke down the riverbank. There's so much going on I don't know where to look. I roll a cigarette for a place to rest my eyes, throw in a crumble of hash — why not? The Ganga flows into the Bhang-ladesh delta...

The holy river is what unites everyone, from the baby being bathed to the corpse being sprinkled to the saddhu leaning back, disappearing underwater, coming up gargling and clearing his sinuses. Further along, near the boats, is an alcove where people covertly wade into the river, where women hoik *saris* up over their knees and squat with their hems barely skimming the water. Not all of them are pissing, I realize. Or shitting. The men simply whip out their dicks and let fly and all this is happening *upstream* from the washer-ladies, the gargling *saddhu*, the — no! Not the fruit *wallahs!*

Having once dissected a putrefied dolphin, my inner biologist stops me from puking — from running down into the river and puking — then rinsing with river water as custom surely dictates. My inner biologist is also given to speculate what kind of diseases might lurk in this river, in what would be technically classified "freshwater"? Cholera, typhoid, giardia, hepatitis....

An epiphany strikes, why the Ganges is holy: every time you touch the river you offer your life.

"Yes, Mr. Ian, you are having questions?"

"Yes, Sammy, thank you. I *am* having questions." It's now after dawn and the sun is on the river. It's the first time I've seen Sammy out in the light. He dips his Lennon sunglasses down on his nose. His twinkling brown eyes are a dare not to smile.

"How many people die of waterborne illnesses here every year?"

He wobbles his head. "Same, same all of India." He grins at me wickedly, walks to the river, scoops up a handful and rinses his mouth. "Little bit drinking, like having vaccine."

"Dude, it's not like that."

"You are now being baptized?"

Never have I been more grateful to have gone river rafting.

"Nah, I did that in Rishikesh, thank you." I jerk my chin toward the *International Silly Straw Experience*, surrounded by excitable children grabbing straws. Lars runs around snapping pictures, changing film. "It's cool what they're doing?"

Sammy shrugs. "Not a problem. Varanasi people are having good time."

Indeed they are, even burning their dead. The mourners nearest us are eating, praying, chatting, laughing. I remember my grandfather's funeral not long ago, the itinerary sheets we got handed beforehand: opening prayer, speech, song, another speech, blessing by the rabbi, cars back to grandpa's. Here, it's all happening at the same time; portable stereos; children running everywhere. It strikes me I haven't seen anyone grieving. A few heartfelt hugs, solemn faces but no crying. That happens somewhere else, once the soul has departed, says Sammy.

"When's that?"

"When the skull of the dead cracking open." He explains how because this *ghat* is informal, it's cool to have women around the cremations but "Big *ghats*, Manikarnika, not having women. They see husband burning, they are jumping and joining them."

Sati, they call it, which two hundred years ago was sometimes enforced — but now is bad etiquette according to Sammy. Distracts the soul leaving the body, same as crying. Makes it remember its earthly attachments.

"Death is not sad thing," Sammy instructs me.

"Death is happening. Hindus, real Hindus, are not fearing Shiva. Why fearing winter when winter is existing?" He hands me a pair of lightweight binoculars.

"You are seeing the boat, very blue, very flat one?"

I focus on a barge way out in the river. A man in white robes is holding his palm over a corpse. It's wrapped-up in rags, or maybe wet newspaper. Another guy pushes it overboard. Small splash. I catch the glint of fins.

"Are there *sharks* here?"

Sammy smiles. "Only catfish. Very big. Very holy. Poor people not having money for wood." Sammy Hindu headshakes. "For them, still *samsara*."

Contrarily, *The Stupid Guide* says many people believe if you die in Varanasi you go straight to nirvana. Murderers, rapists and pedophiles — just die here. The crone and her *moksha*.

"Many, many truths," says Sammy.

Barry and Lars are now on the move, bringing their straw-sucking mob along with them, sculpting and shooting their way down the river. I realize what they're doing: trying to get a small, family pyre into the background.

Sammy starts toward them but I grab his wrist. "You already told them. Let it play out."

If the silver-wrapped corpse with the teak was some rich guy and the body dumped into the river was broke, then the charred half-burned figure half a block away, in a nest of skinny mango logs was, for argument's sake, a plumber. I count fourteen mourners of varying ages. They stand close enough to feel the heat with their palms, the women in their Sunday-best *salwaar kameezes*, the men wearing thickly-embroidered white *kurtas*. Sammy tells me one woman is mourning her father, that the man walking circles around the fire is her elder brother, that he'll walk for three hours until the body is ash.

But I can't take my eyes from the little girl tending the fire.

She's barefoot and wearing a plum-colored dress, her braided pigtails folded into a pretzel. Doesn't look older than ten, missing baby teeth. With a set of iron tongs she turns over a human torso. Bold as brass too, shouting other kids back, pushing cinders and body parts back into the fire, running up the ghats to get more wood from her old man.

She's the most magnificent little girl I've seen in my life.

"Untouchable?" I ask.

Sammy nods. "But not poor." He explains how when millions of people want to burn here, on three hundred kilos of different kinds of wood, when there aren't any forests for miles around, there's profit to be made — but no social standing. The *doms*, like this girl, can't eat in most restaurants, can't enter many temples, can't touch other castes and, if their shadow should fall across a Brahmin? Back in the olden days, that was a death sentence.

The straw Barry's making is simply incredible, a blue crocodile you put your whole head inside, suck Kool-Aid from out of its pink, pointy tongue, through its jack-o-lantern smile — *the most lovely piece of trash...* The crowd, about twenty-five kids and five adults, surges forward, their hands outstretched trying to get at it. They're perilously close to Barry's heat-tongs but he fends them all back with one leg — dude's had practice. Lars chooses a boy swaddled up in batik, hands him the straw and positions the cup. Swivels the bill of his baseball cap backward, motions the crocodile-kid up the *ghats*.

"One stair, just one more — that's it kid. Right there." He swings up his camera, Barry ducks out of frame, but just as his finger comes down on the shutter a little brown palm shoots in front of the lens.

The untouchable girl in the plum-colored dress, run down from the funeral pyre dragging her tongs — clanging, red hot, making everyone scatter. Lars looks up, startled.

She tells him: "No photo."

Back at the Moksha's rooftop restaurant, eating fried paneer with chutney and parathas, the boys say they're bushed and need to crash out. I track down Sammy at reception: "Show me something."

He takes me to a nearby café for *bhang* lassis, in an alley too narrow for cars but not people: flower vendors, people in business suits, beggars, school groups with backpacks on, wandering Nandis. Afterward, we walk to Manoj's Golden Temple. It has twenty foot walls and I can't see inside but it's strictly Hindu's only unless we namedrop. It doesn't feel right and besides I'm too high.

We take an auto-rickshaw ten miles to the Deer Park where Buddha revealed his four noble truths: All life is suffering. With roots in desire. Which can be avoided. By following the eight-fold path. *The first three are free, boys, then you gotta pay*. We walk three times clockwise around the sacred stupa, a three-story conical object made of brick.

"Making good thoughts," Sammy instructs me. "Sending love, being grateful." This takes twenty minutes.

"I could never be Buddhist," I confide to him afterward.

"Why? Very peaceful, vegetarian religion. Making stop suffering, right speech and compassioning. Buddha was very good man, very wise man."

My problem is not with the man, I explain. Nor is compassion for all sentient beings. My problem is that, without having met them, and being so inspired, I'm not bowing down to anyone.

"That being said..." I reach into my belt-bag and pull out my prize from the Burning Man messiah contest. With his cell phone and coffee. *Ska-week!* says the Buddha.

This make Sammy laugh. "You are not understanding. Buddhism, real Buddhism, is only the teachings. Man, woman, rich, poor, cows, monkeys — same-same. Everyone enlightening. Everyone compassioning. Not looking at the Buddha, looking only at the teachings."

I nod toward the monks prostrating before the Buddha statues, foreheads to the ground. "Okay, whatever, man."

Sammy's eyes twinkle. "Always are using rational mind. Very good, Mr. Ian. This is also Buddhist teaching."

The afternoon shoot is a little "same-same." Same crowd of grabby kids, same bemused-looking adults.

The straws are similarly uninspired and repetitive, though probably not for folks who've never seen them. I'm antsy because there's so much more to see — the monkey temple, the rat temple, the main burning *ghats* — but fatigue gets the better of me and it's nap time. This time the boys disappear from the guesthouse. When they return we go out for dinner to a restaurant recommended by both Sammy and Manoj. It has silverware, tablecloths and tilapia on the menu.

"There's no fuckin' way I'm getting fish," remarks Lars.

I smile. "Didn't you see them washing vegetables?"

His face drops.

They ask about the Deer Park, if they should do a shoot there. I tell them there were monks, it might be inappropriate. "Besides, after Egypt I'm kind of spoiled for monuments. It was mostly just ruins."

They glance at each other.

"Listen," says Barry, "this isn't going to work. Don't get me wrong we appreciate all you've done. The itinerary, the research, trying to learn the language…" For a moment I think he's going to cut me from the project.

"Don't worry, it isn't the light," says Lars. "It's just that the people here all look the same — in a cultural way, same clothes like in Rishikesh. Besides all the saddhus and temples and funerals? It's too crowded, man — like you said, inappropriate."

"Crowds are bad," confirms Barry.

Our *thalis* arrive but they scarcely register. *Are they ready to leave Varanasi after only one day?*

"So… what do you want to do?"

"Rajasthan," says Barry. "While you were asleep we

went into a bookstore."

Inside a coffee-table book entitled *Faces of India* they'd seen pictures of turbans, mustaches, mirrored cloth, a Medieval-looking castle in the sand dunes called Jaisalmer — from where we could camel-trek into the desert. To be fair, the trip doesn't sound all that bad, plus would entail a few days in Jaipur, the carbonized heart of India's gem trade where I could learn all about emeralds and sapphires. Still, Jaipur is a long way from Varanasi, the City of Shiva, surrounded by death. Away from Manoj's connections and Sammy — though I'm starting to burn out on Uttar Pradesh. The filth, the smog, the chill, the cramps...

"When are you thinking of leaving?" I ask.

"I'm thinking a first-class sleeper tomorrow." Barry fans out train tickets. "See? I take care of people."

It's New Year's Eve and while the *Experience* avoids other tourists as a point of pride, they admit it'd be nice to drink booze, hear a DJ, chat up some girls and watch midnight fireworks. Sammy — dialed-in and casually westernized with his real-looking, fake-leather jacket and Levis, tourist girls batting him eyes in the restaurant — takes us to a speakeasy, rooftop New Year's Eve party. En route, we stop at the Government Bhang Shop, get in line with the college kids, tour guides and saddhus. At nine o'clock they open their shutters for one hour. Through heavy iron bars, we buy legal marijuana biscuits.

They're heavy and taste of molasses and sawdust. We have to drink water to choke the things down. Within half an hour I'm sorry I did — face down on a table at the back of the disco. I'm rousted by a couple of dolled-up, Hindi girls who sling me unwillingly onto the dance floor where, to the sound of Kula Shaker's, 'Govinda' I bust a few moves of my octopus break-dancing.

Laughing with? Laughing at? Same-same, crowd goes wild.

Afterward, sweaty, but back in control, I step out to the roof for some air and find Lars.

"Those fuckin' bodies, man — this place is intense."

"You want intense? Let's go down to the *real ghats*."

Sammy, leg-locked with a blonde, Scandinavian girl, gives me directions: two lefts, then a right. Lars and I slip out the back into an alley. I have no beef with Lars. In fact, I quite like him. A couple of times I've caught him gaping at the poverty, taking pictures of things that don't involve straws. Privately, I think he's thrilled to see the world but, as a company man, can't let on. Barry had literally plucked him from obscurity — a Fotomat in Rochester complaining about his prints. The guy's shooting Aunt Trudy's second wedding one moment and traipsing across Africa with new lenses the next.

We get a bit lost but follow the firelight, find stairs to a platform overlooking a burning *ghat*. Here, there's no need for little girls with iron tongs — it's a huge, haystack bonfire with a body on top. The ritual cloth has all burned away, leaving a charred but distinguishable corpse. Not fully grown, a young boy I would guess, one hand curling skyward as if clutching an orb. The heat drives us back then recedes. We inch closer. A bare-chested man in a *dhoti*, sitting lotus, looks up, nods and goes back to mumbling prayers. Below him, below the bonfire, the stairs disappear into black, turgid water.

Lars, his eyes bugged, can't stop staring at the body.

I pile it on thick. "They call it the eternal flame. Four thousand years and it's never gone out. They keep little hearths of it burning somewhere."

"How come there's nobody there but that priest? No family or anything?"

"Probably too distraught. Sammy says crying distracts the departing souls. Turns them into angry ghosts — that's a *kid* down there, man."

Then I clock something I should have noticed sooner: a nightclub jutting out over the *ghat*. Like the prow of a ship, on three concrete pillars, lined with pink neon, its windows blacked-out. The pulse of trance techno reverberates the glass. I'm reminded of my dream about the genie electricity, how before humanity learned to rub sticks together, lightning was to fire what father is to daughter. The fire seems like it's *straining* to reach the nightclub while the neon is seemingly taunting the flames. Gloating, perhaps, like it has the upper hand —

Pop! With a shower of sparks, the skull cracks.

January 2, Pink City Express

"Guys, wake up. This is it, we're in Rajasthan."

I hear someone trying to force-close a zipper.

"Get your shit together, you two. I'm going to be hell if this train starts to move."

I roll over and notice Lars busily packing, boxer shorts bunched at the top of his jeans. The train has stopped but I can't hear a station.

"Get up," he says, sharply. "Just *look* at those fields!"

A filthy, white sock tumbles off the bunk above me.

Barry groans. "Jaipur's in another three hours."

"Forget Jaipur — just look out the window."

"Alright, just give me a minute. My head hurts."

I vaguely recall the night before in Varanasi. The train had been late so we'd gobbled our biscuits. For the next several hours we'd sat on the platform, completely immobilized, laughing like idiots. The joke was a dog lying dead on the tracks being picked at by rats being hunted by cats while above this whole food chain a fresh-painted sign declared *Indian rail prides the nation, Cleanliness at every station.* Yeah, that was a good one alright. As funny as who could get the most flies on their *thali*. At least our hilarity kept the natives at bay. There's a healthy respect for madmen in this country.

Barry clambers down from the top bunk in his underwear, to the horror of three women sitting across the aisle. He scratches himself then goes over to join Lars.

"Jesus, that's beautiful. Where the hell are we?"

"Who cares?" says Lars. "Just look at that scene. Hey India Mon, get it in gear!"

India Mon, they've taken to calling me.

Grumbling, I pull my face up to the window.

Outside the train, under cloudless blue skies, lie acre-upon-acre of bright yellow fields. Wading through them, waist deep, several women in orange *saris* are filling their handwoven baskets with mustard flowers.

"Lars," I say, "you're the opposite of color blind. But there's no habitation, no hotels, no nothing. Maybe we get in a shoot but what then?"

"Not important," he says. "It's the shoot of a lifetime." He goes back to hurriedly stuffing his sleeping bag.

"He's lost his mind," I whisper to Barry.

"I got this," he says. "Find out where we are. We'll figure out how to get back here from Jaipur."

I walk down the aisle asking people where we're at but as there's no obvious landmarks in sight, all I receive are a few Hindu headshakes, some what-name-what-countrys and half a pomegranate. Halfway down the carriage, a train whizzes past us and after it's gone clear, we begin chugging forward.

"Noooo!" I can hear Lars howl in the background.

Remember Neel Kanth? Call it karmic retribution.

Midmorning we roll into Jaipur, the Pink City, put on fresh t-shirts and pack away our fleece. The air inhales clean, warm and dry here in Rajasthan, a welcome change from Varanasi's dirty, cold and wet. The usual chaos awaits on the platform: legions of ticket touts, baying for blood: "Hotel-want-restaurant-come-stay-best-gem-shop!" We stride through the station: "*Nain, baba, nain!*"

The temperature's nearly a hundred degrees. We grab the one driver not paying attention and, while the jackals shout curse words behind us, take to the streets in his yellow, three-wheel death can. For the next ninety minutes we hurl around Jaipur, trying to find a room during some kind of trade convention. Lars glowers behind his sunglasses the whole time, the grind of heavy metal pumping out of his Walkman.

By noon we're settled at the Maharaja Guest House,

sipping tea in the garden on padded, wicker chairs. I'm learning that getting around India is hellish — but heavenly once you actually *get* somewhere. After we gripe about being served Lipton in a country with cities named Assam and Darjeeling, Barry wonders aloud if there's time for a shoot. I tell him have fun as I'm going gem hunting. The prospect of wearing precious stones appeals to me, of carrying the burden of wealth on my fingers. Of reminding myself every time I look down how privileged I am to up sticks and go wandering.

"India Mon, at it again," says Barry. "Good luck in finding the *stones of prosperity*."

I push myself back from the table. "You know what? To paraphrase a Buddhist proverb —"

"Oh goody, another one."

" — a person who ignores the divine is like one who returns empty-handed from a land rich in precious stones and *that* is a grievous failure. Enjoy your Lipton."

Rajasthan: home to the warring Rajputs, the Mediaeval-knight clans of the Indian desert. Their history is full of incredible battles over who can build the biggest fortress or grow the biggest mustache. Jaipur, as the capital, has both features aplenty, arising from dark, craggy faces and hills. Being homeless and unable to grow a proper mustache, I see my stay in Rajasthan as being good for my character.

The Pink City's buildings are indeed painted pink, though tastefully peachy rather than shocking, and the streets, though congested, are broad, tree-lined and teeming with colorful turbans and *saris*.

I'm curious about the fortress looming over the city,

its ramparts reflecting in an artificial lake.

"A classic example of Rajput architecture," says *The Stupid Guide*, "which impresses despite its inchoate gigantism."

As I stand on a corner trying to get my bearings, declining offers of film, fake watches and real peanuts, a child surreptitiously starts shining my boots — the pedestrian equivalent of a bum washing your windshield. While I'm stood there, a camel gets hit by a bus and, while I ponder the matter of insurance, a man with a soup-strainer mustache approaches: "Good day to you, sir. That is quite the predicament."

His clipped English accent throws me a bit with its unsubtle hint at the reign of the raj. He looks to be in his mid-to-late thirties, wears a collared white shirt and pleated tan trousers.

"Good day to you too, sir," I say. "Jolly good. What service do I have the pleasure of refusing?"

He snorts, unamused. "Let me ask you a question: Why don't tourists talk with the Indians?"

It's a line straight out of the guidebook's scam section, right next to "buy booze for my sister's wedding."

"Because all I have to do is walk down the street and everyone's jumping out trying to sell me something. Good people, bad people, people like you — I'm in a new city and everyone's coming at me."

"But you look at the buildings," he counters. "The temples. You see the Pink City but what do you see? When you go home to tell your friends about Jaipur what will you say of its people, its history?"

He's got me there. I know jack from Jaipur, minus the little I've read in the guide.

"I'll just have to see how it goes, I guess. But give me a break, baba G. I just got here."

The kid at my feet spits into his cloth, wipes it around and asks for ten rupes. I point out a scuff on my heel, snap my fingers. When it's all good and polished I give him a twenty.

I return my attention to the con-maharajah, who seems rather well-off to be harassing backpackers on street corners.

"You Americans are most suspicious of all," he says. "I just want to talk and still you don't trust me. Invite you to join me for lunch, that is all. I enjoy showing visitors the charm of my city."

We're standing on a curb in the heat of the day, he's local, seems friendly, I am kinda hungry, I *do* want to get to know India's people — yet no-one has ever said that in the history of Los Angeles.

"Let me ask you something, Mr...?"

"Vishy," he says. "No mister, no baba, no G. Just Vishy."

I shake his hand and introduce myself.

"Alright, *Vishy* — how would *you* feel if you were in America, you didn't speak the language and every time you took a step, someone came up to you wanting your money?"

He mulls it over a moment and shrugs.

"If I were in America, I'd be very lucky."

Vishy grew up just outside Jaipur, went to college in London, has a degree in mineralogy, is writing a book about mining in Rajasthan and tells me Jaipur has five thousand gem-cutting factories. As we share our life stories in a crowded café, dipping fresh *chapatis* into hot, curried eggplant, I decide to trust less in the little blue bible — and more in the intuition that brought me here. *Then again who's to say Vishy isn't a con-artist, that my food isn't drugged — no one knows where I am!* — a sweaty paranoia which sinks to my gut and identifies itself as last night's Government-sanctioned marijuana biscuits.

"And you — are you here for business or pleasure?"

I try and act casual. "Little of both. Today I was hoping to look at some emeralds. How 'bout I buy lunch then you point me in the right direction?"

At this, Vishy looses a great, booming laugh, says something in Rajasthani to the cook who laughs harder. "You were on your way to Johari bazaar. Those scoundrels will rob you far worse than any pickpocket. Yes, perhaps later, we can talk stones but *I* will pay for lunch. That's Jaipur hospitality."

He orders us sweets — delicious, raw-honey-things — and afterward, ushers us out of the café, pauses for traffic, and leads me across the street... directly into his family gem shop.

Oh, how very slick these Rajasthani jewel traders, ambassadors of their mid-level merchant caste, Vaishya. Vishy's hustle impresses me more than his mustache which, being eight inches wide, is saying something. After a round of milk *masala chais*, sipped while his nephews fly kites on the roof, we retire to a red-velvet showroom downstairs and recline amid gold-tasseled pillows on the carpet. Here, Vishy lays down a white handkerchief, magnifier, forceps, and a brass, handheld scale. He opens a briefcase filled with tiny manila envelopes and, with a flourish, raises the window shade. A sunbeam falls perfectly onto the handkerchief creating a diamond of light in which to browse. The approach, the lunch, the kites, now this sunbeam — it is, on the whole, a most excellent seduction.

For the next two hours, chasing the sunbeam across the floor, I learn how to handle and value an emerald. The telltale feather-like inclusions of synthetic stones; which faults occur naturally and give a stone character. He coaxes me to go with my heart, to appreciate color and feel as well as clarity. He tests me by mixing up several emeralds and asking me to grade them according to quality.

"When a gem-trader sees you have patience," he says. "Maybe he lets you keep some of your money."

By the time the sunbeam is climbing the wall, I feel confident enough to reveal my intentions, the stones I'd been shown by the Rishikesh palm reader: an oval yellow sapphire and a rectangular emerald.

Vishy twirls his mustache. "Yellow sapphire, very rare." He uses the forceps to resegregate the stones. "You come back day after tomorrow, same time. If you like what I find, we can take them to the gem-testing center."

"Two days? But I might not be here by then. I'm travelling with a photography crew."

"Patience, my friend. To buy gems, must have patience. Since before dinosaurs these stones wait for you."

Back on the streets, feeling vaguely dissatisfied — *I'm buying the fruits of incredible pressure yet the man selling them applies absolutely none?* — I make my way toward the Johari bazaar and get swept away in a street celebration. An ornate Krishna temple has opened its gates. In a heartbeat I'm wearing a necklace of marigolds, setting my freshly-shined boots in the courtyard and chanting *om-hare-Krishna-hare-Ram-hare-Krishna*. It's refreshing to walk on the cold marble floors, being welcomed, included and jostled by the crowd — so unlike a synagogue, mosque or church — both part of the fuss and unsure what it's about.

The crux seems to be an interior shrine. An old woman says it's been shuttered all year. We all circumambulate thrice, holding hands. I'm made to eat sweet rice and get daubed with holy water. When the bare-chested priests with the red-painted faces fling open the shrine doors the crowd whoops and gasps. I glimpse the top of a gold figurine. The crowd surges toward it with palpable excitement. It's a *murti* of Krishna playing the flute, his head poking out of a mountain of flowers, surrounded by figures of courtesan dancers — gargantuan breasts, tiny waists, beehive hairdos. *Send to me one of your milkmaids*, I pray, tossing my marigold necklace to the priest. He winks at me, dangles it off Krishna's flute arm. I'm marked with a *tika* and swirled back into the foyer.

There's a holiness here I can't put my finger on, and all this silly ritual is just a facade: the flowers, gold leaf and repetitive chanting both distract from, and inform of, the existence of God. It's the mushroom conundrum all over again, that moment which seems to confound my every trip: on the brink of discovering the secret of the universe, the wallpaper moves or my foot starts to itch. With these thoughts in mind I encounter a plaque with a quote from the *Bhagavad Gita* in English. As the only white face in a sea of brown bodies, I can't help but wonder if it was placed for my benefit.

It is without and within all beings, it reads, *and constitutes both animate and inanimate creation. By means of its subtlety it is incomprehensible; it is both at hand and far away.*

A few blocks from the temple I enter an observatory created by Jaipur's founding father, Jai Singh. It's an oddball collection of stone sculptures and instruments built to measure star positions and calculate eclipses. I learn the word *gnomon*, "the style of a sundial", which makes me irrationally happy. After that, I fall-in with a band of Aussie yahoos and proceed to the City Palace to browse the royal armory. We eat curry and chips inside the palace grounds, pounding Cobras while the sun disappears into the smog. At the Johari bazaar I learn that my afternoon with Vishy has made me an expert in spotting emeralds beyond my price range. Nobody has yellow sapphires, however — the one from Rishikesh remains all I've seen — but the hunt rejuvenates me with a new sense of purpose: to find and acquire the *stones of prosperity*.

It's well after dark by the time I return, exhausted and grimy, to the Maharaja Guest House. I find the Silly Straw boys on the roof, drinking Coca Colas, plugged into Walkmans.

Lars sets his headphones down on the table.

"India Mon," he gushes in welcome. He looks to be baked halfway out of his skull. "Barry and I were worried about you — thought maybe you'd gone and set yourself on fire."

I tell him not yet — though I appreciate his concern

— and ask if they managed to get into Jaipur.

"Nah, we pretty much kicked it here," says Barry. "I was illin' pretty hard with my stomach."

A gust of hot wind nearly blows Barry's cap off, bringing with it first smell of burning meat I've had in weeks.

"We're getting up at five again tomorrow," says Lars. "Hire a Jeep and get back to those mustard fields."

Lying in bed a half hour later, watching Barry restock his holsters with straws, I remember how Jaime had wanted to go to Rajasthan and start to leak tears I can't talk about with anyone. I feel suddenly lonely out here in Jaipur, sharing a suite with the *Silly Straw Experience*. I wish I could capture the exhilaration of that Krishna temple and carry it around in a bottle, like frankincense. As a balm for the soul I take out my rose oil, apply a few drops to my chest, throat and forehead. Some chalky, red grit comes away on my finger — India Mon is still wearing his *tika*...

...I stand on a gigantic, inchoate fortress overlooking Jaipur, under a galaxy of stars. The gnomon of a moon-dial tells me it's midnight. A hot, desert wind nearly blows me off the ramparts. Nearby is a window, the flicker of candles. I creep my way toward it on rough, yellow stone. I'm barefoot, bare-chested, clad only in jeans. An Indian pan flute is playing a *raga*. When I reach the window and peek over the sill, I find the most beautiful woman inside bathing — like a nymph come to life from one of the temples, waspy waist, dark brown skin, jet-black hair, breasts like melons. A wet, orange *sari* hangs loose around her hips. She's standing knee deep in a polished, copper urn, dragging a sea-sponge over her breasts. Her nipples spring back. I feel myself harden.

She seems to be staring directly at me — but does she see me or her reflection in the window? She steps from the urn, walks backward to the bed, then sits down, knees apart, with her heels under her labia. I spot a loose cobblestone down at my feet. Glance left and right down the ramparts. They're empty. I pick up the stone, test its weight in my hand then send it crashing into the windowpane. The woman makes no move as the glass shatters down. She remains supine, half-smiling on her elbows. I climb through the window. The *raga* gets louder. When I reach her bedside, it rages in crescendo.

Her eyes pull me in just as much as her hips — daring, suggesting, insisting I enter. I open my jeans, cup her neck in one hand and, while still standing, *Om-hare-Krishna-hare-Ram-hare-Krishna...*

January 4, 1998, Jaipur

There's a scene in *Raider's of the Lost Ark* where a Capuchin monkey lies dead on the floor.

"Bad dates," says Dr. Jones' companion, pointing to the half-eaten fruit in its claw.

Now, eating dates at Vishy's cousin's clothing factory, haggling over the price of a neckerchief, I suddenly flash on that scene from the film — followed by a questioning clench of my stomach. Still, the blue neckerchief clashes terrifically with the bright-orange, long-sleeved *kameeze* I've just purchased — along with some flowing, white, tie-at-the-top trousers.

"What do you think? Do I look Rajasthani?"

Lars shakes his palm at the platter of dates. "More

like *Goofasthani*. Please don't wear that back to the hotel. Barry's still pissed about what happened yesterday."

Yesterday was a complete disaster.

We got up at five as Lars had insisted, hired a taxi, explained what we wanted — and got stuck in a queue for an hour buying petrol. Missed the whole sunrise. Lars went mental. While we waited, our driver brought us some tea which he poured from a repurposed motor oil can. At the end of the day, when we needed motor oil, the mechanic poured it into the car from a tea kettle. In between, through a series of misunderstandings, we'd gone to a whorehouse next to a mustard field, followed by a mustard field next to a whorehouse. Sunset we spent in some podunk police station.

In hindsight, it makes perfect sense why my gestures and restaurant Hindi hadn't translated:

"*We want to photograph women in traditional clothing, sucking on Silly Straws — yes, we can pay them.*"

Barry had made a few straws for the girls, all of whom refused to go into the fields. They wouldn't change into their finery either, didn't want to be photographed yet still demanded payment. The cops had shown-up for whatever reason — commotion, or called by the hookers themselves — and after an evening of third world corruption we returned, rupees lighter, to the Maharaja Guest House.

Our problem is a shared Hindu-Muslim practice called *purdah* where women are forbidden to associate with unrelated men, often to the point of being locked in their houses. To put it politely, a baffling custom. This morning for instance, in another small village, we'd approached a few lovelies in pink, with gold nose-rings. They'd run from us, terrified, dropping their baskets, shepherding children and calling for their husbands. Lars sagged in defeat while watching them flee, then resigned himself to photographing men with huge mustaches. It's obvious now if we'd gotten off that train, our subjects would have scattered like doves through the mustard.

At least I'd been able to sneak off to Vishy's and go to the gem-testing center with my stones: a Colombian emerald as green as new willow and a local sapphire in lion's piss gold. All I have to do now is set them in rings but for now they're tucked away in a sandalwood stash box. Jaipur though, has not been kind to the *Experience* and I think I'm about due for another one of Barry's talks.

Back at the guesthouse we gather our gear, head to the restaurant and reunite with Barry. I'm unhappy to find he's ordered us dinner as I'm feeling lightheaded and nauseous already. I force myself to eat some plain rice while Barry informs us the night train is full which is why, in one hour, we're taking the night *bus,* which takes all of thirteen hours to roll into Jaisalmer.

"Excuse me," I say, getting up from the table. I remove my blue neckerchief and drape it over the chair.

"What's up with India Mon?" Barry asks.

"Bad dates," replies Lars. They both bust up laughing.

A friend of mine, Robert, who'd traveled through India gave me some pointers before I left. The one I remember verbatim was, "You *will* puke in India. No doubt about it."

As much as I'd wanted to prove the guy wrong, I knew even then he was speaking the truth which explains why I'm currently doubled over in a flowerbed screaming, "Fuck you, Bob, fuck you!" through the puke. Shivering, I weave my back to the restaurant, the knees of my *dhoti* stained green from the lawn. Change back to a t-shirt and jeans in the bathroom.

"Are you going to be okay?" says Lars.

"*Koi bahd nahim.* No problem."

The first bile goes over the side of the auto-rickshaw. The dry heaves begin at the entrance to the bus station. The bus driver snorts — he's seen this show before — and offers me a *bidi* as if it were medicine. Shaky, spun out, feeling worse than real bad, I stagger toward a landfill across the parking lot. Halfway there, I'm approached by a blonde English nurse, a posh bird named Karen, who'd been talking to Lars.

"You sure you're up to making this trip? It's thirteen—"

"Back off, I know!"

She backpedals. "We saved you a seat by the window. Your fingers are filthy — stop gagging yourself."

The enamel of my molars dissolving with bile, I hack my way back to just before lunch. Wiping my lips, I take a moment to look around and *appreciate* where I have come to throw up. There's six people crouched on six stacks of tires, streaming shit ribbons into the empty holes. There's a cow with a festering gash on in its udder. There are pigs nosing chunks in a oily cesspool. The place is, for puking, in a word, inspirational. India never fails to provide. The ancient, blue government bus honks its horn. I thrust up my chin and — knowing

I'm not finished — nod to the driver and make my way inside.

The passengers are an equal mix of Indians and Westerners. The bus is chock-full save a seat next to Barry. As soon as I'm seated, we pull onto the highway. I pepper my hellos with preemptive apologies. Across from us, Karen and Lars share their histories, already sharing a blanket — dude moves fast. I apologize for being sharp with her earlier. She looks away, red-faced, and says she understands. Without further ado, I open the window and wring my intestines out like a towel — facing forward and having to time every mouthful, lest I lose my head to a branch or lamppost.

On perhaps my best effort, I dodge a tractor-trailer and manage to puke on an unlucky dog. After that, I fall back to my seat in exhaustion. Barry, impressed — like he should be — applauds. What have I done to deserve such bad karma, other than having bad thoughts and bad dates? The fact we're now scanning for women *and* children, assuming the profiles of pedophiles *and* rapists? Or maybe it's the sense of revulsion I feel watching children get greedy and grab for the straws, the annoyance when their parents insist on *baksheesh*, the fact my enthusiasm for this country is wearing off...

Mercifully, Karen gets the bus to pull over. I run down the aisle, out the door and into the bushes. Drop my trousers and shoot a wet pancake into the dirt. Nothing to wipe with. More puking. Convulsions. Barry and Lars confer with one another while the driver and other passengers have a smoke break. There's no light for miles, aside from the highway.

I'm dying, delirious. "Everybody out, two exits!"

"You want to go back to Jaipur?" offers Lars which,

at the time, I find very sweet. He's been so uptight and obsessed with the sun lately. This cute, English nurse might be just what he needs.

"No, that's okay. I'll be sick wherever. On the bus, in the cab. We might as well move. Besides, I got eyes for that French girl behind you."

Lars pats my back. "Major trooper points," he says.

I feel a bit better, have a mouthful of water, clean up with a handful of Karen's alcohol swabs; apologize to the driver in Hindi — which produces some shouts of delight from the Indians. None of them seem all that bothered by the delay, though many a white, western tourist is grumbling. I assume people running off of busses for medical reasons must happen all the time. Their patience is comforting.

A elderly Rajput with a canary-yellow turban leans forward and offers me an anonymous, white pill.

"Good every kind trouble!" he says. I accept and swallow the thing without question.

"Where are you from?" asks a woman in a headscarf.
"California."
"Oh, you sick from the smack?"
"No, just something I ate." I smile weakly.
"He's sick because this is India," says the pill man.

January 5, Entering Jaisalmer

Once a wealthy Rajput trading center on the camel trails between Asia and India, the fort-city of Jaisalmer was hit hard at Partition by the cutting of trade routes between India and Pakistan. Its economy was revived by the Indo-Pak wars which proved its strategic worth as a military base — a historical explanation for my jarring awakening by the twin sonic booms of Indian warplanes. It's a frightening way to come-to on a bus as you rumble along an accident-strewn highway but once the jet noise subsides without violence I'm suffused with small pride at surviving the ride.

Outside the window, in the late-morning sun, a Medieval fortress rises into view. The Golden City it's also known as, for the color the sun imparts on the sandstone. It's a gorgeous fortress, hulking and proud, perched on a hill like a single, gold tooth. Around it, stretches the barren Thar desert, a shimmering expanse of scrubland and sand dunes.

"A city plucked straight from *A Thousand and One Nights*," Karen reads from the British edition of *The Stupid Tourist Guide*. "Unspoiled by tourism and the presence of the military... romantically reminiscent of ancient Afghanistan." She lowers the book and adds, rather Britishly, "What a complete load of shite."

In 1980, the city of Jaisalmer had three hotels to accommodate backpackers. Less than twenty years later: two-hundred-twenty.

"Christ, will you look at that mob," mutters Barry.

The bus rolls to a halt under a date palm, next to a tumbledown roadside café. There's at least two touts for every passenger — a shouting, turbaned mass of My-Hotel-Come-Stays — along with a squadron of uniformed cops wearing arm-bands reading *Tourist Protection Squad*. A couple of them even carry rifles.

"Now I know how it feels to be a rock star," says Lars.

The time to make a decision is *now*, to choose a hotel and stick to our guns. Barry decides on the Swastika Guest House on the premise of avoiding all

Germans and Israelis. The Swastika's also inside the photogenic fort as opposed to below, in the ramshackle town. Despite running on vapors, I offer no resistance. My sole aim in life is to eat a Saltine cracker and keep it down. Karen decides to tag along with us — at least until we arrange our camel trek — so with Lars at the point we pocket our guidebooks and proceed through the touts in a delta "*Nain Baba*" pattern.

"Everywhere full! Changing money? Camel trekking? Five rupees, go anywhere! My guesthouse TV!"

The Indians filter unmolested into town.

"No clean inside fort! Many ghost! Too expensive!"

We hike up the spiraling, steep, tarmac access road, surrounded by touts, sweating buckets, swatting flies until we enter the fortress' signposted *No Harassment Zone*. A phalanx of guards let us pass because we're white. Immediately I get a second wind: it's a place of haunting, military majesty, an eight-hundred-year-old castle of stone with cylindrical turrets, gap-toothed double ramparts and slits to rain arrows on infidel armies. Beyond the front gate is a cobblestone alley which purposefully winds to the top of the fort. We pass under stone arches high enough to pass camels then orient ourselves to the map in the guidebook.

After a few minutes bumbling down cul-de-sacs, past bric-a-brac shops and the Jain Sambhavanthji temple, we manage to locate the Swastika — flags flying — precariously perched atop the western ramparts. A drainage pipe has recently burst, meaning puddles of sewage outside the front door but other than that the place seems well run and Barry is particularly fond of the decor.

"Nothing like neo-Nazi graffiti to make my Jewish friend here feel at home."

There's an awkward moment when the manager, Kopak, a tall bearded man in a preppy-pink robe, announces he's either got two ensuite doubles or one room, with four single beds, in the dorm. Barry grits his teeth. Karen stares at her shoes. We leave it to Lars who decides on the latter. Barry calls whatever bed is closest to the bathroom.

While our room is swept-clean and supplied with fresh linen, Lars presses Kopak for details on camel trekking. Kopak assures us his guides are the best and ready to leave the following morning, if necessary. Lars makes him swear, on his family honor, to get us to places with no other tourists. Barry breaks out the promotional stills. Karen, uncertainly, flips through her guidebook.

"And what if we do it by Jeep?" asks Lars, after Kopak says camels go four miles an hour.

Kopak looks up from the map, "Also good."

Barry bobs his head. "We'd cover more ground."

On the couch with my pack, like an upside-down turtle, I'm further exasperated by the *Experience's* mentality. The thought of us Jeep-blasting village to village seems completely at odds with an aesthetic sensibility.

"We need to slow down to capture the desert. It's just going to be paint-by-numbers in a Jeep."

"We're not here for pleasure," Barry snaps suddenly. "We're not on vacation, remember? Image gathering?"

"You want me to write about the *International Silly Straw Experience*? Well right now it comes across pretty pathetic."

Barry knits his brow. "What's that supposed to mean?"

"It means you're not going to like what I've written."

An uncomfortable silence descends on the office. Kopak rattles keys attached to a piece of wood.

"Should I leave?" says Karen.

"No, you're cool right there," says Lars. "It sounds like *India Mon* has the problem."

"You're right," I say, hauling myself to my feet. "Let's do it by helicopter, carpet-bomb India." I reach out to Kopak who hands me the room keys. "As long as it's all about the children I'm cool with it."

I awaken refreshed, raw-throated and hungry; tentatively eat a Saltine, keep it down. Karen and Lars are both asleep next to me, their beds pushed together, touching at the forearm. I rise and peer out of the narrow, stone windows — archer slits cut in the fortress' walls. The view extends over the castle-side trash piles, past town and airbase, to a desert mirage.

I find Barry alone in the rooftop restaurant, his table pulled flush with the ramparts, without his cap. On the roof of the more-happening guesthouse next door, twenty tourists sit underneath Pepsi umbrellas.

Barry jerks his chin. "*La wai*," he growls, using the Chinese epithet for foreigners. "This place is a fucking major *la wai* town. At least they serve decent coffee."

He kicks a chair out from under the table. I sit down across from him, pick up a menu. We watch two jets land on the airbase's runway. From above, the yellow-brick town looks like a rabbit warren.

"Is Lars awake?" he asks offhandedly.

"Nah, he's crashed out with the nurse. Is that a problem?"

"I hope not, man. I really hope not."

I gently restrain him from lifting his cup. "So, what's the plan for tomorrow?" I ask.

"We're taking a Jeep to *get* to the camels."

I release his wrist. He raises his coffee. "Oh, and later? Like out in the desert? We should have another talk about your role in the project."

I exit the Jaisalmer fort around five, the afternoon sun warm and kind on my skin. Mapless, bookless, two gems in my pocket, I'm on a mission to find Vishy's schoolfriend, the jewelry-maker.

"*Do you know Ram?*" I ask Indian strangers, the equivalent to asking "Do you know God?" It's a query that elicits strange looks, Hindu headshakes and, from the holy men, sly, knowing nods. While browsing stringed instruments for sale on the sidewalk I notice a smart, yellow sign on the fortress: *Government Authorised Bhang Shop* it reads. I order a Bhang Ginger Tea for my stomach.

"*Do you know my friend God?*" I ask the vendor, an unshaven man in a poorly-buttoned shirt.

He puzzles at me like he can't place my face. "Yah, he live other side Patwon Ki Haveli."

I drink the tea with my back to the fort, keeping a paranoid eye on the streets. There's major *la wai* traffic, too many hippies, black-socked-sandaled Germans, click-happy Japanese. It's Heisenberg's uncertainty principle come to life — you can't observe something without changing its properties. *What did those two-hundred-seventeen hotel owners do before our aesthetic transformed their economy?* Jaisalmer town is a maze, a cow burrow, a place to get lost, disappear down the back streets. The *bhang* intensifies my search for Ram, who lives on a row of stone merchant-mansions called *havelis*. The buildings' facades contain intricate carvings of many-armed deities posing in *mudras* — postures symbolic of divine lessons but for tourists they're sculptures out posing for pictures.

"Where is God? Where is God?" I shout at the foreigners.

"*Where is my jeweler friend, Ram?*" I ask street urchins. For the first time since Delhi, I'm out of control and the *bhang* is so strong it burns my eyelids.

A red-turbaned *saddhu* sits begging on a stoop in front of one of the more impressive *havelis*.

"*Ram?*" I ask. He indicates his brass begging bowl. The wheel is the wheel and *baksheesh* is the grease.

I throw down twenty rupes. He points across the street to a blue, plastic sign reading *Ram Krishna Trading*. From there it's a matter of choosing my ring design and promising stacks of Monopoly money: nine grams of gold, a fifth of my budget, which leads me to wonder how far I can stretch it. It's the first time I've asked myself this since I left. My heart quails: *when will I have to go back to America?*

I hoof it back up to the fort for sunset, the sky erupting with purple and orange clouds. Above me, the turrets, the ramparts, the temple-tops — every last brick has been touched by King Midas. I race through the Swastika to retrieve my camera, through the lobby, up the stairs and kick open the door. Two startled faces look up from the bed. Lars' is clean-shaven. Karen's is upside down.

"You're... you're going to have to leave," says Lars.

I cover my eyes but too late, seeing all.

"For crying out loud, you could have thrown the lock."

"And you could have knocked — *Jesus, get out of here!*"

Upstairs in the restaurant, I find Barry moping in front of the greatest sunset on earth. He's wearing headphones and playing a game of solitaire, using the ashtrays to weigh down his Bicycles. About fifty people are up on the rooftops, cooing and snapping the alchemist sun. Even the natives, who've seen thousands like it, seem genuinely impressed by tonight's epic meltdown.

Barry pulls the headphones around his neck. "Did you go into the room?"

"Sure did," I reply. "*Coitus interruptus*. I wish they would have just gotten a double."

"That fucking guy has no class sometimes."

I shrug. "At least he was wearing a condom."

A pregnant pause then we both burst out laughing. The sun dips below the horizon to applause.

January 6, Jaisalmer

Sitting outside the government *bhang* shop, waiting for Kopak to arrive with the Jeep, Barry and I watch, detached and from a distance, while Karen and Lars say goodbye holding fingers. He's wearing a camera bag over one shoulder. She's in a flowing, peach robe, hat to match. The wind nearly blows off her hat but he catches it.

"Welcome to the *Castles of Rajasthan County*."

Unshowered, unshaven, bleary on *bhang*, wearing the same shirt he's worn for six days, Barry sets his *lassi* down on the table and casually dubs in the couple's conversation.

"Karen, my darling, you know I can't stay. The desert calls and there's war in Pakistan."

"I know, my sweet prince. And my work is here. These people must learn to make chipped beef on toast."

Lars swings his camera bag out of the way, wraps up the toe-headed nurse with one arm. He parts the peach veil trailing over her hat brim.

"Oh, Lars, don't go!" Barry moans in falsetto, perfectly timed with Karen's lip movements.

Lars sets a big, meaty paw on her shoulder.

"I wouldn't, but for one thing, my darling. You were a one-night-stand. You mean nothing."

With that, they embrace and we turn them our backs. Barry takes a bow and I give him a golf clap.

"Been a while since you got laid?" I ask.

"Ages." He rubs his bald spot. "Fuck-ing ages."

It's nine a.m. at the *Government Authorised Bhang Shop*, and the grizzled proprietor's already high. As I sip my strong *lassi* in an effort to join him, I read the disclaimer on the back of the menu:

Do not anticipate or analyze, must enjoy. Bhang cannot compare to sedative alcohol, will not make fall off elephant turn you into orange and you will remember most of your experience in the morning.

Barry takes out a tape-recorder and tries to interview the government weed dealer: What is *bhang* exactly?

Where does it come from? Why is it legal to eat but not smoke? The g-man is cagey, Hindu headshakes, won't let us photograph or Xerox the menu.

I peruse *The Stupid Guide's* section on camel treks which recommends all trekkers supplement their food. Barry and I purchase fifteen *bhang* "coukies" accordingly. They come in two types: driver and passenger. When our man Kopak arrives with the Jeep — overflowing with blankets, water bottles and crates of food — we squeeze our pared-down belongings inside and help tie a camel saddle onto the roof. Lars gives Karen a last kiss goodbye then hops in the passenger seat promising to write. When she's safely out of earshot, disappearing into dust, he confides he's never written a letter in his life.

"One hundred fifty kilometers," says Kopak as we spiral down the road to the fortress. "Tourist only allowed *sixty* kilometers. You listen camel driver. I not have permit."

"As long as there's no other tourists," says Lars. "Otherwise no tip, understand? No *baksheesh*."

"You no see tourist," Kopak mutters darkly, adding something unintelligible in Hindi.

I suddenly realize that *I took a nap* while Barry and Lars negotiated this trek and now we're racing west toward the Pakistani border, ninety kilometers from the Tourist Protection Squad. Do bandits still roam the Thar desert at night, slitting traveller's throats with their jewel-bedecked knives? If so, would they mind being photographed with Silly Straws? Or trotting out their women in traditional *saris*?

The terrain is dead flat, mostly hard-pan and pebbles, some low-lying shrubs and abandoned mud dwellings. Three-hundred-sixty-degrees of mirage. The sun is relentless, still climbing. Demonic. We bump through the desert for almost three hours, unloading to cross every sandpit in first gear. No seat belts, no maps, no compass, no roads and a driver whose face shows no sign of recognition. We continue until every vertebrae is pulverized, until my tobacco has spilled on the floor and right when my kidneys are about to shake loose, we pour in more gas and go fifty klicks more.

Finally, like a basketball bouncing into view, a cluster of huts appears on the horizon. Kopak's bearded frown splits into a smile. There's a red-turbaned man coming forward to greet us.

"See, no worry. This Mr. Nigel. You listen what he say, nothing bad happen."

We spill from the Jeep in a cloud of fine dust, blinking our eyes in the terrible sunshine.

"You wanted three days?" I shout over at Lars. "That was four hours, man —you're fucking nuts."

He grins, puts his hands on his knees, coughs a dustball. "Four hours on a camel, man, then you can talk."

Mr. Nigel, our camel guide, looks about thirty with a chalk-eraser mustache, red turban and green flak-jacket; ballooning white trousers tied with a sash and — unlike us with our hiking boots — flip-flops. The beasts of burden appear from the village: five of them led by a gangly, young boy. When they reach the Jeep, the boy raises a leather switch, taps his shoulder and makes kissing noises.

The camels pitch forward, then back, all at once. Come to rest on their knees. We eye them suspiciously. They look almost twice the size of a horse. Do they bite? Do they spit? What do they eat? What do I know about camels, by god, except they can go a long way without drinking? It appears that these are the one-humped variety, they live in the desert and, um, they're mammals...

The camel nearest me cranes its head back, lolls out its wet, bulbous tongue and starts gargling, a noise not unlike a septic tank draining. My first thought is, *Great, the poor creature is dying.*

"Oy!" shouts the camel boy, raising his switch. The beast slurps its tongue back and blinks at him bashfully.

"Camel smelling female," the drover-boy explains.

Dying or horny. I'm not sure what's better.

Our gear is offloaded and distributed atop the camels. Blankets are sloped into cushions on saddles. The boy indicates which three are for riding and motions for us to choose our mounts. Barry chooses first, takes the youngest, fittest camel. I take the tongue-gargler. Lars gets the third. We dangle our daypacks off the saddle horn, swing our legs over — and find there's no stirrups.

"*Huh-huh-huh!*" the camel boy grunts. The beasts cantilever, hind-legs first, to their feet. The motion pitches us forward, then back, effectively smashing our balls into the saddle-horns. The boy jogs over and hands us the reins which attach to wooden pegs through the camels' nostrils. Having spilled all my nerve-calming smokes in the Jeep, I bum a *bidi* off Mr. Nigel.

"This camel garbage." He pats its neck.

"You mean it's no good?"

"No, Garbage his name." He proceeds to Lars' camel and tightens the saddle. The New Yorker clutches his groin with both hands.

"This one Rocket," says Mr. Nigel. "No kick too hard, otherwise much jumping."

"Jumping?" says Lars, his eyes going wide. Mr. Nigel winks and moves on to Barry.

"This one, Mr. John Major," he says, stroking the dromedary's flank with pride. "Racing camel, very fast, you know?" He squints at Barry and covers his eyes.

"What's this you wear? You Hindu?" he asks, indicating the logo on Barry's Los Angeles Bulls hat.

"No," says Barry. "I'm a basketball fan."

Mr. Nigel chews on this for a moment. "Okay, I call you Cowboy."

We wave goodbye to an unsmiling Kopak, hoping we'll see him again in three days. It's surreal, the flat landscape, the village of nothing-fields, the children peeking out of their three-foot-tall doorways. We set off in slow motion across the hard-scrabble while the Jeep disappears in its own trail of dust. *Where are we going? What are we doing? What does anyone live on out here?*

The boy introduces himself as Ramesh. He's twelve-years-old and will be doing all the cooking. When I ask why the camels are all male he replies, "Girl camel causing much trouble, much biting." The heat bakes away my worries, good sense, until I arrive in an odd present tense where I'm riding on top of a camel named Garbage, exclaiming, "Hey guys, we're going camping!"

"Outside cities I just feel... unnatural," says Barry. "Every time I go camping I feel like an invader. Like I wasn't designed to be living out here. The animals don't want me and I don't want to be here."

Lars concurs: "Yeah, I'm New York City all the

way."

"It's a shedding process," I try and explain. "Your house, your car, the trail, your basecamp, your day pack, your clothes — you leave all that behind you. You bathe in a stream at ten thousand feet? A few days of that and you never felt so natural."

We ride for forty-five minutes in silence while Ramesh in his flip-flops walks alongside. We're moving at half the average human walking speed — a trade-off you make for being twelve feet high.

"Mr. Nigel, how do you make camels go faster?"

"You say, 'Son-of-a-bitch fucking camel' and kick it. Not doing now. Desert too hot for running."

At the end of a stretch of rock-strewn, xeric plain, we reach a curtain of spindly acacias — trees with appreciable amounts of DMT. Without warning Garbage steers straight into their branches.

"Hey!" The thorns pierce my jeans, drawing blood. He's scratching an itch, his tongue lolled with relief. Mr. Nigel shouts, "Pull very hard on rope! Say, 'Son-of-a-bitch fucking camel, no do that!'"

"Son-of-a-bitch fucking camel!" I jerk Garbage's nose pegs in opposite directions. He comes out of the acacias looking shocked, as if to say, "Who me? I wasn't doing anything."

We draw to a halt at the base of more thorn trees. It's a hundred degrees and the heat of the day. Ramesh takes the reins, brings the camels to kneel then spreads out some blankets for us in the shade. Lars asks Mr. Nigel what the plan is and can we get into a village by four. Mr. Nigel, who doesn't wear a watch, tells him we're not going to move for the next two hours. Too much heat isn't good for the camels' huge hearts so our movements will tend toward the mornings and evenings. Irritated, the *Experience* takes out their promotionals. Explain that *these* are times we need to be in villages.

This is all news to Mr. Nigel who'd only been told to take us away from the regular tourist track. Regardless, the afternoon sun is too brutal to do anything but eat passenger coukies.

As we lie on the blankets, surrounded by moonscape, something suddenly clicks for Lars.

"This is about the whole process, isn't it?" He blinks at the desert. "We're slowin' it down."

For lunch, Ramesh prepares curried cauliflower, *chapatis*, fried macaroni and chai. Everything is cooked over twigs and dry dung. The *chapatis* are actually laid on the fire.

"Nothing like eating off a piece of burning shit," says Barry. "Anyone want me to piss in their tea?"

"You gotta admit it's pretty impressive," I say. "Considering what he has to work with."

"I hate camping."

We help clean the battered, tin cookware with sand — which we've come to refer to as vitamin S — and after the temperature dips a degree, we saddle-up and continue our trek, heading west. We ride for two hours across the desert, either trotting or walking depending on terrain. I can't imagine the heat here come summertime, seeing how hard it's baking in January. An immense stretch of sand dunes rises in front of us, a Saharan-like expanse of rippling, yellow hills. This, we learn, is to be our first campsite. Looks like dinner will be vitamin-enriched. At the base of the dunes lie a few simple houses and just enough light to pull off a shoot.

We unload the camels, get clearance from Mr. Nigel and, while he and Ramesh gather twigs, the three of us strike off toward the village on foot.

The mud-brick houses, built low to the ground, glow gold like the Jaisalmer fortress at sunset. At the center of town lies a small, shaded well surrounded by empty, wire pens full of goat droppings. Some children approach us, barefoot, in shawls. The houses are shuttered. No adults in view. Barry's heat tongs come out and the children run toward him. They call to each other in a guttural language.

Barry hands out a few basic corkscrews and soon we're surrounded by two dozen children. Lars breaks out cups, Kool-Aid packets and water bottles. Barry sculpts a camel. The children leap for it. I don't like the vibe though, the grabbing, desperation, the conspicuous lack of adult supervision. The older kids notice our watches and cameras. I sense the mob is about to go feral.

A man in a shawl and a loosely-wrapped turban comes out of a hovel. I notice he's drooling. He weaves through the goat pens, eyes crossed, jabbering "baba."

"Mental midget, two o'clock," Lars shouts, which is accurate.

The guy shuffles bowlegged, knocking into children, bouncing his way up to Barry like a pinball. He snatches a purple and green chambered nautilus. We're in Rajasthan's version of East Appalachia.

We've taken it too far…

"Aaack! Guys!" Barry is besieged. "They've got my battery-pack, get them off!"

He tosses a handful of straws in the air. The mob momentarily surges away from him. A dirt-caked young boy gets run down in the melée, skinning his elbow. He starts wailing miserably.

"Where are your mothers?" I shout at the horde, the valve between larynx and brain deteriorating.

Lars keeps his face on the viewfinder. "Good question. Keep your eye out for the orange *saris*."

My Hindi is useless, wrong dialect or something. The mental midget runs up, I offer a handshake but it isn't enough: he wants my gold earrings. He gropes for my face.

"*Nain, baba, nain!*"

Meanwhile, Barry has given up sculpting, he's fighting back kids with his smoldering tongs. No one is posing but Lars keeps on snapping, more children come out of the woodwork. It's chaos. I'm certain the women are watching behind curtains, their husbands out tending the goats in the fields. It's time for a premature Defcon 1 Get Away but there's nowhere to hide in this place. I feel fear.

The children encircle us, jeering. They've got numbers. We back toward the sand dunes calling for Mr. Nigel. A few of the kids are still sucking Silly Straws which makes them appear to be eating huge insects — it's a tough place to be on a passenger coukie. If I had a handgun I'd probably start shooting.

Barry and Lars seem merely annoyed.

"Now you know what it felt like in Africa," says Barry.

"No way," Lars shouts back. "Africa was worse."

Mr. Nigel appears at the top of the dunes, followed by a bug-eyed and dumbstruck Ramesh.

"Help us," I cry. "Make them go away!"

Mr. Nigel trots down and yells at the kids, picks up a

stick to threaten the stubborn ones. Soon they're all running hellbent toward the village, waving their Silly Straws, whooping and hollering.

Barry unplugs his heat tongs. "Good shoot?"

"Nice lighting," says Lars. "Cute kids but no women." He rewinds his film and starts packing away lenses. "Still, that was probably our best shoot in India."

I blink at them both in disbelief. "Are you fucking kidding? That was a disaster. We've moved beyond bizarre into sick."

"Oh, you haven't begun to see sick," says Lars. "Wait 'til the kids start to fist fight — *that's* sick." He reloads his film, makes a mark in his notebook and zips up his camera bag, cool as an ice cap.

Barry makes a sad face. "Awww, look at that. India Mon is starting to crack."

I bite my lip and stare at the horizon. He's right. I'm trembling. I can't take much more of this.

"It happened to Barry in Sobibor," offers Lars. "Happened to me with that parasite in Madagascar. Sooner or later it just gets too much. Both of us have broken down crying in public."

Mr. Nigel returns, palms spread but still smiling. "Cowboy!" he says. "What you are doing? Tonight we have many children, much sneaking. Every day you do this, morning time, afternoon?"

"Every day," says Barry with not a little pride. "Every day for three years around the world."

He does a quickdraw into his holsters and showers us all in a hail of colored straws.

January 7, Thar Desert

I sleep like a bubble trapped under a stone, rolled suddenly free and straining toward the surface, a gurgling mirror getting larger and larger until — I open my eyes to the smell of my own crotch sweat. Our wool saddle blankets have doubled as bedding. There's sand in my boxers, sand on my tongue and, for eternity, sand in my dreadlocks. As I lie here and scribble, fearing the day ahead, I'm urged to get up, get dressed, load my camel.

"Sunrise in thirty-five minutes," says Barry. "Mr. Nigel says it's an hour to the next village."

"This is why we have Jeeps," mutters Lars.

I piss the word *Relax* in the sand, steam coming off it because of the chill. Teeth chattering, I put on some jeans and a t-shirt. In an hour I'll want to strip back to my boxers. Mr. Nigel, I discover, has short, jet black hair which he sets about covering up with his turban — six feet of wet cloth to be wound about his head like a triply complex, spiraling Windsor knot.

Ramesh has made breakfast — *chapatis*, jam and peanut butter — washed down with piping-hot goat's milk *masala chai*. The boy went into the village this morning, milked the goats himself and gathered wood for our fire. While we eat, he jogs off to round up the hobbled camels which have shuffled a few hundred yards away. I'm looking forward to riding again, despite my sore haunches, to put distance on yesterday.

Before saddling up, we eat passenger coukies and Barry makes straw necklaces for everyone's camel. The beasts don't seem to mind the colorful additions and it does make our caravan look rather festive. On Mr. John Major, he places a crown with curly antennas over each ear. Mr. Nigel and Ramesh roar with delight and we set off across the desert in high spirits.

When the sun appears, Lars grows visibly tense. I spur Garbage into a trot to avoid him. We ride north across the plains until we come to a bluff. Below, lies a village surrounded by nothing fields. We urge our mounts down a narrow footpath, a terrifying ordeal for all creatures involved — pitching and yawing, our luggage swinging wildly. I cling for dear life to the creaking saddle horn. When Rocket's straw necklace gets tangled in the reins, Lars makes the mistake of trying to remove it and it's a bad idea to neck-stab a camel picking its way down a rocky embankment. The jab sends Rocket charging to the prairie where it engages in what the experts call "much jumping." Ramesh, who's on foot, runs ahead clucking while Lars, his limbs flying, rides camelback rodeo.

The reins are grabbed and Rocket calms down.

"No more Silly Straws on my camel!" shrieks Lars.

We catch up to him, snickering, bring the camels to kneel. Barry promises not to make any more necklaces.

"This Muslim village," Mr. Nigel explains. "First I go talk, you no straw-making."

"Ask about women in *saris*," says Lars. "They drink from a straw, we give them *baksheesh*."

We put on our sunglasses, slather with sunscreen, prepare cameras and holsters then walk into the village, leaving Ramesh to look after the camels. The village is wealthy by Thar desert standards: firm, adobe houses, wooden doors and red paint. The children are clothed and many wear shoes. A few of them come forward for confident handshakes. A gray-turbaned man sits atop a low wall, *bidi* protruding from under his mustache. He greets Mr. Nigel and summons him over. The two of them chat while we hang back and fidget. After a while, Barry is given the okay. He clicks on his tongs and begins making sculpture. Blue, yellow, brown; flowers, animals, spacecraft. Lars prepares cups of Kool-Aid as usual.

When I ask for a toilet I'm waved into the scrub, which is how things are done here: fully exposed. I add to the desiccated turds on the hardpan, partially hidden by a shifting wall of goats. The village has only thirty residents and Barry decides to make straws for them all, to make infants drink Kool-Aid through red double helicoids; to pay turbaned men to suck Superman soccer balls. Within half an hour all sentient beings, including a good many goats are accessorized with colorful, hard-plastic novelty drinking straws — all sentient beings, of course, except women.

And look, there they are, peering over the shoulders of men stood in doorways, like rare birds in cages. Bedecked in pastel-colored *saris* and headscarves, wearing all the family's wealth in gold bracelets and nose-rings. One of the women has striking blue eyes which I manage to catch through the half-open door. She's clearly intrigued. We ask, but no dice. To be photographed? By unrelated men? For *baksheesh*? Like whores?

"India Mon, move out of the background," says Lars. "Mr. Nigel, ask him to drink on my signal."

I bum another *bidi* off Mr. Nigel. It sits me down hard in the dirt with the goat pellets. Children approach me, grubby hands outstretched, sensing the show is about to be over. Soon they're stuffing their straws in their houses and running back to Barry, begging for another…

Back on the camels, heading further afield, a gun shot rings out from the village behind us. The kids who've been chasing us halt in their tracks and sullenly return to their strict, Muslim households. I'm angry, uncomfortable, slugging warm Kool-Aid, mumbling in French about Roman fucking gladiators. Garbage's necklace has gone soft in the sun. I break and remove it, put the remains in my pocket. Soon it becomes too hot to ride and we look for a place in the shade to rest. Ramesh spots a grove of acacias nearby. We follow him toward it, wilting in our saddles.

Turns out we're not the only ones seeking refuge inside the thorn trees' meager patch of shade. There's two teenage boys, barely older than Ramesh, watering some goats and a bearded, hobbled donkey.

The boys rush to greet us, accost Mr. Nigel. I catch the word *straw*; our reputation has preceded us. We bring the camels to kneel making kissing sounds: Rocket and Garbage and Mr. John Major. The goatherds notice Barry's Los Angeles Bulls hat, run up to him shouting: "One straw! One straw!" Barry takes his hat off, wipes sweat from his brow.

"Is there too much light for a shoot?" he asks Lars.

Photo Man — as Mr. Nigel has dubbed him — appraises the sun, says, "Traditional robes. I should be able to do something with a filter. Take your time, man. Make something far-out."

I dismount and lean against Garbage's flank, gratefully accept Mr. Nigel's proffered *bidi*. Barry's heat tongs get hot in no time. He begins crafting two of his most intricate creations. The end products look like the virus illustrations from out of my college biology textbooks or, with a little imagination, bubbled-out submarine probes from Atlantis.

"Is the blue too much with the sky?" asks Barry.

"Nah, it anchors it to the horizon," says Lars.

"Those are the best you've made yet," I admit.

"Thanks, man. Soft plastic is easier to work with."

The goatherds accept the straws with huge smiles. Seem proud to drink Kool-Aid and pose for the pictures. While Lars shoots, Mr. Nigel chops strange-looking vegetables and Ramesh sets off across the scrub to find firewood. When the *Experience* is done, all the tools put away, Barry and Lars flop down on a blanket. Still holding their contraptions, the goatherds approach, thrust out their hands and demand reparations.

Annoyed, Lars shoos them away with his boot heel. "Get lost, you little punks. Goodbye! *Namaste*! You'd think getting crazy-ass straws was enough."

Mr. Nigel says, "These boys do anything for fifty rupees."

Barry sits up on his elbows and snorts. "The only way they're getting fifty rupees is if they have sex with that ugly-ass donkey." Lars and I glance at the mangy, hobbled beast and, our brains warped by the *bhang*, bust-up laughing.

The goatherds, however, want to know what's so funny. Their ears perk up at the mention of rupees. "*What do we have to do?*" they inquire. Out here, fifty rupes is a whole lot of money. Impishly, shrugging eyebrows, Mr. Nigel explains the straw sculptor's offer of cash for bestiality. Right away, the older kid wants to see the money while his scrawnier friend backs away, looking horrified.

"You're kidding me," says Barry. He unzips his

money belt. "All I got's hundreds. Anyone have change?"

"Nope," says Lars. "You've got all our cash."

"Fuck off. Don't even *think* about asking me."

Barry flips through his cash wad again. "Aw come on — it's not worth a hundred." He frowns dejectedly, asks me why not.

"I'm not paying some kid to have sex with a donkey!"

"Fine." He digs through the rest of his pockets, produces a few crumpled bills and some change. "Mr. Nigel, tell him I've got... thirty-four rupees but he has to put his banana in *the whole way*."

"Holding straw?" says Mr. Nigel.

"Of course," says Barry.

There's a moment of silence. A bit of nervous laughter. We look from Mr. Nigel. To the goatherd. To the donkey. I have a Cartesian moment: *Is this happening? If so, what is the nature of reality?* Mr. Nigel translates Barry's offer to the goatherd who immediately comes over and inspects the money. Still holding the Atlantean space-bubble straw with a blue that anchors it to the horizon, the boy ducks behind a thorn bush for a moment then comes back around and approaches the donkey. At this point I probably should yell "Stop!", pay the kid off, give the *Experience* a lecture but instead I melt deeper into Garbage's shadow. The boy takes his place on an overturned milk bucket.

The beast's pointed ears go up in surprise then it goes back to nibbling a shrub. One thrust and it's done. Barry and Lars howl with laughter and the goatherd withdraws his maybe, please-be, thumb.

Lars puts his camera away. "Got it," he says.

Barry forks over his less-than-a-buck. The other boy starts rousting goats with a stick.

"Cannot believe that just happened," I manage.

"Kid's gotta be at least eighteen, right?" says Lars. He glances around for reassurance. There is none.

"Best money I've spent in India," says Barry.

The goatherds exchange a few words with Mr. Nigel then beat their livestock toward the next patch of shrubs.

After dinner, around a small fire, Mr. Nigel regales us with stories of past treks. Lovers quarrels, dying camels, apocryphal dust storms — but mostly he wants to talk about sex. He's a man of the desert and ruggedly handsome but his mentality's that of a horny teenage boy. He's unmarried, eager to sleep with Western women and keen to know more about one-night-stands and pick-up lines. Barry, who once made a study of pornography as part of his bachelor's degree in psychology, is delighted to engage our aspiring Lothario in what amounts to a cultural-taboo-exchange.

"In America, women have sex with machines. They fill them with batteries and use them for pleasure." He illustrates this with a handy carrot, greatly amusing Ramesh, to my discomfort.

Mr. Nigel, however, becomes deadly serious. "This machine is no good. Woman use, no need man. You send woman with this machine to Rajasthan — plenty of real banana for them here."

Thus encouraged, Barry explains tele-dildonics: special underwear combined with computer-generated porn, meaning virtual sex with all manner of orifice.

Mr. Nigel frowns as he struggles to grasp the

concept. "In desert, we have donkeys and goats."

It takes him a while but he paints the whole picture: with women's virginity heavily guarded, homosexuality sometimes a capital offense and masturbation said to cause madness, bestiality is a common, though unspoken practice — especially amongst adolescents.

"Have you ever had sex with a donkey?" asks Barry.

"Once," he says. "When I was teenage."

We're camped on an expanse of sand dunes again. It feels like there's Vitamin S in my lungs. I try to bum a *bidi* off Mr. Nigel but he's run out of smokes and I feel a twinge of panic. Lars, however, to my amazement, produces a hardpack of unfiltered Camels.

"I carry them around to give away as gifts. Fuck the ethics. Give the people what they want."

I've never been much for big-brand cigarettes but gratefully take one and light it with a twig.

Barry shakes his head. "Harry Buds smoking Camels. Never thought I'd live to see the day. Wait 'til word gets back to the States. What are all your vegetarian hippie friends going to say?"

"And what are all *your* friends going to say, buddy, when they hear about you paying an impoverished goatherd to have sex with a hobbled donkey?"

"Hey, it was probably only his thumb. Besides, you saw him. He did it *theatrically* — sometimes things just degenerate, man. These are some seriously backward-ass people."

I take a head-clearing drag off Camel. Mr. Nigel gets up and starts clearing dishes. Meanwhile the real camels, silhouetted by starlight, gargle their tongues and nibble acacias.

"What are we doing here anyway?" I ask. "Barging

in, making straws, hardly stopping for tea. The kids don't have time to do anything *but* grab. All we did today was inspire people's greed."

Barry sighs tiredly, scratches his neck. "Well, sometimes it's like that. Other times we *do* stop and have tea. You're not in a position to judge the *Experience*, man. You've only been travelling with us for a week."

"And how long were you making straws in Tanzania before you called the whole continent the most pathetic place on earth?"

"Alright, so what are your impressions, Dr. Buds? What would it look like — your intro to the book?" He wriggles his rear in the sand to get comfortable.

"The novel? *The Techno-Pagan Octopus Messiah*?"

"Careful now, don't have a flashback."

Lars shakes his palms between Barry and me. "Look, we just want to know what you're writing — we already know about you and the Serpent."

"Oh, but it goes beyond that — well beyond. DMT and the Serpent were only the catalysts." I produce the amethyst out of my bag, lean forward and rotate it over the flames. Its facets reflect both starlight and embers. "See, after I found this, I took it to India. There, I met a holy man named Naga Baba who gave me a *lingam* to take to Neel Kanth, only I freaked-out and got swept away with... the *Stolen Explorer Lawn Flamingo Project*."

Barry and Lars throw looks at each other.

Lars leans back, smiling. "Go on, make it good."

Ramesh brings us chai and lays down by the fire, adds a few spindly pieces of firewood.

"Now, the *Stolen Explorer Lawn Flamingo* — which

I'll hereby refer to as SELF," I begin, "started as a prank by this high school friend of mine who ripped-off his neighbor's pink flamingo lawn ornament. He was loading the car to go skiing or something, just swiped it off the guy's lawn on a goof. Sitting around having cocoa in the ski lodge, he got the idea to take the flamingo on the slopes. He took a picture of it, right? Standing in skis, wearing ski-goggles and a mask. Posted it back to his neighbor with a caption reading 'Having a great time in Aspen'.

"Well, all his friends thought this was hilarious. He took the flamingo to Europe that summer, posed it in front of the Eiffel tower, the tower of Pisa, the Tower of London. Now my friend is seriously loaded, okay? He's got this, I don't know, Bar Mitzvah trust fund. Decides he's going to make a coffee-table book and take the flamingo to all the world's wonders. He's never been out of the country before and all this travel is blowing his mind. Probably, secretly, he just wants to see the world, but that's something only hippie seekers like to do and the SELF project makes him more serious than *those* losers."

A night wind picks up, sending sparks in the air. I realize I've been talking to the crystal. Looking up, I find Barry and Lars swirling their cups. Ramesh slumbers peacefully.

"Are you done?" says Barry.

"Almost. See, dude's grandfather owns a publishing company, guarantees him his book will see print. He hires marketers, a photographer, even yours truly. Funds the thing past all sense of proportion. He starts seeing the world through flamingo-shaped glasses — people become mannequins, countries become backgrounds. He's determined that everyone, everywhere pose with it: hookers and holy men, nevermind the consequences. What started out as a jokey urban legend becomes a sort of artistic commercial and, in my mind, SELF becomes a metaphor for America spreading its pink, plastic culture.

"Only *now* I'm supposed to be part of the project and write how Indian kids love the flamingo — a flamingo stood next to a sodomized donkey and stopped being funny long before India. It probably stopped being funny in Africa where people said, 'Fuck the flamingo, we're hungry.' This is probably also around the same time they stopped sending photos back to that neighbor guy. See, to me the real story isn't about the flamingo, it's about the two guys taking it around the world. Did they do it for fame, for money, for art? Like I said, it's a cultural metaphor."

Barry throws back the dregs of his chai, fixes my eyes across the fire. "Is that how you're going to write about us in your novel? The flamingo thing instead of the straws?"

"Nah, the flamingo thing doesn't quite work. If I'm doing Silly Straws, I'm doing Silly Straws."

Lars glances at Barry. "All I gotta say is Barry's straws are *original*, man, not some bullshit pieces of plastic. And everywhere we do a shoot? I get pictures of people smiling — thousands of them."

"Lars, no-one's saying the straws aren't incredible — or that people don't smile when they see them, they do. Or that your photos aren't amazing either — but the *story* isn't about the straw sculptures. The story, at least from where I'm sitting, is you two."

Barry rocks to his feet. "Well let me tell *you* a story, okay? About this friend of mine I knew back in college. He was a biology major who wrote a column about growing and smoking hydroponic marijuana. He started experimenting with this fucked-up super drug on the advice of the author of the *Magic Mushroom Grower's Guide*. Then he went to this naked hippie drug fest where someone convinced him he was the Messiah. He smokes more super-drug and decides he's a serpent who's somehow now *gracing* the earth in human form. He flies to Egypt to find a magic crystal and starts taking dream-altering malaria drugs.

"The next time I see him he's staying at a yoga ashram, all hippied out with dreadlocks and shit. He's putting on oils, praying at Shiva temples and spending the last of his money on emeralds. I try to reach out to the guy, bring him back. Give him a chance to get paid for his writing. But Silly Straws in India aren't funny enough. He wants more than that, he wants his own religion." He flash his palms. "Listen man, it's late. We've been on the road for what feels like forever, we're tired, we're miserable, we want to go home. The last thing we need is a spiritual lecture from *India Mon* about some fucking flamingo."

Lars stands as well and moves closer to Barry. "Those stones you bought, man? *Slave kids* cut those. It's not like they popped all perfect from the earth. You act like you're fucking above it all."

Barry frowns and kicks at the sand. "If you're the Messiah then what's your message? Isn't a Messiah supposed to have a message?"

"I don't know," I reply, feeling suddenly unsure. "It's not like there's a guidebook showing me what to do. A messiah, I think, saves themselves plus one person."

"What-the-fuck-ever," says Barry. "Keep looking."

Mr. Nigel returns with more wood for the fire. He covers Ramesh with an extra blanket. Sensing the tension, he produces a corked liquor bottle. "Good for gas." He doesn't say whether relieving or producing.

The bottle is full of horrible palm wine, replete with fibrous chunks of debris. When it's empty I stagger out into the dunes and drunkenly piss the word *Quest* with a question mark. Returning to the fire I find Barry and Lars have moved their bedding to the far side of camp. My time with the *Experience* appears to be ending. Looks like I'm not going to be writing funny captions. What I need to do now is get back in the saddle, back on the camel and back to the real story. The one that I'll have to start over tomorrow, as if I just landed, from the beginning…

VI. BEGINNINGS

January 9, Jaisalmer Fort

Lying back on a gold-tasseled pillow on the balcony, sipping an iced, ginger tea laced with *bhang*, I observe the comings and goings of the restaurant as reflected by low-hanging, miniature disco balls. There's a half-dozen tourists reclined at low tables, writing postcards, reading guidebooks and eating early dinners. At the bar sits an Englishman wearing a clip-on, joke turban and a t-shirt reading *Vincent's Asia Tour '98*.

I rub my hand over the faux-Persian rug and gaze through the balcony's railings at Jaisalmer. Far below me, a government bus sits at idle, discoloring the air with a plume of black diesel. My heart goes out to Barry, seat thirteen, the same seat I'd puked from on the ride up. I left him there over an hour ago — after slipping a packet of Imodium to Lars — complaining about something he'd eaten for lunch.

This morning, Lars told me, they'd gone on a shoot. Kopak had arranged for a woman to model — or, rather, a man in an orange sari hiding a proper Rajput mustache under his headscarf. Barry apparently did not find this funny, stalked out in disgust, did a sculpt in the street, got mobbed and assaulted, had a rare, violent freakout and accidentally kicked a small child in the face. Next thing, the *Experience* was running for their lives, trailing a mob of angry Rajasthanis and it wasn't until they were safe inside the fort that Barry discovered one heat-tong was missing.

When the bus pulls away, heading east across the desert, I poke my head over the railing and wave. From Jaipur they'll be taking the train to Calcutta and finally a flight, transiting Berlin, to LA. If anyone needs to go home it's those guys. Hello and goodbye my compatriots. *Namaste.*

I order half a papaya in Hindi, eat it with a spoon, including the seeds. Paint my toenails a fabulous, beetle-wing green and, while they're drying, admire my new rings. One has an emerald, square cut, no inclusions, one is a slightly-chipped, oval, yellow sapphire and the last, my late grandfather's simple gold wedding band, removed from his cold, dead finger by the coroner. *We are all rich in this restaurant friends, we all have the taste of yellow gold in our teeth — no point in hiding it beneath a dirty backpack. We are all rich by virtue of us being here.* I roll up a joint from a new pack of Drum, generously seasoned with the last of my hash. A striking young couple soon motions me to join them, both with blue eyes and blonde manes, deeply tanned.

"*S'il te plait*, share your smoke?" inquires the woman.

Their names are Bertrand and Monique Montpelier. French-speaking Belgian schoolteachers, just married, on honeymoon, and *itching* to discuss the ethics of camel trekking. They're recently back from three days in the Tourist Zone which they claim was overridden with trash and souvenir vendors. They tell me they felt *"comme voyeurs"*, like poverty watchers, pockmarking the dunes with their cat-holes and campfire craters.

"Trust me, it could have been worse," I assure them. "Things can get ugly out there in the desert."

The Belgians don't press which is probably for the best. I ask them how long they've been together.

"*Six ans,*" says Betrand.

Just like me and Jaime.

How long before my heart doesn't ache at the slightest reminder she didn't come with me? She and I used to sit like that, touching at the shoulders. We used to bird-whistle to find each other in crowds. We used to engage single travellers for sport, just like the Belgians are doing to me now.

"*Alors, voyages-tu maintenant?*" asks Monique. She pinches the joint like a fine-china teacup.

I drum my fingers on the table. "*Bon question.* All I know for sure is I have to leave Jaisalmer."

I explain how the queue at the bank had been monstrous, how purchasing gold would have used all my cash, how I'd asked a young jeweler named after a god if he'd like to barter, perhaps for my camera. All at once, the young shopkeep — let's call him Ram-esh — confessed that his wife had lost interest in sex and before I could have second thoughts on the matter I'd promised the world in a bottle of essence.

"Rose oil from Egypt and ylang-ylang — not cheap."

"This works?" says Monique.

"Who knows? I read somewhere it might. Whatever the case, he'll know by tomorrow and I'd rather not get thrown out of the country."

The Montpeliers fall about roaring with laughter. At least it appears I've endeared to new friends. They tell me they're leaving for Pushkar in an hour and, if there's room on the bus, I should join them.

And what do you know, there's one seat left on the night bus to Pushkar which leaves in one hour: seat thirty-four, behind the two Belgians and next to a lovely and slender young tourist girl. She wears an earth tone, hemp-and-cotton chemise, has long, russet hair just as straight as her posture, pale, freckled skin and a pink, sunburned nose. She's the hot girl-next-door to a cornfield in Iowa.

"Are you French, then?" she asks in an Australian accent, derailing my whole Midwesterner theory. She must have overheard me talking to the Belgians.

Monique whispers, "*La jolie jeune fille te donne un compliment.*"

As the bus rolls away from the Jaisalmer fort, I feel like a seed released from a pod. At the mercy of the wind, being blown somewhere new, across the gold desert and into mirage.

The girl next to me is named Melanie, from Melbourne, a former ballerina for the Australian ballet. Twenty-two, she's recovering from career-ending foot surgery, absconding to India on an open-ended holiday. I ask if she's travelling alone, fingers crossed. She tells me she's meeting her sister's friend in Pushkar — and hanging out with the redhead up front in the meantime.

"The girl with the lumberjack snore and two seats?"

"Valium," says Melanie. "I took two myself. You can buy them here right at the chemist — would you like some?"

"Sure," I reply, feeling game. "What size?"

"I think these are twenties."

"You mean as in *milligrams*?"

"I guess…" She rummages through a mirrored-cloth handbag and pulls out a bottle of peanut-sized pills. Dips her head like an apologetic swan. "How many would you like?"

"Just one, I think. Thank you."

We both settle in for a night on the road, casually sharing a blanket, no fuss. At three hundred rupees per seat, air-conditioning, there isn't a single brown face, save the driver. There's safety in numbers from guilt over wealth here. Looking around at all the other westerners I realize that *this* is the backpacker's main circuit and Pushkar might be an even bigger *la wai* town than Jaisalmer.

The Goa of Rajasthan, reads *The Stupid Tourist Guide, where shoppers can peruse the desert's finest wares. Home to the only Brahma temple in India, as well as the world-famous Pushkar camel fair.*

I'll be missing the camel fair crowds by two months and have no desire to buy any more *wares* but something about the temple intrigues me — in a nation with over a million temples can there really be only one to the Creator?

"Everybody up, this is it. We're in Ajmer," an Aussie woman's voice shouts us awake in the dark.

Ajmer? I smack at my lips. *Never heard of it.*

"Up everyone, chop-chop! Five minutes!"

The lights flicker on. We collectively groan. A German voice croaks, "But we go to Pushkar."

"Not on this bus you don't, sweetie pie. I've taken this miserable trip fifteen times. *This* bus only goes as far as Ajmer — it's a scam for the bus people to get money off the rickshaw drivers."

Rubbing the chemical sleep from my eyes, I peer down the aisle with the rest of the passengers. The voice belongs to a short, busty redhead and we're all thinking, *Who died and made you our tour guide?* Rolls of white flesh spilling out where it shouldn't but mostly between her halter top and skirt, she wears her hair bobbed and a startling amount of make-up.

Monique whispers, "*Who is zees horrible woman?*"

Melanie meanwhile stays asleep on my chest, one arm around my neck, the other on my thigh. Her hair is intoxicating, like honey and hay and frankly, the best thing I've smelled in a while.

"Melanie, wake up." I pat her on the cheek.

She flutters her eyelids and says to me, "Mama?"

I prop her against the seat. She falls back — so tranquilized she would have spooned with my luggage.

The flame-headed maven of Ajmer approaches. I dimly recall her as Melanie's companion. She grips the seatbacks as if climbing a ladder. I make a mental note: eleven hours, twenty milligrams.

"What have you done to my Mel?" she demands, staring me down with unflinching green eyes.

"Maybe I slipped something into her drink?"

"Overdid it, didn't you?"

"Depends what you like."

The woman tosses her head back and cackles. "I am Euphoria *LeGrande*, pleased to meet you. Here, allow me, you're not doing it right." She leans over and seizes the ballerina by the shoulders. "You bitch!" she bellows, shaking her violently. "Three days you made me ride that shite camel! I should leave you here with the rapist —he seems nice."

Melanie comes to with a start, disentangles.

"If it makes you feel better, I've never been convicted."

"I know you — you're the French guy from California."

"Mr. C!" cries Euphoria. "That's what I'm calling you!"

Our charter bus parks at the side of the road, in the middle of nowhere, at four in the morning. No buildings or lights for what seem to be miles, though the scrubland is lousy with pylons and high-tension wires. As soon as we step from the bus we're surrounded, as Euphoria said, by a crush of auto-rickshaws. The *wallahs* want two hundred rupees per passenger.

Euphoria wags her finger at the bus driver. "You ought to be ashamed of yourself!"

The driver grins and Hindu headshakes.

"But madam," he says. "This *is* Ajmer stop."

"Bollocks. The real station's half a mile that way."

She locates her pack, helps Melanie find hers and tucks her head under the dancer's armpit. "Bullies!" she shouts, shouldering past the rickshaws. "Come on everyone. The city bus only costs five rupees."

A few other tourists shrug and follow suit but the majority stay to haggle with the drivers.

"Zat woman, *elle est vraiment horrible*," says Bertrand. "But her friend, you like. Very sexy, I think."

"*Je m'en fou*," I say, pulling my pack from the pile. "But I do think the redhead knows where she's going."

The three of us gear-up and head after the Aussies. We crest a small rise and sure enough: there's the station. When we get there, a window on bus seven slides open.

"Over here, Mr. C!" calls Euphoria, triumphant.

We pay our five rupes, thread past all the locals and sit where the Aussies have created a tourist section — Melanie already asleep on her pack. The seats around us fill with rice sacks and children.

"What are you staring at?" Euphoria demands of a man in white, cotton pajamas and skullcap. He blushes, looks down at his feet then looks back.

"Yes, these are breasts," she says, jiggling, "and there's two of them."

With that, she sits down next to slumbering Mel and begins to chatter to no-one in particular about Planet Hollywood, Sydney, where she works, name-dropping Madonna, Demi Moore and Mick Jagger.

The bus climbs through hills which get gradually steeper, passing trucks on blind curves. The driver looks bored. My standard third world mountain terror takes over: *whatever you do, don't look out the windshield.* Nearby me, a little boy catches my eye.

I nod. "*Namaste.*"

"One pen," he replies.

And brother, right there is the unsalted nut-meat — my soul for your stuff. I give him a pencil.

We arrive in Pushkar an hour before dawn on a wide, concrete street lined with baby-blue buildings. My libido is desperate to trail after Melanie but etiquette dictates I stick with the Belgians. Lucky for me, Euphoria announces they're meeting Mel's friend at the Mercury Hotel which allows me to hug nonchalant *au revoirs.* I promise the Aussies I'll drop by some morning.

The Montpeliers and I end up at the Darshan Guest

House, a collection of terraced blue rooms with blue stairs, where my blue-painted cell has a baby-blue bed, under a poster of ol' blue-skinned Brahma. It's the first time I've seen the Creator depicted: a white-bearded Biblical god on an island. His mount is the tortoise, *darshan* a divine vision and B is for bright, blue beginnings by Brahma.

January 11, Pushkar

This morning I wake with a bulge on my lip, meaning my amorous pursuits are now over. In a week I'll be smiling through bloody, yellow crust. The virus has sensed fluctuations in my hormones. No rear-guard action can halt the advance of a cold sore, the symptoms, like herpes itself, are unstoppable. I put on some rose oil and pout at the mirror. *Unless you're in a land where anything is possible...*

Last night, I went to bed drunk on two women: Melanie and her older sister's best friend, Charlene. Physically, the ballerina embodies perfection but Pushkar is made of the substance of dreams. This is Brahma's town, home of *brahmacharya*, the vow of the Hindu ascetic, the celibate. It's also a place with a gluttonous food supply, promiscuous Westerners and fifty brands of cigarettes. Signs on the lakeshore inform it's forbidden for the opposite sex to hold hands in public — which hadn't stopped Melanie taking mine after dinner. I'm thinking this bulge on my lip must be karmic.

Yesterday had started promisingly enough, buying breakfast and narcotics with my Belgian companions. For myself, papaya muesli and three grams of *charas*

— brittle, green flakes that smoke like strong hash — while Bertrand and Monique went for vegan chocolate crepes, a marble of opium and some questionable ecstasy tablets. While we ate and got baked in the safety of the restaurant, a floppy-eared bunny begged food, licked our legs — a good vegetarian pet is a bunny for another town that's outlawed all meat, including eggs. After breakfast, the Belgians went off to browse wares and I bumped into Melanie, feeding cows in the street. She showed me the surgery scars on her metatarsals. I asked if she'd like to come with me to the Brahma temple.

The town is centered around an artificial lake, two thousand years old and said to have healing properties. The *mandir* is a blue-frosted, seven-tiered wedding cake, in mild disrepair, with a banyan tree poking out of it. After paying our respects to the porcelain *murtis* of Brahma and some of his much younger consorts, we discovered some secretive stairs at the back which led to a balcony overlooking the lakefront. There, with our brown paper baggies of offerings, we pelted each other with sweet rice and marigolds then sat side by side, trying not to laugh, forbidden to touch and dripping orange petals.

"See, Brahma is both creator and creation," I said. "The oversoul to which all our *atmans* belong and, because all is embodied by Brahma, he's also the Preserver and Destroyer by default. It's basically monotheism."

The girl had done nothing but smile at me, bashfully. She was movement and not philosophical discussion. It would go where it went, to the tune of its own music — but not there, where a stern-looking priest had just noticed us.

Afterward, we'd gone down to the water and had *baksheesh brahmins* perform *puja* rituals; break coconuts, chant prayers and affix red, string bracelets. The latter, worn by everyone, are called Pushkar passports. These, we were told, carried the blessings of Brahma, were bad luck to remove and must drop off naturally. The passports also allowed us free access to temples not explicitly marked Hindus Only.

Our foreheads anointed with lake-water *tikas* we proceeded to the obligatory *Sunset Café* which is where I met Melanie's sister's friend, Charlene, an olive-skinned Aussie with silver-tipped braids. Mel and I joined her and Euphoria at a table on the floor.

"Aye, so you're Mr. C," she said warily. "What do you know about the Monterey Bay? LeGrande here tells me you're from California."

"Well, I studied marine biology at Santa Cruz. Lived on the Monterey Bay for four years."

"Santa Cruz? You wouldn't happen to know Professor Newbury?"

"Actually, he was my college advisor —"

"He is so beautiful," said Euphoria with a sigh. She waved her slim cigarette toward the kitchen. "Just *look* at that man — but don't make it obvious. Do you think he'd mind if I used him for sex?"

I turned around and looked over the restaurant — a carpeted acre of hippies at feed — half-expecting to see my zoology prof but no, she'd been talking about one of the waiters. A Nepali late-teenage boy by the pastry rack. He had long, jet-black hair and an '*om*' symbol necklace. Charlene had reached out with a Pushkar-blue fingernail and playfully prodded Euphoria's shoulder.

"You've been staring at him for two hours, LeGrande. Why don't you bring him Mel and Mr. C's orders?"

Euphoria found this a bully idea and quickly snatched menus off neighboring tables. "Hurry, hurry. The pasta is good — or try the veg burgers."

"Veg burger and chips, please," said Mel, without looking.

"Mr. C?"

"*Saag paneer*, jasmine rice, two *chapatis*. On second thought, scratch the chapatis — *parathas*. And an iced ginger-lemongrass tea if they've got one."

Charlene had cracked up which I'd found rather fetching.

"Why do you have to be difficult?" hissed Euphoria.

"You're the one calls yourself 'waitress to the stars.' I was just thinking you'd want to impress him."

Euphoria blinked as if seeing me for the first time. "And if there's no lemongrass, what do you want?"

I grinned. "Whatever your man recommends."

And off she'd sashayed, hip by hip, across the restaurant.

"That woman has no fear," said Mel. She plucked a marigold petal from her hair, spun it around and tucked it in her diary — a perfectly studied and elegant gesture.

Charlene rapped the table. "Anyway, Todd Newberry. I'm doing my masters in micro-zoology. When it comes to invertebrates, he is the *man*."

"The guys knows his tunicates, that's for sure. You know he carries one encased in plastic on his keychain?"

"Does he now!"

"What's a tunicate?" asked Melanie.

"And the *reason* he carries one — tell her Charlene."

She leaned back and pounded her heels on the carpet. "So when people ask him what tunicates are *he can take out his keychain and show them!* Call me Charlie."

By drawing on napkins we'd tried to show Melanie how tunicates, sea squirts, which superficially resemble sponges, by virtue of their larvae possessing what's called a notochord, are directly related to all living vertebrates. When Mel tuned us out in favor of doodling, Charlie and I moved on to octopuses which I'd kept as pets since I was fifteen while the rest of my classmates went surfing or had girlfriends.

"What I find fascinating is how they communicate," said Charlie. "Color and posture and movement — even texture. It's like they *are* what they're trying to say."

"Holy shit, you've been reading McKenna."

Actually no, she'd been reading Patrick Moynihan's *Communication and Noncommunication by Cephalopods* — a book recommended to me by McKenna not two months ago in an e-mail, as it happens. I relayed to her Terence's theory on the octopus being humanity's next totem animal as their brains are arranged in a non-localized neural network, analogous to the organization of the internet.

"In the eighteen hundreds our totem was the horse because we were shaping our world with our engines. The train, moving freight over distance — you know, horsepower. The Native Americans called it the Iron Horse. In the nineteen hundreds our totem was the eagle. Fighter jets and airplanes, death from above. America being the last superpower. The next phase is all about visual communication."

"Well this is a bit hippy-dippy," said Charlie. "You're not going to talk about chakras now, are you? That bead on your neck and the jewelry's a worry, mate."

I decided to steer clear of my DMT experiences.

Our food had arrived, taking Mel's full attention — poor girl had been starving herself for a decade — and, while she groaned and tucked into her burger and Euphoria continued to flirt with the waiter, Charlie informed me, in breathless G'day-mate that a type of colonial, phosphorescent tunicate that moves through the water like a long plastic bag got mistaken for a torpedo in the Gulf of Tonkin.

"And kicked off the Viet Nam war, how 'bout that?"

After dinner, while walking the Sheilas back home, Melanie, ignoring the signs, took my hand. Did it so natural I almost hadn't noticed — and her being the loveliest foreigner in Rajasthan. There was chemistry there but I think I got greedy. I wanted the soulmate and not just the fling so after a minute of neurotic second-guessing, I'd wriggled my hand free to fiddle with my rings.

At the Mercury's gate, the girls made me promise to come back and wake them this morning at five. There's a hilltop temple a few miles away and Euphoria had a notion of catching the sunrise...

The gate to the Mercury's courtyard is locked. When nobody heeds my rattles and calls, I pick my way under the barbed-wire fence and vault myself over a glass-studded wall. In front of me stands a U-shaped longhouse with five unmarked but different-colored doors. Using my headlamp I locate the red one, knock a few times but nobody stirs. Not wanting to disturb other residents further, I return to the wall and consider my angles.

"What you want doing here now?" a man snarls.

It's an Indian guy with a meat-carving knife which, in a town full of vegetables, is preposterous.

Backing toward the gate I pick up a rock. "We don't have to do this. I'm a tourist. I'm invited."

Thankfully, Euphoria opens the red door. "It's okay, Ratu. It's just Mr. California."

Ratu lowers his knife, but keeps his gaze frosty. "Next time you sneak, tourist man, I kill you."

Euphoria yawns and goes back to her bedchambers.

The three Aussie women are sharing a double which they sleep on together, alternating the middlewoman. Their belongings are heaped in three piles around the bed. Jittery, feeling ruthless, I switch on the overhead.

"Why are you here so ear-ly?" groans Charlie.

"You made me promise to wake you at five."

"I don't recall any such thing," says Euphoria.

I grab a callused foot and hear Melanie giggle.

"I can't believe you guys aren't up yet. I almost got knifed to get you this wake-up call."

"Ratu wouldn't knife a poached egg," says Euphoria.

"Alright, whatever, I'm going to the temple." A hand shoots out and grabs hold of my shirt, another grabs my arm, pulls me down to the bed. The light is switched off and my boots are unlaced. I make a spurious effort to resist.

"Be quiet and sleep 'til a reasonable hour," says Charlie. "You're not about to make us feel guilty — and *behave*." She rattles a bottle of Valium before sandwiching me between her and Melanie.

Hours later, I awaken on the edge of the mattress to find Charlie pouting in front of the mirror. Her legs are short, though shapely and strong, giving rise to a perfectly rounded *derrière*. To further enflame me, she's up on her tiptoes wearing only some lacy silk shorts and a t-shirt. She touches her lip and winces, stamps her foot. "I cannot *believe* I'm getting a cold sore."

Simultaneously gripped by lust and compassion, I rummage my bag for the essence of rose — the essential essential for both these conditions.

"Do not underestimate the power of placebo."

Charlene rubs a drop on her lip — "Bonzer smell, mate" — slips on some gauzy white trousers and studies me.

"It's supposed to be good for the skin," I say awkwardly.

She tells me she's never met a straight man so feminine.

We adjourn to the Mercury's garden for tea, to sit under umbrellas or bask in the sun, surrounded by waxy, green tropical plants, accented by laughter, sitar music and birdsong. It's a miniature Eden contained by blue walls, centered around a sizable bo tree. Beneath the tree are hammocks, wicker tables and shade, that most precious of desert phenomenon.

Behind the tree, an orange-robed *saddhu* is quietly tending a black, knee-high *lingam*. I break from the group, approach him deferentially and introduce myself in Hindi.

The man shakes his head. "There is no need. More

people speak English than Hindi in Pushkar."

He regards me through bloodshot, brown eyes, his chin raised. I have a quick flash on the ash-covered Naga Baba. This *saddhu*, however, looks near my same age, wears a trim beard and has oil-combed, black hair. His accent is also all over the place, as if he learned English from ten different masters.

"I see you are wearing your Pushkar Passport. How much did you pay for that silly piece of string?"

"Fifty rupes — which included not one but two coconuts."

"You got ripped-off, man. You must be American."

He chuckles, returns to attending the lingam, anointing the phallus with lashings of *ghee*. He wears silver rings on each of his fingers and sports a king cobra tattoo down one forearm.

"You don't seem like your typical *saddhu*," I say.

"Why do you think I'm a *saddhu*?" He smiles.

"I don't know... the *tika*, the *naga*, your robe, the fact that you're buttering a lingam — come on, G."

"A *saddhu* is an ascetic, my friend. The rest" — he flutters his hands —"meaning nothing."

He pats himself down and produces a cigarette. "How much did you pay for the sapphire? It's worthless."

The *not-a-saddhu* goes by the name Jimmy Baba. A former gem trader and Vedic astrologer. He wants to know where I was born and what time. He asks where I'm staying; seems pleased by the Darshan.

"So this is a *gem-cutter's* flaw in the sapphire?"

He takes hold of my hand. "Yes, but this emerald is better than most. For your first time in Jaipur, I think you've done well. We often sell good stones along with the bad. For karma. It makes us feel better about ourselves."

He studies my palm, looks up at the *rudraksha* bead, asks where I got it, who told me to wear it and when I explain the whole business of Rishikesh he questions me all the way back to McKenna.

"How are you certain you saw the Lord Shiva?"

"I went to a temple and looked at the statues."

He steeples his fingers. "Where, in New Delhi?"

"Uh, no." I shuffle my feet. "Back in Malibu."

Jimmy Baba snorts — whether amused or dismissive I can't tell. Waves with the back of his hand at the Aussies.

"Which one do you fancy?"

"Charlene, although Melanie —"

"This is not a good place to chase women," he cautions. "For that go to Udaipur, honeymoon city."

Melanie leans back and tosses a grape. Catches it laughing and high fives Euphoria. I realize her profile reminds me of Jaime's.

"Funny thing, Jimmy, but less than a year ago? I planned to bring my ex-girlfriend to Udaipur. Find the right castle and ask her to marry me."

"You are a poet and a fool," he says."You get married anywhere if the love is right."

For a moment, a sense of despair overwhelms me. "I know, man. I just wanted it to be perfect. "

Rejoining the group where I'm called Mr. C, where the soft drugs and vibes of new friendship are flowing, where the ice in our smoothies is made with bottled water, where everyone's wearing a new piece of clothing... I observe the arrival of Swiss-guy Enrique:

blonde, leather bracelets and an action-figure's torso. Returning from a rave in the desert he'd helped organize. Confident. Firm handshake. Surprisingly soft-spoken.

He tells us he'd hiked to the temple this morning. "Incredible sunrise, sad you guys missed it."

I smile self-consciously, just one of the girls, with my earrings, painted toenails, rose oil and fruit salad.

"I'm going to go on a fast," announces Charlie. "And stop smoking fags. And give up on puff." Somebody scrambles to pack her a *chillum* which she expertly smokes through her fist. "And *charas*."

"There are better places to stop," says Enrique, stroking his dimpled and perfect square jaw. "In Pushkar, there's too much good food, temptation. You want to fast, you go to the mountains."

"That's not fasting, that's *starving*," says Charlie, shaking her head with a clatter of silver beads. "I'm talking about an act of willpower, getting rid of the built-up shite in your body."

She passes the *chillum* along to Euphoria who accepts it while also holding a cigarette.

"I reckon if you can quit fags around this lot. You'll never be tempted to smoke back in Melbourne."

"So who's with me?" says Charlie. She bangs the table. "We've feasted for almost three days, it's enough. Who wants to cleanse and be pure for *one day*? Mel? Mr. C? Enrique? *LeGrande*?"

Ratu appears, bearing a spiral-bound notebook.

"Sorry, love, " says Euphoria. "Please may I have chips?"

"And me," Mel says meekly. "With mayonnaise and curry?"

"One more," says Enrique.

Charlie scowls. "*I'm serious!*" She locks eyes and squints at me over the table; instantly crawls her way under my skin. "Loving the gems, white man dreads, by the way. Does that stuff mean anything or are they just... *totems*?"

Never having fasted for more than Yom Kippur — always a miserable day until Mona — I consider the chance to out-macho Enrique.

"One day? That's a cakewalk without the cake. Let's do three."

"Drinking juice?"

I shrug. "For the first two days, fine."

She extends for a handshake.

"And no smoking either, mate."

We hike to the temple in late afternoon, Charlie, Mel and myself, while Euphoria shops — she's after an elephant tea cozy whatever that is, a pair of velvet "flares" and a couple of "jumpers". The path winds its way up a conical hill to a Nepalese stupa radiating prayer flags. We find a small terrace overlooking town and spread ourselves out on a couple of blankets. Below us, the lake is an olive-green gem, surrounded by buildings of pale, Brahmin blue — the reverse of the poster over my bed where Brahma sits on an island in the ocean.

There's ten other tourists on top of the hill, a captive audience for ol' Hilltop Baba who jabbers about not spending money in Pushkar and ascending instead, through our third eyes, to the true heart of Brahma. After the sermon he passes a donation bucket, our coin has the desired effect of him leaving and while Melanie sketches a mandala in her diary, Charlene asks me what do I do for a living.

"Outdoor education. Place called Emerald Bay. I teach groups of teenagers hands-on marine science."

"And *why* does that make you so sad?" she asks.

I stare down another miraculous sunset.

"I don't know, really. The job is idyllic. Snorkeling with kids on a small, desert island…"

"And?" Charlie says, gently bumping my shoulder.

"And I don't want to go back — there, you happy? I'm tired of getting high looking over the water, wondering what else I could do with my life. I *wanted* to be a writer but then I got fancy, met this McKenna guy. Now I'm in India…"

She narrows her eyes. "Have you done a lot of drugs?"

"That's not exactly the point but sure, psychedelics."

"Have you thought about quitting?"

"Fuck, girl, who are you?"

She raises her palms. "I'm just an observer, mate."

I hang my head and mumble an apology. She reaches over and tousles my dreads.

"Not really sure where that came from," I manage.

"I think we should both quit everything together."

She tells me she'd recently split with her boyfriend. They'd partied a lot. He'd gotten into coke. Her best friend, Sandra, Melanie's older sister, suggested she check out what Australia lacked, namely culture. She'd taken a semester off to go travelling — from Kerala all the way up to Nepal. Now, halfway through, she wanted a detox.

"Plus, travelling here's a bit mental."

"You reckon?"

I glance back at Melanie, silently sketching, completely tuned-out of the whole conversation. I ask Charlie how long she's been smoking cigarettes.

"Seven years and it's bloody expensive. You know, Jimmy said you're a Gemini too — not that I'm into astrology, mind — but two marine scientists meeting in the desert?"

"It's like you're the barrier reef to my kelp forest."

She locks eyes with me and my heart does a flutter. I think hers does too until —

"That's not what I meant." Abruptly, she stands, brushes dust off her skirt. "Come on, we should go before it gets dark." Reluctantly, Melanie closes her notebook, says she has to wee and tiptoes behind a boulder. Charlie and I begin folding blankets.

"Soooooo... why should I give up cigarettes?" I ask. "Three roll-ups a day isn't really a problem."

"Because it's absolute, they're bloody killing you, mate. Why did you drop the atom bomb on Nagasaki?"

"Come on, that's not fair. I wasn't alive at the time."

"Come off it, mate. You know what I mean. The Japanese had already surrendered — or would have. Why bomb Nagasaki after Hiroshima?"

The brass bell rings in the temple behind us. She crosses her arms. I become agitated.

"Because... they started it. They bombed Pearl Harbor. It was dropped as a warning to all of humanity."

She snorts. "Sometimes you're very American. The truth, in your heart, is there is no good reason."

We descend under darkening skies back to Pushkar, picking our way down the boulder-strewn path. When I ask Melanie what she thinks about fasting, she says no big deal, she used to be anorexic.

Charlie avoids me the rest of the evening, although she does say to enjoy my last meal, trailing her fingertips over my shoulder before sitting down to teach Enrique to play the didgeridoo. Craving potatoes I order them all — french fries, *parathas, aloo saag, aloo channa* — and afterward compliment Ratu on his cooking. He gives me a throat-slitting gesture: "All poison."

"Alright, enough." I chase the man down, grab him by his apron and pull him to the grass. Wrap up and tickle him into submission.

"Not poison, not poison!"

"Next time you want to kill me, get up earlier."

Jimmy Baba appears — it's unclear where he sleeps — and starts a small fire in a barrel on the roof. I realize I haven't seen Melanie in a while so I slink off and poke my head into the Aussie's room.

I find her alone at the edge of the bed, crying. I crouch in front of her, ask her what's wrong.

"My feet hurt and I'm not supposed to take painkillers. Can I have a hug, please?"

"Course you can, darlin'."

I know the feeling of being sad in India and not having anyone around to stroke your head. I hold her a good minute longer than necessary, savoring the peach-flambé warmth of her skin. Once more I feel gripped by both lust and compassion, only this time the answer is sweet almond oil, massaging it into her scarred, ballerina feet. Wanting to go further. Not wanting to get caught. In the end she falls asleep and I slip the whole party, leaving a note saying *Hungry for tomorrow* —

octopus style, cloud of ink and I'm gone — then head back to my little blue room at the Darshan.

Riding a one-gear bicycle home, rented for a week from the hustling Ratu, I wonder which girl I'd rather make love to, in a rosewater bath, in a haveli, in Udaipur. It's the wrong thing to do because there's that stray thought and suddenly — *click!* — the power goes out, plunging the street into moonless darkness. That's Pushkar for you, the ultimate taskmaster. Now there's no time for venereal fantasies, fasting or Jaime or quitting cigarettes because right now it's all about shop carts, pot-holes and not wiping out in a pile of cow shit. I stop the bike with a fishtail skid and stand in the middle of the street breathing hard. With dead batteries in my headlamp it takes presence of mind to find my way home by light of a borrowed candle.

January 9, Pushkar

I wake up hungry and wanting to smoke, remember the fast and decide to sleep in but amplified chants — one of the *hare-hare-ram* derivatives — from a nearby temple rhythmically thunder me up out of bed. While ascending the Escher-like flights of blue stairs, I get lost and end up in a courtyard full of laundry. There, I encounter the Darshan's proprietor, a jolly-keen, bearded and plump, grinning Brahmin.

"Full power, twenty-four hour," he says. "No toilet, no shower, no *chapati* flour!"

He smiles, looking pleased with himself. I smile back. "Good to know," I say, thinking, *Brother, you are nuts*. Duck into the shower and find, while the light works, all the hot water has been used up. Emerging to shiver and drip in a sunbeam, I find the proprietor lurking outside.

I secure my towel. "Yes? Is there a problem?"

"No honey, no money, no tourist, no funny!"

"Also good to know." I quickly step past him.

After putting on *T-shirt, Part Two: the Clean One,* I placate my lip with the essence of rose then head next door to check on the Belgians. I find them strung out after two days of opium. Wild-haired, Monique says she's *mal à la tête* which literally translates to *bad of the head* and asks me to buy her a bottle of water, a bar of milk chocolate and some soluble aspirin. Heading down to the convenience-snack-plumbing-supply cart I pass the proprietor's wife in the courtyard.

"*Namaskar*," I say bowing, my fingertips touching.

"Hello, mellow yellow." She blushes like a schoolgirl.

I look down and my shirt does happens to be yellow, full-power-twenty-four-hour-no-shower can easily be chalked-up to last night's power outage but how to explain the convenience cart vendor pulling a packet of Drum from his wagon?

"Smoke, tok, choke, croak." He collapses into a fit of the giggles.

I bristle with goosebumps. "No thanks," I say warily. "Tobacco. It makes the lungs blacko. Or something."

The scent of conspiracy thick in the air, I play the Aquarius — bring the Belgians their water — then cross to the restaurant with the wannabe-dog bunny and sit down to order my breakfast from the drug dealer.

"No hurry, no worry, no chicken, no curry," he says, coming forward to hand me a menu.

"Thanks, but I've heard it before, Baba G."

He doesn't skip a beat. "So sorry."

I put down the menu and study him, frowning.

"Is there some kind of festival going on today? Everyone's acting weird — including you."

He Hindu headshakes. "Grapes... or crepes?"

I remember the fast. "No thanks, just some juice."

After taking on fluids I take to the streets, intending to clear out my head by the lake only to find the "full-power-twenty-four-hour" nonsense has replaced all the usual "You-big-*puja*-makings." I watch as a *saddhu*, smoking a *chillum* greets a Korean couple with this ditty and even though one of the shopkeeps informs me that all this is standard post-blackout protocol, I can't shake the feeling that I'm being mocked; that India's trying to challenge my sanity.

At a flower-stand next to the main Krishna Temple I buy garlands of marigolds to give to the girls then duck my head into a yoga retreat center where a potbellied, Buddha-baba asks my experience level. I tell him I'd learned a few basics in Rishikesh, my instructor was named G and I just started fasting.

"Beginners are winners, sinners eat dinners." He smiles munificently.

I decide not to ask.

The tables have all been pushed together in the Mercury's garden, under the boh tree. Jimmy-Baba and Charlie are in heated discussion while Enrique's gone totally bobo over Melanie. There are plates in front of everyone save for Charlene and it pleases me thinking we both haven't eaten. I creep forward silently, feeling invisible, until I'm standing directly behind her.

She notices me with a start. "There you are — Jimmy and I were just talking about you." She seems glad to see me but also mistrustful. Her lower lip, like mine, looks painful and bruised.

"Full power, twenty-four hour," I say. "I hope there's no sugar in that glass of juice."

"Liquids are fine, mate. Even sweetened. You haven't smoked anything recently, have you?"

"Not so much as a hit since last night." I lasso the ladies with garlands of flowers. "Have the Indians been rhyming at any of you lately?"

"No more than usual," Charlie says. "Why?"

Jimmy Baba stands and offers his chair. "Please, these people have questions for you." He wears the same orange robe as before, white lines and red *tilak* freshly-painted on his forehead and yet, with his slicked-back long hair and goatee — he looks like a *saddhu* from out of GQ magazine.

The moment I'm seated, conversation stops and I find the whole company staring me down. Two girls with shaved heads wearing sleeveless, batik dresses float over to join us from out of the garden.

"What's going on?" I say to Charlene.

"Ask the *astrologer*." She thumbs at Jimmy Baba. "Apparently someone found a crystal at the pyramids after free-basing *ayahuasca*."

"I came to Pushkar to find someone," says Jimmy. "After a dream I had last new moon. I knew that this person would be Gemini, a foreigner — show them the amethyst."

"How much did you tell them?"

"Why, everything," he says. "Surely not a problem. You said you were hoping to publish your journal."

"I... uh..."

He appropriates everyone's marigolds for the shrine. "We will talk later, my friend. *Bom shankur.*"

He wanders off humming *Dil to Pagle Hai,* leaving me stuck at the head of the table. All eyes on me, I produce the knotted handkerchief.

"And you found this *where*?" inquires Enrique.

"Halfway up the pyramid of Chepren. I was in Egypt about five weeks ago." I take out the amethyst, remembering Mohammed Number Two: "You fool!" he'd said. "This purple rock is everywhere!"

"And what was the job you were doing before?" says Charlie. "Sheepdogging children around some small island? The job you chucked in so you could go to Egypt?"

"These are all loaded questions — *what's going on?*"

Euphoria leans forward, waves everyone quiet with a motion not unlike drying wet nails. "Have you ever heard of a book called *The Alchemist?*"

The bald, batik women lean closer to hear.

"No, but the name rings a bell. Why, is it something I should read?"

Everyone at the table starts gibbering at once — turns out the only one who hasn't read it is Enrique.

Even Ratu can't quite believe his ears: "Yes, yes, Mr. C. It is something you should read."

Euphoria leaps up in a flash of blue velvet. "I'm going to do you a favor," she declares. She runs pigeon-toed to her room, bell-bottoms swishing. I now understand what she means by "flares."

Meanwhile, the bald girls take hold of the crystal,

start pressing it up to their foreheads and ohming — I'm starting to feel like clown number one spilling out of an Age of Aquarius clown car. Euphoria returns with her hands behind her back, inspects my fingers to see if they're clean then produces Paulo Coelho's, *The Alchemist*. She makes me swear not to take it from Mercury. The cover features a boy with a staff walking a path toward a trio of pyramids but what strikes me most is the book's purple background: nearly the exact same color as my amethyst. *Now* I remember seeing it for sale in the Esalen bookstore during McKenna's conference.

Charlie stands. "Well, I don't believe you. How do we know you're not making this up?"

"Ya, it means nothing unless you can prove it," says Enrique.

Melanie frowns. "But what would he gain?"

"Maybe it helps him pull," says Euphoria.

"Then again," says Charlie, "maybe it doesn't."

She wrestles the crystal away from Euphoria, eyeballs it, sets it back down on the handkerchief. "That's an incredible story there, mate. Find me next time you want to talk about invertebrates."

She blows me a kiss and I laugh with the others but fact is, I'm unsettled by the range of people's reactions. Ratu fetches a pitcher of what looks like pond-water — his legendary lime-ginger-watermelon bhang juice — pours me a glass and points me toward the hammocks.

The Alchemist — "*a fable about following your dream*" — concerns an Andalusian shepherd boy who dreams of finding buried treasure at the pyramids. He leaves his homeland as well as his flock and is helped on his way by a king and an alchemist. I put the book down a hundred pages from the end, at which point the bald, batik women approach — two doe-eyed, nineteen-year-old Canadian lesbians it turns out.

"Is it about you?" they ask me in stereo.

"Well, I did leave my home, my job and my flock… haven't met a king but I did meet an alchemist. *And* dream of finding a treasure at the pyramids."

"I can't believe you're so calm," says the taller one.

"I know, I've been totally scooped by this guy."

"What? You're fulfilling the journey of the Tarot."

"Darlin', you're not making things better —"

"Have you ever heard of the *Celestine Prophecy*?"

I go down to the lake, watch the egrets hunt frogs and come back to find everyone packing for an overnight: a nine-mile hike to a temple oasis. Enrique has organized booze and a sound system. They invite me along but I'm lazy from fasting and this is day one out of three — where's Charlene? She's putting a daypack together, swapping outfits. Running around like she doesn't even see me.

I return to the hammock, watch everyone bail.

"See you tomorrow, crystal man," says Enrique. He slings a guitar case over his shoulder, grabs up some blankets and trots after Melanie.

The courtyard grows quiet. I doze, wake up coughing. Accept some more bhang, this time in a lassi. Roll a cigarette, thinking the buzz will be wicked but only succeed in a wicked-bad headache. An Englishman, Jonathan, arrives from Jaipur. I notice he's wearing a yellow sapphire on his thumb. He tells me a palm reader told him to wear it. When I show him the gem-cutter's flaw, he cracks up.

He asks if I know where to score decent *charas*. I hand him my Drum and the rest of my stash, confess I've been stoned every day for ten years.

"Are you sure? This is kind of a lot —"

"Dude, just take it."

There will be no more smoking. No food for three sunsets. No more marijuana in any of its forms. I will purify, cleanse, figure out what I'm doing here. Be ascetic for once — *the rest, meaning nothing.* Of course, I'm more crippled than I was back in Amsterdam chain-smoking booyahs the size of Magic-Markers but some of the ideas you have on marijuana? The next day, a few of them sometimes hold water.

When Jonathan leaves Jimmy Baba takes his chair. "I looked at your charts," he says matter-of-factly. "Have you heard of what's called your Saturn returning?"

"Have you ever heard of a book called *The Alchemist?*"

"You joke, yet you're here in the place of beginnings and you could be anywhere — anywhere in the world. Why do you think you envisioned the *naga*? The Muse, as you call it, the size of a mountain?"

It suddenly clicks: *A poet and a fool.*

"You told all those people to rhyme at me, didn't you?"

He Hindu headshakes as if the matter has no consequence. "Pay attention — a new phase of your life is beginning: it takes three-hundred-sixty-five-and-one-quarter days for the earth to complete one orbit around the sun. This, we are calling a year — do you follow?"

"There's no way you got to the guy at the yoga center."

Jimmy Baba snaps his bejeweled fingers between us, tells me Saturn's orbit takes twenty-eight years and when it re-enters your zodiac sign, that was what's known as your Saturn Returning. Because of the planet's elliptical orbit, a Returning can last from weeks to several months. Mine would be on the longer side of things. He then echoes the phrasing of Sammy's comment at the Deer Park.

"Forget the astrology, remember the lesson: the first phase of life is for gathering blocks. What you like, what you don't, your friendships, allergies. Athletics, learning music, degrees — think of Lego. When Saturn returns, this is done, no more gathering." He dusts off his hands, taps his finger on the table. "*Now* you are putting the blocks together, *now* you are building the starship, the hospital. The transition is challenging, often uncomfortable. This second phase of your life is called 'homeowner.'"

"And if you keep gathering Lego?" I ask, plucking a grape from a bunch on the table. I eat it before I realize what I'm doing.

"Most will die young, before Saturn's next returning."

The company reappears unexpectedly at midnight, just as I'm finishing my first rhyming poem. Entitled *The Prologue* it tries to explain in a linear fashion what brought me to India. It doesn't look right on the page but it *sounds* right, at least when I read it out loud to myself. More meant to be heard, like a song or a spell — performed, focused into a chant like G's yoga.

Which is better than Jimmy-Baba blabbing it to everyone.

Melanie is the first of the Aussies to find me. She sets down her pack in a fluid, backhand motion.

"I can't believe you're still sitting here," she says. "Your lip looks much better, by the way. Have you eaten?"

I shake out my dreads and ask her what happened.

She pulls up a chair. "We didn't even dance. The flying squad nicked two Pommies with disco biscuits."

Translation: the cops caught two Brits selling ecstasy.

The men had been handcuffed and taken away while the Mercury crowd, at Enrique's insistence, had consumed all their contraband, jumped in a Jeep and bashed their way back to Pushkar on a camel trail.

"I'm so off my head I can barely see," says Mel. "And don't even bother talking to Charlie."

"How come?"

"Mental nicotine cravings, you wally. She was the only one of us not smoking."

Still, before taking my leave of the Mercury, I knock, duck my head past the red-painted door, find the girls in various states of undress, trying on clothes in front of the mirror.

"Goodnight, all you lovelies."

As one they turn toward me, strike provocative poses and bust-up laughing.

"Goodnight, Mr. C!"

I return to the Darshan, my lower lip pulsing. Besotted, conflicted. They might as well be Sirens.

January 10, Pushkar

One winter I lived in the hills of Mendocino looking after a modest, indoor marijuana farm. The Lord's work we called it, growing the good stuff. Getting caught was a ten-year mandatory minimum. My cabin was chilly and draped with green moss, the grow-house underground and powered by diesel. Hydroponic as well, which was of course madness — outside was rich topsoil and plenty of sunshine. One afternoon, I'd returned from a run, wearing headphones and throwing a stick for the dog, when over the trees came a low-flying helicopter, shining a spotlight and bristling with guns —

I wake with a start and find my sheets drenched, as if I were trying to sweat out the memories. The first thing I see is the poster of Brahma, that most Judaeo-Christian of all the Hindu deities. Gray-haired and white-bearded, sat lotus on a tortoise, retired to Pushkar because it's a dry heat, no longer concerned with the fate of world for he is the Creator and his work is done here.

Coming out of my room I encounter Bertrand.

"You are well?" he asks, looking anything but. Sunken eyes, unkempt hair, open sores from mosquito bites.

Before I can reply, he runs into the bathroom.

"Holy Brahma, holy Pushkar, I big *puja* making," I call as I ride Ratu's bike past the *ghats*. "Me, my whole family, big donation giving!" For this is the prayer of the *baksheesh* lake Brahmins.

Famished, I weave between delicious-smelling market stalls, splattering cow dung over my sandals. In the Mercury's courtyard, Melanie hugs me good morning. Like the sunrise, she has a beautiful way of not saying anything. I invite the three Aussies to join me for yoga. They dress in loose fitting, yet revealing cotton garb. On the way to the ashram, Euphoria gushes about how *in love* she is with her waiter boy.

Charlie rolls her eyes. "Just jump him, LeGrande."

"I've never done anything so crazy in my life. Oh, Mr. C, it's like you with your crystal. He and I were *destined* to be together."

We're met at the gate by the Baba from yesterday: barefoot, rotund with a mane of gray hair. He leads us through hedgerows of pink and orange bougainvillea to a green patch of grass in front of a gazebo. There's six other Westerners limbering up, behind them Brahma's temple reflected in the lake. Buddha-baba informs us he has a bad back and the class will be taught by a middle-aged Spanish woman.

Her credentials are having done yoga six months and attained a certificate. Her English is poor. She confuses left and right, doesn't say when to breathe. People apologize for banging into each other. Meanwhile Buddha-Baba sits crosslegged in the gazebo — *Jesus, the guy is not even trying.* He's picking his nose and falling asleep and here I am woozy, thirty-six hours without food, Melanie's in mustard-colored tights right in front of me, doing Angry Cat, Forward Bend, and Downward Dog. Her figure is lithe and maddeningly flexible, the loose pants I'm wearing don't hide my erection and after two hours of sweaty embarrassment we're told to lie back and "Listen to the teachings."

"Smoking is... very bad," intones Buddha Baba, deigning to come down from off his high gazebo. "Smoking makes cardiac... of the lungs. With smoking, one simple breath... becomes difficult. Some of you are trying... not to smoke. Brahma is happy... people not smoking. Brahma is happy... not getting emphesemen. *Ohmmmm... Ohmmmm... Ohmmmm...*"

I roll my head over and peek at Charlene at the same time she rolls her head toward mine. We screw up our faces, trying not to laugh.

"How did he know?"

I give my best headshake.

Back at the Mercury, Charlene joins me in the hammock, lays her head on my chest with surprising affection. Says she's sorry for brushing me off yesterday.

"I've been in a strop since we went to that temple."

She's wearing a flowing, maroon, cotton kaftan with the letters OCI picked out in embroidery. Inhibitions eroded, I toy with her braids. "Nice, white-girl weave here. You're beautiful Charlie."

"Don't." She bats my hand away playfully, tells me my story had opened a can of worms — her ex-boyfriend, before getting hooked on cocaine, had smoked weed every day and been big into acid.

I tell her DMT is most likely endogenous, that there's precursors found in the human pineal. "That's why you smoke it — it breaks down with MAO. You body knows exactly how to metabolize it. But Charlie, it's different in other ways too. Not so much a drug as a vehicle to a *place*, a place many people describe the same way — and after four times it told me not to take it."

"Drugs." She sighs. "It's a clumsy word, isn't it?"

"You wanna drop some acetylsalicylic acid?"

"Actually, I prefer ibuprofen."

"Then stop lumping chimpanzees in with the sponges."

Before long we're chatting about sequential hermaphrodism, how wrasses go female to male, unlike clownfish and speaking of wrasses had I seen the mating display of the orange-and-silver-striped harlequin tuskfish?

"Why don't you come with us to the *Om Shiva*?" she asks, meaning the forty-rupe all-you-can-eat buffet.

"I thought we were fasting three days — it's day two."

"We were... then I had to do a runner from that rave." Cringing, she confesses how before returning to the Mercury, everyone had gone to the Sunset Café.

"I ordered some juice like a good little girl —"

"But oh-just-some-crackers-soup-big-buffet-wipe-out? Charlie, how could you? I'm starving over here!"

She hammers my chest. "Hey, I threw away my fags."

"How many were left in the pack?"

"Okay, two — you're a right cheeky monkey, Mr. California." She stands up and smooths down the folds of her dress. "Anyway, I heard you haven't been fasting either. A little bird told me you ate a *grape*."

"You know, for a holy man that guy's pretty indiscreet."

"Come on, break your fast with us. Otherwise I'll feel bad."

I affect the accent: "No worries there, mate. But I might go for dinner if you'd be my date."

She says she'd be honored and offers to pay.

We agree to meet up again just before sunset.

"By the way what does OCI stand for?"

"Osho Commune International. Why?"

I stare at her blankly. "I'm sorry, come again?"

"In Pune — they rebuilt the original ashram. Don't give me that look, mate, I'm not a disciple."

I swing my legs out of the hammock. "*You're kidding me.* And you think I'm crazy for smoking DMT?"

"They happen to have a very nice pool and it's also a good place to get tested for HIV." She crosses her arms. "Have you ever been tested?"

"Tested?" I splutter. "I've never been *exposed*."

She flicks her braids over one shoulder. "Honestly? What about oral sex?"

"Thank you, I'd love some."

Euphoria appears, looking scandalous as always. "Change of plans, ladies. We're going to the Sunset."

The two of them depart — Melanie trotting after them — a raucous procession of colorful outfits, leaving me shaking my head in the courtyard with no-one around but Ratu and the peacocks.

Osho Commune International — good lord. Formerly known as Rajneeshpuram, a now-defunct free-love commune back in Oregon, shuttered amid accusations of vote-rigging and a dash of intentional salad bar poisoning. At the head of the cult: the late Bhagwan Rajneesh, a gray-bearded, hypnotic Indian mystic. People were rumored to have signed away everything at his ecstasy-fueled, latex-glove-wearing orgies where people wore orange, swapped partners, did tantra — while security guards prowled the compound with semi-automatics.

What Bhagwan Rajneesh was most infamous for was his fleet of Rolls Royces which numbered in the nineties, followed by how, when the dragnet came down, he'd been caught by authorities en route Bermuda with something like fifty-eight grand and a clutch of platinum timepieces. After a brief stint in jail he was deported and died of mysterious causes in 1990 but not before changing his name to Osho — and his followers robes to maroon, apparently.

How could someone of Charlie's intelligence be wearing the garb of an off-beat sex cult? I wonder if she's some kind of nymphomaniac who'd gone down to Pune for a clarified-butter romp. The thought makes me angry, not in a possessive way — polyamory being part of the mammalian condition, correlated to the average weight ratio between the sexes — but because I can't stand — can't abide — being squeamish. Maybe I *should* bring the drama of my first HIV test to Osho's front gate, face the terror head-on. Mona had spun me around like a top — could you really contract HIV from going down?

Jonathan, the Englishman I'd given my *charas* to, sits down with a handful of magazine clippings, suggests before we buy any more gems — get hoodwinked again — we bone-up on palmistry.

"You can tell if a person is honest," he declares, "based on the relative straightness of their pinkies."

"Let's do this," I say, digging into the pile. "What else can you tell?"

"That you're sexually frustrated, mate."

Marilyn Monroe has long, tapered pinkies. There's short arcing stubby ones on Saddam Hussein but the best ones of all are Baroness Margaret Thatcher's, with more kinks and joints than a bicycle chain. I hold out my pinkies and find them straight enough, with a slight inward curve for artistic license.

"Is it *that* obvious?" I ask, feeling drowsy.

"Geez, you're surrounded by fit birds in knickers."

Sinking deeper in the hammock, I relax my "whooooooole bo-dy", find mad, fractal patterns behind my eyelids; hear the bumblebee-trapped-under-cellophane noise, last heard in Rishikesh, and drift into... somewhere. This time there's a mountain inside of a tunnel, a figure on top waving four... many arms. He's snake-dancing faster than hummingbird wings, yet perfectly still *which cannot be possible.* It occurs to me here, where each passing second is thousands of lifetimes, his arms are a blur but I, being mortal, am not of this place. Every second is a second and my perspective is mine own. I try to make sense of it, fly faster down the tunnel. Receding, he beckons me, one arm outstretched and I have the sensation, or thought, or remembrance that, *Why are you rushing? The mountain is Death.*

The vision abruptly dissolves with a poke from a kindly, young man who once threatened to kill me.

"Your friend, he go." Ratu sets down glasses. "He pays for you sitting here, not buying anything."

"*Bom shankur*," says Jimmy Baba, making me jump. He's perched crosslegged on one of the stools.

"I've decided to give up on bhang," I tell him.

"If no longer sick, stop taking the medicine."

Ratu reappears with a pitcher of water. "Okay, no more juice, tourist man. Proper fasting." He pours us each glasses then swiftly departs.

It's time for more light to shine into my darkness.

I study each item of Jimmy-Baba's jewelry: the ruby in his right ear, the diamond in his left, the nine precious stones set in gold on his thumb, the quartz crystal hung by a thong around his neck.

"Where are you really from, *saddhu*?" I ask, not caring a whit about his asceticism.

"Originally from Mysore." He widens his eyes. "You'll find we are both coming here for beginnings."

It strikes, like the cobra tattoo on his forearm. "If you're fifty-six how come you look thirty?"

"Good vegetarian diet, meditation. Much love in my homeowner phase — and no children."

"Are you married?"

"I met a woman here once, she was English. She died of lung cancer a few months ago. I stayed with her, loved her until she was gone."

"Jimmy, I'm sorry —"

"Shhhh, it was beautiful." His eyes remain dry but a cloud passes over them. "Later I learn she is leaving me everything. I will build an ashram, I think, in her name. My heart is unclear. Somewhere by the ocean."

He explains how when Saturn returns a second time, you sweep all the Legos away from the table. Give anything left to family or charity. Devote your attention to matters of the spirit.

"If you took up the orange then why keep the jewelry? Why the goatee?"

"Americans." He sighs. "Not giving up *everything*, now, all at once."

"And this dream you had — coming to Pushkar to find me?"

"Or someone like you." He taps his red *tika*. "I think we are similar spirits, you and I. My fate line, like yours, comes out of my moon. It makes us both travellers, both wanderers, never satisfied. One day you too will help someone in your position." He flutters his hand at the garden, the boh tree, the sunbathing travellers, the blue walls and peacocks. My ears pop and for the first time while sober, I experience a vertical shift of my consciousness.

"All the great artists and mystics come to India," he says. "Jesus and Buddha, Madonna and Beatles. They come to find truth they can put into teachings, truth they can put into music. India is materially poor in the way the West is poor of the spirit. You bring us money, computers, technology, we give you *brahma*. It is the way of things.

"Your fast right now is a means of letting go and the things you drop are unnecessary, like your stool. Your desires, bad habits, distractions, attachments — perhaps your very life you may wish to let go. You have heard, no doubt, of the *gurus* in Kashmir who sit in their caves for centuries, without food? They do not even breath, their hearts do not beat, only their hair continues to grow. You have been to Varanasi?"

I nod my head yes.

"Also to Hardiwar for Kumbh Mela?"

"I wanted to stay but it all got too much. I had to leave before the Mela started..."

"This is unimportant. What matters is your heart. It has led you to some of the holiest places on earth. There are people, these girls, who will be afraid of you, because you follow your truth. Let them run. Each person is born with everything they need, a vessel to hold their soul, their *atman*. Connect it to *brahma*, you will need no one else, but still you will give freely because *that*? That is love."

He reaches into a pouch around his waist and pulls out a small, folded square of white paper.

"The choices you make now affect your whole life. I give you this aquamarine to remember."

I steeple my hands, bring my thumbs to my nose, lean out of the hammock and unfold the paper. The gem is the same pale-blue color as Pushkar. It also looks flawless, some five or six karats. A fortuitous gift from a relative stranger.

"You're just going to *give* this to me?" I blurt out. "No offense but, *Baba*, this is so unlike India."

He raises his eyebrows. "Have you not learned *baksheesh*?"

"Of course, but how much?"

His laugh fills the courtyard.

"Two lifetimes' karma!" He raises his palm, displaying a henna tattoo of an *om*. "The gem must be set in both silver and gold. Your challenge this lifetime, Gemini, is balance."

I manage a thank you, stare down at the aqua and have the awareness *my past is behind me* — not as a linear progression to this point but more as a mattress holding aloft my identity. My father's pragmatism, preventing me from letting go but also keeping me grounded, observant. My mother's anxiety, her capacity to love, giving rise to a feminine need for companionship. My best friend, David Holthouse, starting that newspaper, telling me I should be sharing my stories, the wilderness, octopuses, dreams and psychedelics that eventually steered me away from the sciences. And then of course Jaime, being my everything, allowing *me* to dissolve into *us* until finally, McKenna tapping my shoulder and providing the catalyst that brought me to Egypt and now India...

Misting up at how long it had taken to get here, I close my hand over the aquamarine. When the tear trickles off my chin to my chest, I remove the late Mickey Herkus' gold wedding ring.

"This is the gold," I say to the *saddhu*. "I got it from the morgue when my grandfather died. As for the silver, I'm guessing you know a place?"

"*Acha*, we go to Ajmer," he replies.

TWO STONES

Not far from the bustling Ajmer bus stop
Stands a building-supply-kitchen-curio shop
Selling cutlery, candlesticks, hammers and brass
Metal pipes, antique lanterns, cut keys and stained glass
Where way at the back, through a dingy, brown curtain
Up two, maybe three flights of stairs — I'm not certain
You'll find a steel door where a knock from Bombay
(the theme to the hit movie Dil To Pagle Hai)
Opens into a room with a red, Persian carpet
Upon which are men taking gemstones to market.

Now this place is wholesale — not up for discussion
The buyers from everywhere, the sellers mostly Muslim
But if you're a friend of former gem trader
Who's willing to pull a few strings, call a favor
You might get to sit and sip tea for an hour
Talk cricket and whiskey and nuclear power
With a dapper old man in a salwaar kameeze
Who won't sell you nephrite and claim it's Burmese…

And maybe you've come to buy gems, maybe not
Maybe later, just looking, no thanks — wha'chu got?
And after the velvet is laid on the cushion
The spotlight moved into its proper position
The dapper old man in the salwaar kameeze
Pretending he's not sure which one of his keys

Will open a briefcase of miniature hopes:
A thousand and one tiny, white paper envelopes...

He'll show you some hematite, petrified mud
(the former's apparently good for the blood)
Tourmaline, malachite, agate and jasper
(you'll set one aside just to make things go faster)
Past a pearlescent, olive-sized labradorite
(with a naturally-occurring om symbol? Yeah, right...)
On to peridots, amethyst, citrines, and garnets
(the best are the orange Sri Lankans called gomeds)
A tanzanite pock-marked with chips on the surface
More tea will arrive and you'll start to get nervous
For this is where poker begins to be played
Where stones become precious and carefully weighed
The unfaceted sold by carat and gram
Princesses, octillions by haggle and scam
Him hoping you're foolish enough or pathetic
To buy something fatally-flawed or synthetic
You praying your eyebrows don't rise and betray
The gemstone you have to have now, right away
For your lover, your girlfriend, your man or your mistress
For you it's romance but for him it's just business...

And that's when he'll lay on the velvet
Two rubies
Opaque cabochons, hemispheric —
Real beauties
Star rubies they're called, because in the presence
Of spotlight, inside of their adularescence
A six-pointed asterisk appears in the stone
And moves through the matrix like sunlight on chrome

And you'll suck in your breath at the one that seems flawless
(exposing your busted-heart flush in the process)
Why? Because some things are better than rupees
Requited true love, good health, certain rubies
So ignoring the smirk on the dapper old man
Your trader friend sighing and throwing his hands
You'll pick up the seen-to-believe-it star-ruby
With the same expert care you'd take pinching a doobie
To find that this dazzling stone you've selected
Weighs quite a bit less than you had expected
Unblemished, no chips on the rounded, red surface
The star moves around every axis with purpose
And yet... there'll be something that's hard to explain
It's oxymoronic but regular strain?
Too perfect, like maybe a gem from a lab
But nobody wants to make star rubies that bad...

So you'll put the one down and pick up the other
(its two-carats-heavier, pigeon's-blood brother)
And find yourself holding a riveting stone
Some natural rough on the edge, darker tone
A mysterious gem, full of cumulus, wonder
Though not for the Gem Trader Magazine cover...
Unlike the first, which was love at first sight
This second one doesn't rush into the light
Both beautiful, yes, but to each their own ways
Despite the same finish and asterisk rays
So you'll set them back down, side by side on the velvet
(have a dram of the gem-trader's whiskey, the hell with it)
And he'll ask where you're from, any kids, what you do
You'll say Mississippi, fifteen, how 'bout you?

Then acting indifferent you'll ask him, "How much?"
"For each or for both?" he'll say, calling your bluff.
"For this one," you'll say pointing down at the perfect
"Same-same," he'll say, wobbling his head for effect
And he'll quote you a price you can't possibly pay
You'll offer a third, he'll tell you no way
And acting insulted you'll haggle it down
To a place where you both feel ripped-off fifty crowns…
But aye, here's the rub, you can't pay with no card
The market is closing, the bank is too far
And you'll only have cash for the one or the other
(along with the gomeds you picked for your mother)
At which point it's left up to you to decide
Which stone might be worth this particular ride
The rarest commodity out there, perfection?
Or an intrigue which comes upon further inspection?
Same angle of incidence, same of refraction
But which one will bring you the most satisfaction?

For with gems, as with people or stories or art
Their worth is the shiver they cause in your heart
And so, needing air, you'll head down to the street
Through the curio shop and stare at your feet
Thinking which stone to discard and which one to keep
One perfect and shallow
And one flawed and deep.

January 10, afternoon, Pushkar

Returning from Ajmer, I shower and shave, get my sideburns as sharp as the actual razor. Put on masculine smells — myrrh, cedar and sage — then head down and settle my bill at the Darshan. On my way out, I stop by the Montpelier's. Their door is ajar, with a key hanging out of it. Inside is a mattress on the floor, candy wrappers, a few burned out candles but otherwise no sign of them.

Feeling light on my feet I head to the Mercury and wait for Charlene to finish getting ready. While I sit in the hammock, Melanie glides up with a handful of objects and asks me to pick one.

"This rock's made out of fossilized mud. Or maybe it's this one... hell, I don't know. But this one I found in Bali last summer." I select an orange seashell and she floats over to the lesbians. They're precious, her stones, these mementos from her travels, because she treats them as if it were so.

Is this what I've done with the amethyst crystal? Imbued it with meaning to make it more valuable?

Finally, Charlie comes out of the bathroom. She's wearing a figure-hugging OCI dress tied at the waist with a gold lamé rope. Her silver-tipped braids, still wet from the shower, trail water marks over her tanned back and shoulders.

"Wow, Charlie, you look fantastic. Praise Osho."

"Thanks." She toys with her glittering red bindi. "I don't know why, but I felt like dressing up. That top there's a corker, mate. Where did you get it?"

I chuckle. "A clothing warehouse in Jaipur. Be thankful I didn't wear the neckerchief."

I gather my belt-bag, journal and books, shuffling around like a feeble old man. We decide to go down to the *ghats* before dinner, sit under a sign which prohibits holding hands. The lake reflects planets and stars in the middle; temples and shops along the perimeter. Charlie narrows her eyes at the Sunset Café, its Pepsi signs blazing.

"What's wrong with this picture?"

"It does rather stick out at night," I admit. "You know in Varanasi there's a goddamn techno club jutting-out over where they burn the bodies? We can't get away from taking it all with us."

"That's where I want to go next: Varanasi."

"Oh really? I thought you might want to go south."

She arches an eyebrow. "What did you have in mind?"

"Udaipur. Two or three days. Just the two of us. Rent a nice haveli. Have a look around."

Her jaw drops. She covers her mouth with one hand. "Ian, I'm flattered and don't take this the wrong way but… I always thought you were interested in Melanie."

"Melanie *is* incredibly attractive."

She shakes her head, laughs. "Mate, don't I know it."

"But we can't really talk — we have nothing in common. I'm not interested in having a fling, Charlie. I miss the feeling of being in love."

She taps the inside of her cheek with her tongue. "That's a bold proposition, mate. Really impressed. Must have been hard for you, giving this a go."

"So what do you think?"

"Well, I haven't said no yet."

I lean forward to kiss her, right there on the *ghats,* but before we can touch, in the road right behind us, two kids on a bike hit a rock and just *stack*, sending the boy on the handlebars flying. The evening erupts into wailing and bloodshed. Charlie and I are up in a flash, break out my first aid kit, apply half the band-aids. By the time we're all finished a small crowd has gathered.

"This is why we have to go to Udaipur," I grumble. "You can't get away with *anything* in this town."

"And what make you think I'd have kissed you?" she says. "Just because you're the guy from *The Alchemist* doesn't mean I fancy you."

We return to the *ghats* and collect our shoes.

"You just need a spark in this country, Charlene. You have to admit there's a glimmer between us. I have Indian friends who got married last month? Before even touching each other, or dating — let alone shacking-up for six years, backing out — and the Indian divorce rate's the same as in the west."

"So now you're asking me to *marry* you? Crikey."

"Well, we are from the caste of biology."

"That's good." She points up at the no-hand-holding sign. "Alrighty then, Pushkar." She offers me her elbow. "I'm not saying no, I just need a day to think about it. Come on, let me buy your first meal at the Sunset. Besides, I can't wait to get the juice on Euphoria — you know the next step is her meeting his *mother*?"

And, just like that, the magic is gone, the moment was blown when the kid skinned his knees. She's eager to get back to the safety of her friends, away from the octopus and all his intensity.

I touch her lightly on the arm. "Actually, you know what? I'm going to keep fasting — but thank you for helping me choose the right Lego. Jimmy says I've got two months left to gather them."

She looks at me cockeyed. "You going to be alright?"

"Oh, wait, one more thing." I reach into my pocket. "Whatever you decide, I want you to have this." And with that I hand her a sandalwood stash box.

VII. THE JOURNAL INVERSE

CASTLES IN THE SKY

Day three of my fast in the town of Pushkar
Surrounded by deserts as hot as the Thar
Travelling with three Australian lovelies
All of them hotter than ninety degrees
Euphoria, redheaded waitress from hell
Zoologist Charlene, ballet-dancing Mel
Big eyes, no surprise, for man of my size
Here in Pushkar, a town painted blue like the skies
Blue-painted buildings, blue-painted ghats
Blue as in air as in God as in thoughts…
A place in the heavens, no feet on the ground
Taboo to hold hands in this blue, Brahmin town
Home of Brahma, Creator, Creation, Begin
The long road to Shiva, Destroyer, The End
And I'm hoping to find somewhere in between
A partner who's willing to flesh out the dream
Which is why the day after I smoked my last doobie
I invited Charlene, with a cabochon ruby
To an actual castle, one that's on land
To Udaipur, tomorrow, where we can hold hands
Because these last days I've seen in her eyes
A spark of attraction, a hint of a fire
And if the girl's willing, then I'm not afraid
To open my heart and have it filleted

In the city of lovers, a bus ride away
But will she accept? I find out today…

Sleep like a stone in the watery deep —
I'll say one thing for Pushkar, it's easy to sleep —
Wake up and catch the first sliver of dawn
Dizzy from fasting but sober, turned on
Cold bucket shower while singing and cursing
(the octopus rap/song I might be rehearsing)
Hotel-man apologizes for the cold water
I smile like it's nothing say, "It's cool, I'm Brahmin."
The highest of all of the Indian castes
Acquired by birthright and deeds, lifetimes past
And he looks at me funny like, "Who the hell are you?"
But why can't this white man proclaim himself Hindu?
The caste system's bunk and I'm callin' it out
Untouchable people — what's that all about?
Naw, I'm a mutt, a religious mix breed
Jewish by birth, Hindu by dream
Christian by passport, Science by degree
The Techno-Pagan Octopus Messiah, indeed.

Dress in my jeans and a baby blue shirt
(my get-up from somewhere I used to call work)
Strap on my belt knife, lace up my boots
Today only juice for this sayer of sooth
Writing poetry — no! — for the very first time
My journal a hiss from the Serpent of Rhyme
And sure, it's pretentious but hell, it's a serpent
Brainwashing me good with its venom detergent
And it slithers me into the streets of Pushkar
Sidewinds me through alleys too narrow for cars
Uncoils me next to Brahma's holy lake

Where I take off my shoes and a "Big puja make!"
Using flowers, ablutions, a coconut shell
A priest of baksheesh and a sandalwood smell
And the priest puts a tika mark bang on my forehead
"For fifty rupees, your karma now sorted."
Releases me back to the Mercury hotel
"Um, hey there, Charlene," I say, awkward as hell
"Have you seen Jimmy Baba?"
"He's under his tree."
"Have you thought about —"
"Not until after my coffee."
And she smiles, ruby-lipped, plaited hair and petite
With her thirty-year-old single traveller mystique
And I find Jimmy solemnly tending his shrine
Adorning a lingam with marigold vines
His robe like the petals, the same color orange
He clocks my expression says, "Don't be discouraged
These three Aussie women are not what they seem
They're castles in the sky, not real, just a dream."
Like Euphoria stringing her young Nepalese
Along for her little girl play fantasies
Always takin' a cluster of friends, chaperones
Pretending she's planning to take the boy home
But it's all just for fun and it's all just for show
She says that she's falling in love, but we know…

Auto-rickshaw with Jimmy down to Ajmer
To pick up my late grandpa's ring from the jeweler
Reforged with an aquamarine, set in gold
With two silver bands alongside it — behold!
An ancestral symbol, my grandfather's ring
Like Pushkar itself, an ethereal thing
Reflecting the marriage he had to Pauline

Their daughters — Aunt Jill and my mother, Arlene
And the aqua, a gift from the Baba himself
A former gem trader, renouncing his wealth
To become an ascetic, a wandering sage
At fifty-six years, nearly twice my own age
And he says to me, "Poet, this stone is no fake
Like your family ring, solid gold and not plate
But Pushkar? A cow wouldn't drink from that lake
It's a castle in the sky."
And he Hindu headshakes.

Return to the scene at the Mercury Hotel
Enrique, Ratu, Vicky, Charlie and Mel
Charlie, still mulling on my proposition
Avoiding eye-contact as much as decision
Gathers her yoga mat, gives me a hug
Kisses my cheek, says "We'll talk later, love."
And after she's gone, Jimmy sighs and looks skyward
Knows and sees everything that has tran-spi-red…
Asks if I fancy the girl, I say yes
A tear leaves my eye and rolls onto my chest
'Cause I don't have calories left to pretend
That it's not going to hurt if she says, "Let's be friends."
With her rational mind, her wash-and-go hair
Her marine science background, her perfect derrière
But I'm leaving Pushkar, of that much I'm sure
For who knows what mischief awaits me in Udaipur?
But if Charlie comes, we should go it alone
Not take the crew with us to play chaperone
Because I am not that Nepalese guy
Penned up in some castle she's built in the sky…

Depart from the garden, following whim
Grandpa's ring on my finger and thinking of him
His great, booming laugh, his great, barrel chest
His terrible jokes, his green, woolen vest
Sit down at the Shri Shiva Juice Center Stand
Say what's up to Shiva 'cause he's my main man
And he whips me a juice in his two holster blender
"For you only vegetable water, bom shankur!"
Then the Aussies appear with flamboyant Euphoria
Charlie's tight-lipped, it's same old sad story and
Mel's got a toothache, looks hurt and depressed
Euphoria's hair is a post-party mess
And Charlie gets bhang juice, says she doesn't care
That we'd quit together, it's her life, don't stare…
And it's clear that the older and wiser girl's spooked
Biologists in particular can't handle the truth
That life is not only about flesh and genes
And rational reasons, it's half love and dreams...

Palm Jimmy a couple American bills
Not a fee, just baksheesh, it means 'greasing the wheels'
And he pockets the cash while chilluming hash
Doesn't count nothing — heck, don't even ask
And for good minute there, nobody speaks
Not a sound from the garden of travelling freaks
No turning of pages, no clinking of glasses
The air becomes heavy and thick, like molasses
As if we were dreaming, as if nothing mattered —
Then a peacock cries out and the silence is shattered:
Enrique says "Checkmate in five" to Ratu
Somebody breaks out a didgeridoo
Charlie and Mel start applying mud masks
With rose petals stuck the gooey, brown mash

And Euphoria adds, "But he's painfully shy…"
To Jimmy, who nods and says, "Castles…"

The afternoon springs a surprise Hindu festival
Hundreds of women lined up by the temple
More women then even a warlord could want
But they don't work in gift shops, hotels, restaurants
They're hidden indoors, many rules to obey
Double standards, except for this one holy day
When they put their rakish & Rajasthan best
Orange and pink and pastel-colored dress
Sashay through the streets with clay pots on their heads
While the menfolk throw flowers at ones they would bed
But does Charlie notice, during the parade
The petals I rain on her silver-tipped braids?
"Wait here," she says, breathlessly, "I need my camera."
Comes back with Ratu, Mel, Enrique, Euphoria…
Poor Mel, with an ice-pack, "My tooth's getting worse."
"Hold on," says Charlene, "I've got pills in my purse."
And it's suddenly lonely inside of that crowd
"Can we talk please?" I say just a little too loud…
Charlie sighs and says, "Alright, mate, let's talk alone."
Leads me down to the ghats onto blue-painted stone
Where she tells me they're all headed back to New Delhi
Their friendship means everything, Mel's got this toothache…
And it strikes me like lightning: The dancer's been fakin'
Pretending this business about her tooth-achin'
But I hold my breath and let Charlie explain

How sensitive people rub her the wrong way
And there's no way that she can be nice all the time
To which I reply, "It's about being kind."
"I'm sorry," she says, "you're a wonderful guy
Thanks for the ruby but this is goodbye."
Hugs me and leaves me right there in the street
The perfect rejection, abrupt, bittersweet
'Cause we're both all or nothing, now or never, she and I
Only I said, "All now"
"Nothing never," she replied...

Feeling less like a Serpent and more like Tofurkey
I quietly gather my things from the Mercury
Head back to my room, say a prayer to Ganesh
Pack up my bags, put on rose oil, get dressed
And when it gets dark, on a sad moment's spur
I purchase a one-way ticket to Udaipur...

Leave my bags at the station, return to the ghats
Decide to make puja right there and why not?
Shooing away baksheesh Brahmins like flies
"Just back the fuck up so I can pray, guys."
Saying Brahma, please bring me true love, epic sex
A compelling, bestselling and runaway success...
Empty the bucket of wants in my head
Invoke all the names of my family dead
My grandfather Mickey, who I loved the most
"You'd be proud of me Grandpa for not smoking dope"
Dip the aquamarine in the lake, not sure why
Under a darkening aquamarine sky
Jimmy's stone in the only ring Grandpa wore
Handed to me at the hospital morgue

The day after he toppled like some mighty oak
On the tennis court after one last mighty stroke
Then lacing my boots thinking, Pushkar goodbye
I come face to face with an Indian child
He asks me the usual questions, ho-hum
"What name? How long Pushkar? What country come from?"
And I answer him patiently, line after line
Wondering what India wants from me this time
But after he's done, as I'm turning to leave
The kid grabs my arm says, "You take something please"
Reaches into his faded, ripped, knock-off blue jeans
Pulls out a harmonica, gives it to me
Doesn't say why, doesn't ask for baksheesh
An act as rare as me lacking for speech
Then he runs to his mom, leaving me streaming tears
Connected, at large, at peace, without fears
'Cause the one thing I haven't heard since the man died:
The harmonica Grandpa kept at his side...

Break my fast at a café, not hungry for much
Fruit, rice and parathas, then head to my bus
Where the bus-wallahs tell me I've got a bad ticket
Too weary to tell them where they can all stick it
But a truck driver says I can ride in his cab
Along with six natives, three cigarettes, not too bad...
I won't get to read, I won't get to sleep
(and I sure as hell won't get to tilt back my seat)
But we'll make it to Udaipur sometime next morning
And right now, driver man, that's all that's important
So I cram myself next to a shrieking young child
Try to forget I have legs for a while

And the baggage boy turns, elbows me in the head
Many travellers I know would lash-out but instead
I find myself filled with a great, rolling mirth
I've left the sky castle and come back to earth…

NOT SMOKING

The man at the table next to me has Drum
But I don't need a cigarette, don't even want one...
Don't want to dip the blue packet with zeal
Roll up a chiefy after my meal
Don't want to dangle that smoke off my lips
Strike up a match, take that first hit
Get a headrush, grab a chair, have to sit —
But Drum is my brand and I hate to admit
That seeing it makes my fingertips itch
Eight days and still craving, ain't that a bitch?
And the smoke, it floats up and drifts through the air
Enters my nose but hell, I don't care!
'Cause I spent too long under the nicotine knife
Slicing the last precious days off my life
But I know how that first ragged rush's gone' feel
Real fuckin' good 'cause that's nicotine's deal
With a let down worse than the one after sex
The smell of your clothes, the lung-butter flecks
And the smoker he sees me says, "Hey man, what's happenin'?"
Offers his pack and I just want to smack him
'Cause what's happenin' is you fag-wielding prick
Is I could kill for that smoking stick!
But I chill 'cause one thing is only one thing
And the trick to not smoking is just that:
Not smoking.

JAIME WOULD HAVE LOVED RAJASTHAN

Another bad night, another bad dream
Of Jaime, the woman I let drift downstream
With freckles, blue eyes and dark, curly hair
Innocence trusted and lost in my care
The first woman I'd ever told those three words:
"Wanna take mushrooms?" We'd flown like two birds
Over the Umqua and onto the Rogue
Down to the beaches through evergreen groves
And half of our twenties went by in a blur
She said she loved me, I said I loved her
And we talked about travelling the whole world together
Until something pulled out the rug on forever...

Three months since I seen her and feeling uncertain
I head to the window and throw back the curtain
On Udaipur, glittering, her kind of city
Bit hokey, bit loud, undeniably pretty
With mirrors embedded in colorful cloth
A place to buy trinkets, a place to get lost
A place couples splurge on a couple's massage
Rent opulent rooms, become part of the Raj
Overlooking the lake and the marble Lake Palace
She'd want to eat lunch there — I'd go feeling callous
Pretending we lived there, as if we belonged

Where they filmed Octopussy, the worst of James Bond
Her eyes growing moist as the lepers begged alms
Her groan at the muezzins who welcome the dawn
Or the weddings — sweet Lord — like an endless parade
Of whinnying horses, braying bridesmaids
And if I had a rupee for each time they played
That Bollywood song — I am Dil To Pagle Hai-ed
And yet...

If we had been born only one generation
Before what we were, we'd have sent invitations
And it would be us renting horses and carriage
Convinced by convention to call it a marriage
Neverminding the unspoken, fraught intuition
That we were too young to make such a decision
More siblings who bickered and loved one another
No way she should marry her first-ever lover...
Which is what I keep telling myself —'cause I'm right
But it sure as hell don't help me sleep through the night
Because I know exactly where I'd have proposed
That haveli, there, on one knee, with a rose
And a gem that I'd secretly bought in Jaipur
Could I really have come to Udaipur without her?

Yes, friend, I have and I'm packing to leave
Trying to keep busy, trying not to grieve
About coming alone to the honeymoon city
And spending a week with my fucking self-pity...
So I'm up and out of this place she would love
To fly like the hawk who'd devoured the dove
Away from where Juliet rides on a camel
Away to the south, to the land of the Tamils

Away from the rooftop where I would have asked
Sweet Jaime the ultimate question at last
Away from the place she might have agreed
To share the whole rest of her life, yes indeed…
And right now you're probably with a new man
But Jaime? You would have loved Rajasthan.

OSHO COMMUNE INTERNATIONAL

1. Fear

Now these words have never reached anyone's ears
And they speak of the Octopus Messiah's greatest fear
The scariest thing under the Sun God, Osiris —
The Human Immunodeficiency Virus...
Now I've never shot drugs with needles before
Never let anyone in the back door
Never received tainted blood, yes it's true
Never sucked dick for money to buy glue
But I did last October have sex with a stripper
On the Jewish high-holy day of Yom Kippur...

Red-haired and petite was the woman who found
My broke-hearted body on the rebound
And while my ex-lover had a nervous breakdown
I drove to the redhead's apartment 'cross town
And she was a friend but oh, what a body
The kind of woman men pay to see naked, a hottie
With freckles all over her taut, silken flesh
Nipples like imported sweets on her breasts
And I knew she was loose and had many lovers
(probably should have put on double rubbers)
But she tantalized me with a clacking tongue pierce
And whispered the dirtiest things in my ears
And maybe I shouldn'a gone down on that muffin

But sometimes you just gotta taste what yer stuffin'
And after the shower (and after the breath mint)
I realized that it was the Day of Atonement
The day that gave the world the Scapegoat
To take all our sins and a knife to the throat
And even though I'm not a practicing Jew
I knew that it was the wrong day to screw
But now I guess there's nothing I can do
'Cept hope that my litmus test comes back blue...

So I get on a bus, headed to Pune
Hopin' I didn't get plagued from bad...
For in Pune resides the cult of Osho, Rajneesh
The late priest of spiritual bliss for baksheesh
And in a land so full of religious choices
Why not a guru with fleets of Rolls Royces?
For money is manifest energy, buddy
And I respect Osho for every fleeced yuppy
At his famous full-moon parties, orange Kool-Aid
Spiked with some pure, pharmaceutical grade
Ecstasy, also called MDMA
First you feel love then you sign it away...
(Allegedly)

But Osho, he wrote some damn righteous books
Provocative, accessible — yeah, I had a look
His words full of truth and often quite funny
My favorite? "Learn to transform your poisons into hon-ey"
But what I love/hate about Osho the best
Is his commune's mandatory HIV test
Results the next day, not next week or next month
Never been tested, braced for the punch

And so I continue my pilgrimage south
Wondering am I the devil or Faust
Fearing an ugly scene at the gate
If my test turns up positive — "Sorry there, mate…"
Ruing the day that I slept with that stripper
On the Jewish high-holy day of Yom Kippur…

2. The Test

Sipping juice at the ashram, admit that I'm scared
And it's not just the test, it's the vibe in the air
It's the overpriced food at the overpriced bakery
Are these genuine smiles or Osho-style fakery?
Surrounded by floods of young studs with clean blood
Maroon shirts, maroon pants, maroon robes, maroon love…
And at the front desk I fill in the forms
(my asshole sure itches, I hope it's not worms)
And when the needle bears down, I sigh in relief —
Give me death, give me life, I just gotta know, chief!
And my blood's the same color as the ruby I wear
I hope it protects me but try not to care
And the alchemist, McKenna, once said these words true:
"Worry assumes you understand the situation and what are the chances you actually do?"
But I don't like the sound of the Octopus Messiah
Octo-crucified by the world's viral fire
'Cause octopus have no conception of cheating
Their mating is more like a handshake, a greeting
And… isn't that the way things work here at Osho?
The part of me that wants to stay awhile sure hopes so
'Cause these women are gorgeous in their maroon robes

Everyone huggin' like anything goes
But oy, Rabbi Leibowitz, I fucked that damn stripper
On the Jewish high-holy day of Yom Kippur
And while we await the results to arrive
We watch a short film about life on the inside
Where folks shout and dance wearing white and maroon pants
Under screens of the late Chandra Mohan, entranced
But I'm not a follower, Bhagwan, I'm a leader
What the gays you refuse to admit call a breeder
And if I have AIDS? Well, I'll search for a cure
But don't make me do it, let my blood be pure
'Cause I've had enough adventure, that's for damn sure
And they give us a badge, take us on a tour
And inside the Osho cult's hive of maroon
I see restaurants? A wet bar? A swimming lagoon?
Traditional, folk, trance-chant, crystal healing
It's gorgeous and green but it gives me this feeling
Like I don't belong among this odd throng
Of spiritual seekers playing ping-pong
Bowing down to the late-great Bhagwan
And this is my take and it might be wrong:
That this perfect commune is a lot like heroin
You're nervous about it until you jump in
And suddenly your family wonders where you been
And it starts with a needle tucked under your skin...

But Osho, it proves to be my salvation
And I'll try anything once this vacation
Offered my life, Shiva said, "You may live."
'Cause baby, I tested HIV negative...
The moment of truth was weeks long and hard
Girl took her damn time finding my card

Said, "Go get this stamped in that line over there."
I said, "Give me a moment I just need to stand here..."
And back on the streets, I buy my two robes
Tomorrow's camouflage for joining the fold
And I have a slight fever, it might be a cold
Might be malaria, so I've been told
Got an itch on my ass, got an infected cut
Might have aneurysm, get a fatal headrush
But one thing that's not plaguin' me Baba-G
Is the thrilla', world-killa', Godzilla HIV...

3. The Buddhafield

Alarm wakes me from a fitful night's sleep
At four in the morning — enough with the beeps!
Malarial maybe, but on medication
I arrive just in time for the morning meditation
Get a sticker, a locker, get primed for the show
Enter Buddha's Pavilion, where posters of Osho
Hang bearded, beguilin', silk robes he be stylin'
Sufi eyes smilin', a man, not an island...
Only one path into love he insists:
"Create a religion, become religious!"
Be Buddha, his message, don't be a Buddhist
Be Christ, not a Christian — you gettin' the gist?
And yet he inspired this massive commune
Where everyone wears non-conformist maroon
Sayin', Look where I'm pointing, don't look at my finger
But he points at your wallet and that's the humdinger...

A thousand of us stand in front of his chair
Some bowin', some sobbin': "He used to sit there!"

Then people in black tell us, "Just let it out!"
Gibberish, laughter: come on, man, just shout!
So hey, what the hell, Coyote Man? Howl!
Shriek like a monkey, hoot like an owl
Throw open the valve between body and brain
Everyone lookin' and doin' the same
And out on the streets they'd call us insane
Lock us up and we'd never be heard from a-gain...
Part crazy fun and part hella scary
In an Indian cult doing primal scream therapy
And it's dark while we bark in the Buddha theme-park
Letting it go from atoms to quarks
'Til the people in black tell us, "Jump up and down!
Raise-up and cry, Osho!" (feel like a clown)
Bangin' the drums until someone yells, "Stop!"
Then a man up on stage does an actual pin-drop...

Ten minutes we stand there frozen in place
Until music starts and they say, "Celebrate!"
Which, to me, looks a lot like we dance
While inside my mind, to Shiva I chant
Help me see through this maroonist confusion
Lend me your power to destroy illusion...

4. Choices

It seems that no one wants to play
With the Octopus Messiah today
"May I join your game of hoops?" I say
They take their ball and walk away
"May I join you here for lunch?"
Seat's been taken? Had a hunch
But pasta fresh and salad green?

Organic soy and tangerines?
In India?

After lunch, trés cher but good
Explore the Osho neighborhood
Past post and sports facilities
Black pyramids as tall as trees
Approach a brooch of golden hands
Around the neck of one who stands
Behind a marble desk, does she
Offering free therapy...
Sit down and start to tell my story
In all its crystal, astral glory
She yawns and says, "Now hold your horses
And let me tell you of these courses
In thirty different therapies
From Reike, Zen to alchemy
On how to sit and how to eat
The pressure points along your feet
Mysticism, Transformation
Martial Arts and Meditation
Primal Screaming, Psychic Healing,
Tarot cards, Pulsation feeling
Shock Release, Neo Feng Shui
Fresh Beginnings, one-two-three
Self-hypnosis, de-hypnosis
Rid yourself of that psychosis
Aura Soma, Aum and then
Love Yourself be Born Again
And after that expand your ken...
With New-Mind-Pulse-Fresh-Juice-Zazen."

The woman smiles and raises eyes

A stunned and awkward pause then I
Say, "Yes in all that litany
Is there a space for poetry?
And not two thousand rupes a class..."
The woman has a pleasant laugh
Tells me not to get uptight
"Just find a place to sit and write
But just to help my concentration
Do some working meditation
Sweep the road or chop some carrots
Help the office staple pamphlets
Run the gift shop, 'scape the land
It's your commune so lend a hand
Oh, and Osho didn't die of AIDS
They poisoned him back in the states
Two weeks in prison, radiation
Under the reign of Ronald Reagan
And never once Osho, did he
Condone the use of ecstasy
So never mind those things you heard
You're at the source and that's the word
But hey, before you up and cruise
Which course, if you would have to choose...?"

"Oh, I don't know about all that
First I think I'll take a nap
Lay down in the garden sun
And what to do surely will come..."
After all, I follow dreams
And many wonders I have seen
And so I lay down on a bench
Near a couple speaking French
In a copse of green bamboo

Big leafy trees, wildflowers too
And suddenly, I have the answer
Don't walk to the front gate, I canter
Use my heart and not my brain
And buy a seat on the next train
'Cause I came to find my own damn self
Not buy it, add to Osho's wealth
For India to me does call
And this ain't India at all
'Cause Bharat sings a dirty ballad
Ancient, brown, can't eat the salad
Beggar boys and Shiva's phallus
It's time to leave this pyrite palace…

VIII. THE REDEMPTION OF ENGLISH AL

February 28, Mysore

It's been seven weeks since I last had a cigarette, same-same since I last smoked a joint or ate *bhang* and it's not like I'm losing my mind or anything, not like I'm a wood-gnawing-desperate dope fiend but my sense of humor is starting to crumble, especially in the face of What-name-what-country? Today in the bank during the daily, seemingly mandatory power outage which shut down the fans and the Visa machine, some simpleton standing in line grabbed my forearm and asked me straight-up whether I was married.

On impulse, I snapped in his face, "Seven wives. Why do you have no sense of privacy?" and right there my day, which had started with yoga began, along with my mood, to deteriorate.

Instead of my cash advance taking an hour, I fended off curious natives for three and when I finally emerged with my stapled sheaf of rupees — they actually *staple* the money in this country — who but English Al should be waiting to greet me.

"Hullo, mate," he says, penguin-waddling toward me — Bermuda shorts, knee-high white socks, dirty trainers. "Lovely day, if you can stand the heat. They're showing the cricket on telly, care to join me?"

I knew English Al would find me in Mysore for he is the avatar — the physical embodiment — of my loneliness. The guy's been shadowing me ever since Pune where we'd met at a guesthouse near to the commune. Al is a twenty-two-year-old video-game technician from Blackpool. He has cupped, sunburned ears, buck-teeth and bad hair but what bothers me most is his lack of initiative beyond the cheap charter that brought him to India. He'd landed in Bombay and frozen right there, at budget hotel number three in *The Stupid Guide*, met a few Brits who were heading to Pune, jumped like a tick and latched on for the ride. When I met him his friends had moved on to Hampi but my feeling was they'd probably ditched him. All he did was hang out in the guesthouse café, ogle the girls and watch sports on television.

Pune is a nasty, chaotic metropolis half a day's ride from the horror of Bombay. All its attractions, gardens and temples can easily be sightseen in less than a day. In short, I could see no reason to be a tourist in Pune *except* to join the cult of Rajneesh. Hang out with the beautiful people by the pool. Play a bit of "Zennis". Eat some raw greens. That, and bow down to the *Bhagwan*'s empty Lay-Z-Boy, dance with a thousand disciples called *sannyasins*, watch Osho give "*darshan*" on videocassette and wonder, *If dude were alive, would I follow him?*

I wondered this solely because of videos. The guy talked a good game and dressed like a pimp, distilled ancient wisdom into spiritual McNuggets — like the difference between being alone and loneliness. Loneliness, he said, was the absence of other while being alone was the presence of self. I wonder what he would have made of English Al, the loneliest presence I've ever encountered.

"So do people shag all the time in there?" he once asked me, stood with an Osho brochure in my doorway.

"I'm sure they do *somewhere*." I swallowed my Mefloquin, a horse-pill both bitter and difficult to swallow. "But you gotta believe, you can't just wear maroon. It's like how dogs can smell fear, you know? These *sannyasin* women can tell when you're bullshitting."

"And this... dynamic meditation at five in the morning? Does everyone really just jump around screaming?"

I sighed and swatted a mosquito off my cheek. "Al, you've been asking me these questions for three days. If you're so goddamn curious, go get a membership."

He inhaled sharply. "Not bloody likely! I... I don't need to join a... a *cult* just to act like a bleedin' monkey. I can do that whenever I want."

"Then go for it, Al. Just fucking *freak out*. Go totally primal, show me your freedom." His pie-pan-flat face had flushed red as a three-ball.

"What I thought." I switched on my travel alarm clock.

"You're... you're becoming one of them, aren't you?"

"Al, you're too cool for this place. Now shut the door, man, you're lettin' the bugs in."

I lay back on my pillow. He pulled the door closed.

"Uh, Al?"

"Mate?"

"From the *outside*."

A week later I found myself bumbling through Bangalore — the cleanest, most modern Indian city I've seen yet — but just as I stepped from an Internet café, who should be crossing the street but Prince Albert.

He was zigzagging, jogging through five lanes traffic, a raggedy beggar-kid hot on his tail. The kid was chanting "*Chapati! Chapati!*" which meant he'd get lost for a measly rupee but Al would have none of it, choosing instead to dash in front of on-coming buses without warning. It looked like he was trying to pick the kid off and though it was horrible, I burst out laughing. Sometimes you just can't shake the little buggers.

Al was in Bangalore because of its "pub-scene," a phenomenon said to have sprung up in recent months, and that night, feeling lonely, not merely alone, I'd joined him for drinks at a place in the guidebook.

Never have I felt more desperate and pathetic than while accompanying English Al to the Bangalore pubs. Over ninety percent of the patrons were men — mostly tech-students and sweaty businessmen — frantically scanning the crowd for lay-options in a haze of secondhand smoke and testosterone. They'd clearly bought into the Western notion of a bar as a place to pickup chicks, take 'em home, but the only attractive woman I saw was a Punjabi singer with six beefy bodyguards. The worst of it was, Al and I fit right in, two lonely no-hopers drinking beer laced with glycerin and afterward, drunk, with gas and heart pain, locked in the messy birdcage of my hostel, I decided to skip having breakfast with Al and jumped on the morning's first train into Mysore.

Now here we are, watching cricket on telly, away from the blistering heat of Mysore's streets. It's been a restless few weeks in South India, made worse by the fact no one speaks Hindi. The language can change with a bus ride down here — Kannada, Malayam, Tamil, Gujarati — and while I'd kept up in the northern part of India, I don't have the will to make flashcards in this humidity.

"So, Al, done any yoga lately?" I drawl.

"Not likely. I did play some five-a-side footy with the lads."

"Have you at least *tried* a *masala dosa* yet?"

He screws up his face. "Those hot curry pizza wraps?"

"They're fermented lentil pancakes filled with chilies and potatoes. I eat them like three times a day — it's a regional specialty."

"Mmm, I dunno, this place makes a good korma."

"Fuck that, we're leaving. You're having a *dosa*."

We pay for our drinks then head down the road to a place near the Ashtanga Yoga Academy.

"Al, have you noticed you've *always* got beggar kids?" I glance at the flock trailing us to the café. Scabby, half-naked, hot-footing across the pavement. "They only follow you because you're so stingy."

"They can all just piss off, mate. Especially those free."

By this point I know he means to say *three* which is either a speech impediment or a bad case of Cockney. Whatever it is, it's getting on my nerves. In fact, everything about English Al just *bugs* me. Firstly, there's Blackpool, some English resort town. He *brags* about their one-third scale Eiffel tower replica. Their regional specialty? Boiled whelks with vinegar. It *hurts* my eyes to look at his sunburn. Wherever I go, he turns up and follows, he orders what I do but then never eats it and now, once again, he's brought his own beggars despite the fact he *never baksheeshes.*

I originally came to Mysore to buy essential oils, try some *ashtanga* and learn to charm cobras and while I've succeeded in all but the latter, the further I go south, the more I lose focus. Ever since Jimmy explained my Saturn Returning, I've been hopping trains every week, buying bric-a-brac. From Udaipur to Gujarat, Pune to Mysore. Bagging South India like a man with a checklist: The Caves of Ajanta, the temples of Hampi, the tribal Karnatakan dancers, Shiva Ratri. I've got jasmine and sandalwood oil up the yin-yang, shot ten rolls of film, *click-click,* Kodak whoopee but the question is not only when to stop gathering but how do I stop English Al from following me?

At least the *ashtanga* is keeping me humble. Never have I seen such sinewy bodies — Indian, Western, men, women, all ages — united in one single purpose: *dehydrating.* Up north in the foothills the practice was all about generating inner heat, deep stretches and chanting. In Mysore it's already hotter than hell, no need for a shawl or to crank up your inner radiator so instead you bow down to the sun fifty times and sweat yourself into a puddle of cartilage. Even the classroom is built like an oven, a walled-in brick courtyard where the mats melt like cheese. If you don't make the six a.m. session, you're *toast.* In Sanskrit, *ashtanga* means "go back to Rishikesh, Mr. C."

Still, I'm impressed by how yoga adapts, like cuisine or fashion or architecture, to the climate — the ultimate expression of which is Lord Shiva: pure meditation, half-frozen on a mountain top. For weeks now, in keeping my promise to G, I've been developing my own daily practice, thinking if terrible yoga can be taught, like the class back in Pushkar, I might as well do my own thing with the basics. The goal, said one *yogini*, is to tire the body enough to sit still with a clear mind, unthinking, and the best way to get there is to focus your practice — unlike your career — on what you do poorly. For me this means anything done on one leg — "Your challenge this lifetime, Gemini, is balance" — as well as not looking around at other people, or trying to impress anyone with my scorpion.

"Met any fit birds?" English Al inquires. He pokes at the seeds in his coconut *sambar*. "I've seen a few lookers wandering 'bout town. I was you, I'd be chatting-up one of them instructors."

He's hit another sore spot — that seems to be his way — my deteriorating success with the ladies. Ever since Jaime, Mona aside, the whole female universe has conspired against me. The baker in Amsterdam, the Egyptian student, the irate Jewish Frenchwoman, the Australian biologist. I couldn't even get laid at a free love commune for chrissakes. Strangest of all though, I can't seem to masturbate. No matter who I think about, memories or fantasies, my erections are bored and immune to further stimulus. In fact, I haven't had an orgasm since Jaipur when I dream-shagged that brown, bathing goddess in the fortress.

"Al, I've decided to take *bramacharya*."

He stares at me vacantly.

"The Hindu vow of celibacy?"

"You mean, all official like — *ph-woar,* I can't eat this. Does this place do curry and chips?"

"Eat the pancake." I swallow my anger, the lesson of Neves. "That's why I'm wearing this bracelet, the white one."

Again, the blank stare.

"I got it last night during *Shiva Ratri.* The big, noisy festival? Fireworks? Shiva's birthday?"

"Naw, musta missed it, mate. Had in me earplugs."

"Al, we're not leaving 'til you *eat the fucking pancake.*"

Back at the hotel I pack up my things, head to the market and locate the snake charmer — I made the mistake of telling Al where I was staying which means he'll be down in the lobby come dinner time. Three hours later, via rickety bus, a white-knuckle motorbike ride and a hike I arrive at a village, all sticks, with no plumbing, throw down my pack and start beating the shrubbery.

In Hindu mythology — and also on postcards — there's a *naga,* a cobra, around Shiva's neck. It represents his mastery of *kundalini* energy, the feminine, serpentine power of the universe. *Kundalini*, say the mystics, can be accessed and harnessed through disciplined yoga and non-orgasmic sex. Barring that, it sleeps at the base of your spine, mostly ignored until the moment of death. *Then*, it shoots out the top of your skull — which to me sounds a lot like my last DMT trip. Charming cobras, some say, awakens *kundalini* without all the messy attachments to other people, bringing you closer not only to Shiva but personal power — i.e. what the fuck you're supposed to be doing.

Next thing you know, it's anything-is-possible-in-India and, after practicing with the defanged variety for two days, I'm bobbing my fist in front of a lidless basket, coming face-to-face with my first deadly cobra. There's dozens of villagers crowded around me, the snake-charmer's playing his flute in my ear and since cobras react to movement, not sound, I'm trying to mesmerize the thing with my rings. When it strikes, I snatch hold of its hood with my free hand. The tail encircles my arm like a whip. Afterward, I sob on the bus back to Mysore, ashamed at how cavalier and stupid I'd just been.

My latest absurd notion is flying to Lhasa and hitchhiking hundreds of miles to Mt. Kailash, a pipe dream given it's early March and the passes stay frozen until early summer. Bottom line is I'm down to my last thousand dollars, whirlpooling back to my life in the States. To going home broke to my Naturalists at Large gig — the life of a glorified camp counselor again. I suppose I've stopped smoking and started doing yoga, but how long is that going to last around old friends? No car, no phone, no girl, no home base, no answer for "What do you do for a living?" Fumbling for lip balm I squeak the squeak-Buddha.

To think I was chosen messiah of the Techno Pagans…

March 3, Mysore

Returning to my original hotel in Mysore, I find English Al has taken my old room. Before long we're back at the café eating dosas, the same band of beggar kids crouched on the sidewalk. When I toss them some rupees they scurry to find shade — or else to pay off their Dickensian masters — but it buys us an hour's respite from their staring, like lunch buys an hour in front of the air-conditioner.

"So Al, done any yoga lately?"

"Not likely. But I did have look at that temple like you said. Couple a priests in the yard, playing footy — turns out they bof' support bloody Arsenal."

We order some Cokes, suck them down through cracked straws — I haven't had a functional straw since Jaipur — and after our Cokes we get ice cream, then tea. Finally, I can bear it no longer.

"So Al, where ya headed?" I ask through grit teeth, knowing he's waiting to see my next move.

"Dunno, mate — 'ave you 'eard of this place called Kerala?" He points to a page in his *Stupid English Tourist Book*. "Says 'ere it's the home of the world's first democra'ically-elected communist government. Wonder what that's all about."

My hands become fists because Al doesn't give a toss about Kerala's politics, birdlife, high literacy rate or even surf. Kerala to him means drinking cheap lager while plying the estuaries on paddleboats with the Commonwealthers. I can give him the herk-and-jerk, wrong bus, ding-dong-ditch but I've already done that three times and for what? To escape from the sense my whole trip's been a failure aside from some rocks and a dime-store harmonica? Quitting weed means I can't really hang with the stoners — which cuts my camaraderie options considerably on this circuit — couples depress me, single women won't have me and all the Indians want is my money.

"What name? What country? Come stay my guesthouse?"

For a good twenty minutes we sit there in stalemate, flipping through guidebooks, complaining about the service. We order more tea to keep out of the heat. While we're waiting, the beggars return to the sidewalk.

"I'm leaving Mysore tomorrow," I declare. "I'm going to the Mudulamai wildlife sanctuary." It's the first that either of us have heard of this plan. I'm hoping to shake him with a surprise-attack itinerary.

"Now there's an idea, mate. The jungle, that's *muuch* better!"

"I thought you were planning to go to Kerala."

Al turns beet red. "Well, I was... I am... but you're right, it'd be nice to do something *zoological*." He says he was planning to leave Mysore anyway then goes on to marvel how one of the roads to Kerala runs directly through the Mudulamai sanctuary.

I feel like I've just kicked a badly-groomed puppy. *Christ, what's the harm in more time with this nitwit? Not like I'm the world's greatest travelling companion either — and who's going to tell him his ears need more sunscreen?* With a deep yogic breath, I channel the Osho Zen spirit of learning to transform my poisons into honey.

"Al, just shut the fuck up already. I'll see you tomorrow at six at the bus station."

March 4, Mudulamai Wildlife Sanctuary

Mudulamai borders three Indian states, Karnataka, Tamil Nadu and Kerala. *The Stupid Guide* even devotes it a picture, predictably that of a roaring Bengal tiger.

I've been meaning to go to a national park, get a glimpse of indigenous flora and fauna. In fact, this whole trip is the first time I've travelled where my sole intention hasn't been seeing animals. The plan, as Al and I hop the morning bus — full to bursting, no honkeys on board, several chickens — is to rent a simple room near a simple café and spend a few days taking hikes through the jungle. After three nauseating hours however, the plan falls apart outside the park office where, after waving goodbye to the bus, we find ourselves under a huge metal signpost: *For Your Own Safety...*

No one is allowed inside the park unless they're on one of the minibus tours and, as I'm trying to reconcile this with *hiking*, the morning's first minibus hauls into view. Even from two hundred yards away, I can hear the whiny treble of *Dil To Pagle Hai*. When the door hisses open, some three dozen college students — all of them men — tumble out and start smoking. The last people out are a heavyset white couple. The woman immediately plops on the ground. Hyperventilates into a handkerchief.

"Did you see any wildlife?" English Al calls out.

"Ja," says the ruddy-faced man. "Vee saw deer."

I clunk my head again the office window.

The building is locked — though the sign says it's open. Inside, the walls are covered with tiger posters. After scanning a chalkboard which lists accommodation options I hoist my ridiculous pack to my shoulders. It's heavy, lopsided and makes me spin circles; full of books, bolts of silk, snorkel gear, leaking oils; warm clothing I haven't washed or worn for two months. I join English Al in the parking lot with the Germans.

"Zee elephant ride is too short," says the man. "Bus ride is nothing, just for show, ja? No one sees animals, just a big party." He gestures to the students who blessedly ignore us.

Before we can press him he runs to his wife who's now throwing up in some ornamental flower bushes. Al and I follow a thin, gravel trail down an oily, green brook running next to the highway. The mosquitos are aggressive. Outside a log dormitory we find a man in a sarong sullenly dragging a rake through some leaves. Turns out he's the manager, yes he has beds but we've got a few hours to kill before they're free. We enter the café — the only café — play a few games of go-fish while we're waiting and after half an hour, the same guy reappears, sets down his rake and puts on a dirty apron.

"Only have toast. Only have tea. Only serve between ten o'clock and one."

"You do serve dinner, though?" says Al optimistically.

The manager scowls. "There no woman, only me!"

"But the book…"

"Yaar, I know book. This is *off-season*."

A thirty-something Australian couple enters the café and orders some tea in a combative manner. Turns out they're the ones vacating the dorm. Birdwatchers, I assume, from their khakis and binoculars.

"How'dja like it here?" says Al, his voice breaking.

"We hate it," says the woman. "It's India at its worst. You're not allowed to go into the jungle unless you're on that dodgy tour bus and the only thing anyone sees is deer — the same two deer — and they're likely drugged."

Her boyfriend is quick to pick up the thread: how you have to beg food, how the manager's a "peeping psychopath", how no-one's seen tigers around for "blaady years" and how, once they've finished this last cup of tea, they're taking the next bus in either direction.

I stand abruptly. "I'm going for a walk."

"Good luck, mate," says the Aussie guy. "You can't *go* anywhere."

"Bollocks. I'm going find me a tiger. Watch my pack, Al. I'm headed downriver."

I toss a few *rupes* on the table for toast then purposefully distance myself from what's happening. I just need to stretch my legs, get some air, donate some blood to the swarming mosquitoes. *For my own safety* — my ass, baba-G. That sign needs to be on the back of every car. There's a million more chances to die trying to get here than there is of being mauled by the last Bengal tiger.

Women are washing their clothes in the brook, filling the slow-moving pools with pink suds. One of them calls out something as I pass, alerting a uniformed guard in a hut.

"Oy, where you going, tourist man," he shouts. "Not allowed, walking alone in jungle."

"Alright, come with me!" I continue downstream. Suddenly it's like I've disturbed an ant colony.

Rangers appear from every direction, blowing plastic whistles and waving old rifles, jabbering in broken English about cobras, tigers, spiders, smugglers and all the other heebie-jeebies of the jungle. When one of them mentions the deer on the minibus, I throw back my head and laugh like a madman — like someone's who's completely lost their sense of humor — and there, far above me, I notice... a seagull.

Once more I ask myself "*What do you want?*", the defining question of my journey to India. It dawns on me I don't want anything so much as spending a day being physically comfortable. No backache from riding the bus, no mosquitos, no stepping in things, no chapati children, no praying for mercy every time I hit the toilet and *nobody touching my arm for any reason*. I sink to my knees in the dirt like a drama queen. I am broken by, giving up on and exiting India.

"Okay, okay, put your guns down, soldier boys. I'm not going hiking. I'm going to Goa."

March 5, Konkan Express

Hopped the first train heading north out of Mangalore, straight off the overnight bus, low on sleep. It's a newly-installed line, only three weeks old, and everyone we pass seems happy to see us. Little kids flying kites, farmers tending fields, more defecating grandmothers, teenagers playing cricket — all of them stop what they're doing and wave. Your arm would fall off if you waved back at everyone.

For the first time in months I can see, taste the ocean, its negative ions aloft in the breeze. I haven't seen ocean since leaving Los Angeles which makes this the longest I've ever been away from it. Soon I'll be entering paradise, praise Shiva. Coconut palms, fresh fish and white sand. Until then I'll be sitting in an unreserved railcar with fifty-six seats and some two hundred Indians:

And they sit and they stand and they lie and they squat
On luggage racks, floors, all conceivable spots
Men, women, children, infants and crones
On their way somewhere else or on their way home
And I'll miserably tell you what's wrong with this place
There's too many people and not enough space
For all of them, each with a bag or suitcase
Staring mere inches from this Western face…

Across from me, Al sits reading his book, a naturalist adventure by Gerald Durrell. He's reading the thing for the very third time — not just in his life, but since he left Blackpool. As soon as he's finished, he'll start it again. When I ask how he likes it the third time around, he says, "It's o'right, but I already know what happens." He says this without the slightest trace of irony.

I tried to get rid of him, good Lord, I did, in the kindliest, gentlest tone I could manage: "Hey, so I'm done with this Mudulamai place, have a great time in Kerala — here's my e-mail. Who me? I'm just gonna flop on some beach, do some reading and you've only got that one little book there…"

That's when the Australians had helpfully chimed in how Kerala was ten degrees hotter than Mysore and, since I would be heading to Goa, I should check out this gem of a beach called Palolem — before it explodes with the arrival of the train line. Twenty-two hours later and here's English Al and I making a hasty retreat out of India. Once more, his presence serves as a reminder: I look in his blue, bovine eyes and feel beaten.

The state of Goa might technically be part of India but it's also the avatar of a cop-out — a former

Portuguese colony where the restaurants serve pork and forty percent of the population are Christian. People like Al go to Goa on charter flights direct from Paris, Hamburg or London, lured by the thought of a drunken moon rave, a romp on the beach and a curry at poolside. Messiahs-in-training don't go to Goa — We take to the mountains! We seek out the wise men! — but here I am not only going but craving it: Westernized food and bikini beach hedonism.

I console myself by noting this Palolem place gets only passing mention in *The Stupid Guide*. If it's any good though, the next edition will kill it, condemn it to death-by-hotel in '99.

The guy to my left is a Mangalore cab driver on a luggage-free jaunt to Calingut, central Goa. No matter how far I slide toward the window, he makes sure we're touching from ankle to elbow.

"How many Indians in Washington?" he asks me, after a barrage of what-name-what-countrys. He wears a pink, plastic diamond on his pinkie of the type often sold as sex-charms by street-vendors.

"Washington state or Washington D.C?"

He Hindu headshakes. Same-same either way.

"Fourteen billion," I say with a sigh. "How many Americans in Kashmir, asshole?"

English Al snickers behind his Durrell. Grinding my teeth, I return to my journal. Unfazed, the man offers me soot-covered peanuts, thrusting the bag between eyeballs and paper. To appease him, I pick out and shell a sad specimen and soon have a horrible paste on my tongue.

"Why are you going to Goa?" I ask.

Without batting an eye, he says, "German women."

"Binoculars?"

"No — but bringing good camera!"

It's no secret that Indian men prowl the beaches for eyefuls of scantily-clad western women. The circuit is rife with tales of topless blondes waking up from beach naps with lenses trained on them. Usually, I end up feeling sorry for the blondes — that's terrible honey, you're just so *oppressed* — but here I can't help but feel sorry for this guy with his half-open shirt, plastic ring and bad peanuts. Twelve hours each way for the privilege of walking in polyester trousers on some crowded beach, alienating women and their boyfriends alike before crashing on the sand for a furious meat-beat. If he's lucky, he'll convince some poor woman to pose with him, perhaps get a shot with his arm around her waist, then tell all his buddies back home she's his girlfriend. The adventures of Hindu Jim, the thirty-year-old teenager.

He starts to grill Al about whether he's married, how many siblings and where he went to school. The air is as hot as a rectal thermometer. Al suddenly snaps: "Just leave me alone!"

The Indians clustered around us crack-up and it feels like the train begins to lose speed. The taxi guy claps his hand on my neck. "Your friend here is simple boy, you clever man."

I'm torn between whether to laugh or look mean, end up doing both 'cause it's true and it's rude but I'm nearing the end of my rope with these people. English Al just says, "Cheers, mate." What else can he do?

Upon arrival at the station, we spill from the carriage, relieved Hindu Jim decides not to follow. I'm surprised to find ten other tourists on the platform.

Word is getting around about Palolem. We miss the first wave of auto-rickshaws — and become the only two people to get stranded at the station. It's a time when I'd normally sit on my pack, roll and smoke a well-earned cigarette. Instead, I swallow the last of my water, cut a hole in the bottle so it can't be resold. When Al asks me how long I'm planning to stay, I dip my sunglasses down on my nose.

"Al-bert." I draw out his name, making it sound all American cowboy. "As soon as these feet hit the sand, you're on your own. Good luck to you, brother. Been real nice knowing you."

A lone auto-rickshaw returns to the station, spirits us under the tracks, along rice fields, through coconut palms, down a knick-knack-shack road and deposits us onto a small, sandy cul-de-sac. In front of us lies a broad arc of beach, some heavy, wooden dinghies and a green, waveless sea. Open-air cafés either side of the road sprout faded umbrellas reading *Limca* and *Pepsi*. There's carts selling fruit, a few mopeds and cars, a dozen or so tourists in bathing suits buying postcards and while it might not exactly be wilderness, the far ends of the beach appear to be deserted. I turn to see Al arguing with the touts, a beggar kid already tugging his sleeve. He looks nothing so much as an overgrown Boy Scout with his green Army pack, knee-high socks and knobby knees.

An Indian youth approaches me with a business card. I like the smile on his sun-darkened face.

"On beach?" he says, and that's all I need to hear.

"Lead the way — and no bullshit, it's been a long journey."

"Oy, did you find one?" English Al shouts.

I don't even turn around.

The youth draws up short. "Only one hut. You can maybe share with friend?"

"Not likely."

He takes my hand and we walk into the sunset.

PIG TOILET

Learned somethin' new, not afraid to admit
That the beast we call pig will eat human shit
'Cause this mornin' I squat, and looked down though my feet
And eatin' my stool was the Other White Meat...
For the toilets in Goa are built 'round the pig
Poop chute through the bamboo door feedin'-trough rig
And with paper in hand, the pigs see you comin'
For a queue at the loo they come snortin' and runnin'
And this is for real, friend, I swear I'm not funnin'
But I aim for, hit snout when I do my tail-gunnin'...
And this mornin' I'm loose, I'm not ploppin', I'm hosin'
Which doesn't deter their noisy brown nosin'
And stateside they're havin' a hell of a time
Ad-campaigns tryin' to reinvent swine
Sayin' how smart, much-maligned and how clean
How pork chops and ham hocks are high in protein
But in Goa you glean why the pig is obscene
Understand what the Kosher and Muslim laws mean...
Even here though you still find pork on the menu
At just about every food-servin' venue
Pork curry, why worry? Eat pork vindaloo
Next mornin' the pigs'll eat that shit too
And Marvin, I won't touch no swine 'less I'm starvin'
Won't see veggie-me Christmas honey-ham carvin'

'Cause this mornin' I squat, and looked down through my feet
And eatin' my stool was the other white meat.

March 10, Palolem Beach

Five days I've been cooling my heels on this beach, a place so idyllic it's making me depressed. Either that or it's the Mefloquin, rumored to cause mood swings — overheard a guy yesterday saying it was used to treat mania. Yesterday, I called my best friend, David Hothouse — a music reporter in Phoenix, Arizona — to confess how miserable I was here in paradise. How the Messiah got lost. How much I missed Jaime.

"David!" I cried, when I heard the man's voice for the first time in months crackle over the rent-a-phone.

"Ian!"

"David!"

"Ian!"

"Get a pen. I only have cash for two minutes — call me back, here's the number."

But the bastard had failed to locate a pen. I could hear him in the background tearing his room apart. When he came to phone he was breathless: "Just tell me." The world-famous journalist who couldn't find a pen. The phone call had ended with me shouting numbers.

English Al had found this particularly funny. Furious, I'd stalked up the beach to my cabin, written Jaime a take-me-back postcard — woe is me — tore the thing up and threw it on the campfire. I'm starting to think this emotional rollercoaster has something to do with quitting marijuana — although it's a huge relief not to be carrying and I've noticed no physical effects of withdrawal.

Today I wake up feeling restless as usual, well before dawn, when the house rooster calls. I'm in a thatch hut on a beach in Southern Goa. I hear ocean, seagulls and the wind through the palms. Above me, the geckos peer down from the rafters, darting to feast on my-blood-engorged mosquitos. I wonder how long before they cut out the middle man, go right to the source and become vampire lizards. The thought makes me smile and I feel a bit better; vow not to make the same mistakes as yesterday. Might even be nice and play footy with Al — though it wouldn't surprise me if he didn't show up today.

I rise and light the Nag Champa and candles surrounding the shrine to Ganesh on my nightstand, his sandalwood *murti* ringed with semi-precious stones, beach-glass, stray feathers and pieces of driftwood. Closing my eyes, I concentrate on his image — a man with an elephant's head, on one foot — until suddenly I see him and it doesn't feel imagined. Four arms, one hand holding what looks like a seashell. There's light radiating from his upraised left toe, where Jimmy had told me to focus devotion. The raised toe represents Ganesh's next move: hopping forward to dance, staying still to maintain balance, raising up for a kick, stepping back for defense. It's the place where the future comes out of the present.

Afterward, I tidy the shrine of old flowers, take a deep breath and blow out the candles, daub myself with Mysore's best sandalwood oil and head to pig-feeding station, or "toilet." The first time I saw it I immediately thought of some American pork brand's *The Other White Meat* campaign. "You know, it's like chicken" — only no, guys, it's not.

Chickens don't follow you clucking to the shit-house.

I return to my shack, one of six on the property, maintained by a quiet, always-smiling, Goan family; change into my swim-trunks, grab snorkelling equipment and lock my door with a thin, wire cable. The predawn air is lukewarm and agreeable. Barefoot, not wearing a shirt, I get goosebumps. It's low tide so I walk on the wet, exposed sand, scaring the fiddler crabs into their burrows. On the beach's northern end lies a shallow lagoon, a good hundred yards from the last batch of guesthouses. After wading across a warm, tidal outflow, I head to a patch of hard sand among the boulders. Further up the beach is a serious yoga class, four hours a day and open to anyone, but the instructor is a leathery old man in a g-string and, at this hour, I prefer the crack of dawn.

By the time I've rotated all of my joints, the sun appears, blindingly, over the palms. I perform several rounds of sun salutations, then move on to animals, warriors and headstands. Afterward, sweaty, I lie on the sand, tense every muscle then sag into corpse. Several minutes go by, my heartbeat slows down and I soak-up the *prana* — in Sanskrit, vital air.

When I hear someone crossing the river I sit up. A shapely brunette woman peeks through the boulders. I shake sand from my dreadlocks and frown at her, confused. I don't have a watch or anything on me.

"*Namaste*," she says. "I hope I'm not bothering you. I've seen you here the past few days." She's wearing a blue, one-piece bathing suit, sarong to match. Determined brown eyes. Her accent is Israeli.

"It's flat here," I say, "and it faces the sun. There's a class going on further up the beach."

"I know, but I've never done yoga before. I was wondering if you could teach me."

I neurotically jabber about how I just learned, have only been doing my own practice a few weeks, would feel terrible if she got injured or something and how I can barely touch my own feet. After I finish, she shrugs and says nothing, still standing in the water, clutching the hem of her sarong. There's courage involved in approaching some weird hippie, alone on the sand, doing slow-motion fish-flops.

"Excuse me. What I meant to say was, 'Why don't we start with sun salutations.'"

I spend the next hour taking Hannah through poses, spotting the tougher ones, saying when to breathe. She's solidly built, with a bicyclist's thighs; makes up for in balance what she lacks in flexibility. Afterwards, I learn she's a business student from Tel Aviv, recently finished her two required years in the military. It's a common pilgrimage for many Israelis, to seek peace in India after training to kill their many enemies. We don't exchange much information beyond that: where we're from, where we've been, how long we've been here, what we do. I'm reminded that this is what everyone wonders, not solely the pestering masses of India.

She invites me to breakfast with her and her fiancé. My heart sinks a bit but not bad. I decline. Show her my ridiculous free-diving fins, which I've only used twice but have been carrying all this time.

"Gotta get in shape." I strap them on and shuffle backward. "Who knows, I might climb a mountain in Tibet."

Hannah tells me she very much enjoyed her first lesson and arranges to me meet tomorrow for the next one.

I cross the tide-rippled sand into the surf, spit in my mask then stick it on my face. It's a welcoming feeling that brings back good memories: spearfishing sea bass on Catalina Island, showing kids their first octopus under the kelp canopy. I swim to a small offshore reef I found yesterday; dive to see urchins, gorgonians and puffer fish. The visibility is terrible, I only get glimpses but am pleased to remember a few Latin names. I emerge sometime later, in front of my beach-shack, have a cold rinse then retreat to the shade. The teenager, Krishna, who'd met me on arrival, appears bearing porridge with chunks of papaya. His smile is infectious, like he knows some great secret.

After breakfast, several pigs run by, headed for the john. Inspired, I retire to the hammock with my journal: a clothbound number I picked up in Udaipur. It releases pressed dandelion petals as I scribble.

English Al appears in a pair of red Speedos. His flat, vapid face lights up when he sees me. Someone has shaved off his bowl-job, I notice. Dude's got a passable crew-cut this morning. I wave him over, make fun of his grape-smugglers, tell him I'd taught my first yoga class this morning. Ask if he'd like to learn a new card game — I could teach him, like, Rummy 500 or something.

"And I'm taking away that Gerald Durrell book. I've got something by Bhagwan Rajneesh you can read."

He's delighted to learn to play Rummy 500, though *Sing, Dance, Rejoice* makes him cringe and say, "Blimey."

I break out the Bicycles, teach him the rules and proceed to beat the living snot out of him, baiting with aces, seeding the draw pile. It's the only way he's going to learn, I figure. When the score is three hundred to negative fifty a little girl comes by selling ropes of marigolds. English Al tenses to shoo her away but before he can do so, I beckon her over.

I fall asleep with the flowers draped around my neck, wake up refreshed a few hours later. Amazingly, English Al has departed, leaving *Sing, Dance, Rejoice* behind on the table. For a moment I actually find myself missing him then perish the thought and scope the beach for women. I have a stray heartache about Jaime and her boyfriends but Krishna interrupts me wanting to play frisbee. We go down to the water, one native, one tourist, and become two young men tossing a yellow disc. We get into a rhythm that's nearly aerobic, floating it over the beach-walkers' heads. When we've both had enough and he comes over to shake my hand, I pick him up and dump him in the ocean. We splash 'til we're soaked then retreat for bucket showers. Lunch is plain rice and a fiery fish curry.

I know what it means to hunt fish in their element, to open their skin with my trident-tipped spear, to slit their gills on the way to the surface, to help them die quickly, to gut and fillet them. There's trauma involved in taking a life and I eat fish because I've experienced killing them. Few things strike me as more hopeless and irresponsible than a squeamish person eating a fast-food hamburger.

English Al returns with an intense, balding Brit with glacial blue eyes, introduces him as Chris. They apparently have a mutual friend in Manchester, another fly in the Indian web of coincidence. When Chris finds out I grew up in LA, he and I get to talking about the cinema. I tell him my pet theory of how blockbuster movies are the modern-day equivalent of the Egyptian pyramids. Everyone pays their five bucks a head to watch million dollar magic performed in a temple. Chris laughs, says he never thought of himself as a priest — turns out he's the director of some British soap I've never heard of. Al, however, is what they call "gobsmacked" and asks for gossip about the cast. When Chris asks me what do I do for a living, I tell him I'm a performance poet. Say it like I mean it.

"Really?" He laughs like he's in on the joke. "Go on then, mate. Show us your stuff."

I pick up my journal and read him 'Pig Toilet' along with a couple of poems from Osho.

"That's quite good," he says. "Where do you perform?"

"Actually, that was my first reading."

"You're kidding! Well done, mate. I'm really impressed. Have you thought about performing poetry in Britain?"

"Oy, you should go to London," says Al. "It's the *lit-tri-chur* capital of the world, innit?"

"You think I could make a living?" I ask.

"Don't know," says Chris. "But I'll buy you a beer."

I pass on the beer but accept some fresh juice and together we watch fishermen haul in their nets. Most of the catch are no bigger than anchovies which the women — wrapped in colorful cloth — separate by size into wicker baskets. We make plans to meet up for dinner tomorrow. Chris says he hopes to hear more of my poetry, adding if I can make it to London, he might know some people in the media who can help me.

Feeling *chuffed*, which is British for stoked, like a fire, I decide to go for an afternoon run; find myself sprinting faster then ever before, hurdling sandcastles, doing cariocas. My intestines are no longer withered by dysentery, my cuts have all healed, I've gained a few pounds. I'm twenty-seven-years-old, in the summer of my life, feeling alive and primed for any mountain.

Back at the guesthouse, I take my third bucket then put on my vest from the Cairo bazaar. I remember the one-eyed tailor who'd made it and wished me good luck for a hundred-fifty years. English Al arrives while I'm putting on oil — tonight, the antidepressant geranium. I make him rub sandalwood into his forehead: "To moisten your third eye in preparation for our card game." I'm not sure what I believe anymore, but the oils smell nice and it's fun to have a play. Looking down at my rings — there's five of them now — I wonder what happened to that love potion I made.

We go out to Palolem's finest beach shack, where two-hundred rupes gets a five-course meal. When Al discovers how much I love seafood he calls me a "fish-and-chipocrite" which I find hilarious. After dinner, we order mint tea and play cards. To my chagrin he wins the first couple of hands. He's no longer my Rummy 500 whipping boy, he's a hundred points ahead and I have to pay attention.

As I'm frowning down at the treacherous draw pile, trying to remember who discarded the queen, I overhear two women whispering behind me about how, "Oh no, we've no money for tea." The waiter arrives, a cool cat in a polo shirt. The women explain they've forgotten their purses. Both of their accents sound European but I find the whole bothersome business distracting. Without thinking I take out a fifty rupee note, turn with it scissored between my fingers. Suddenly I'm facing a lovely, tan woman with golden-brown hair in a lime green bikini. Her eyes are chatoyant, like cat's-eye, but green. Over the bikini, a sheer cotton blouse.

"That is so sweet of you," she says, clearly French. She accepts the bill gratefully, without faking protest, and offers it up to the waiter like a butterfly.

"You didn't have to do that," she says. She sweeps her hair onto one shoulder. Big smile.

Her friend, a shy, mousy woman with bangs says, "Don't forget to tell us where you're staying."

Realizing they're waiting for me to reply, I mumble something awkward about a gentleman's duty. The waiter retreats to make change, refill tea. I hear English Al clear his throat behind me.

The Frenchwoman tilts her head slightly to the side, an acknowledgment of the gawk that must be on my face.

"I should probably get back to my game," I say, spellbound.

"I know," she says, but she doesn't look away.

Reluctantly, I return to the Rummy, my concentration shattered to bits. Force myself to consider my hand. Decide to go for broke and discard the queen of diamonds.

"Lovely," says Al. He snatches the whole pile. Chuckles victorious. Lays down two straights. He's beaten me, handily. Shamelessly even. With my own goddamn deck at my own goddamn game.

We bring our chairs around to sit with the ladies, exchanging our names and countries of origin. The Frenchwoman introduces herself as Ma Deva Anugraha which, an obvious name-change for a Westerner, can only mean she's an Osho *sannyasin*. When Al cracks a smile and says, "So then, *Ma Deva...*" I kick him so hard on the ankle he squeals.

"Al and I met in Pune," I explain.

"And what did you think of our commune?" asks Anugraha.

I throw Al a look that says, *Blow this for me, you'll be eating those cards and playing Rummy with the pigs.*

"He had a great voice and some good stuff to say."

"But he's not the reason you came to India."

For the first time I *briefly, coherently* touch on the dreams and visions that brought me to Egypt and how, after three months racing around India, I've come to Palolem to get my thoughts together.

Anugraha nods. "Your journey is so Osho. Sometimes be the bee. Sometimes be the flower."

"So *don't* seek and you shall find?" quips Al.

"Mmm," she agrees, her eyes fixed upon me.

I'm uncomfortable hearing Osho used as an adjective but the way she says it sounds thought-out and meaningful. She's older than I by I'd guess half a decade. A professional photographer. A grown-up. A woman. Her companion, Julie, however, is salt of the earth. An English schoolteacher she'd met on the ferry. It seems synchronistic that while I've got Al, Anugraha is travelling with a shy Brit named Julie.

The ladies invite us to the world-famous Anjuna flea market, share the cost of cab for a day-trip tomorrow. I politely decline saying I've found a quiet rhythm I'd rather not disrupt with crowds and car travel. English Al concurs. I'm amazed I haven't leapt at a chance to spend time with a gorgeous French *sannyasin* but in truth I'm content to remain on this beach and experience another perfect day just like this one. When everyone stands to go back to their huts, I invite them to join us for dinner tomorrow. English Al says that Chris the director of *East Enders* will be there. Julie's jaw drops. She asks about some actor-guy named Pearson.

"See you tomorrow, same time then?" says Al.

"Consider it a rematch. Prepare for revenge."

We shake hands on the sand in front of the restaurant and return to our guesthouses in opposite directions.

Back in my shack, unperturbed by mosquitoes, I tear off my little white bracelet from Mysore. Light a candle and take out my mirrored, clothbound journal only to find myself lost, lost for words. I'm in the realm of the Serpent again, past the power of description where language doesn't stick. I'd been that thing once, the many-armed cobra. It was stone, like a mountain, but also in movement.

Sing, says the Muse *and I will dance. Ascend to the peak of your craft, fall in love.*

In the back of the journal, in careful letters, I write *Ma Deva Anugraha*. It's a name I want to be sure to remember.

IX. THE DREAM

RAREFIED AIR

Flashback to a back-alley shack in Mysore
The ultimate pure-essence sandalwood store
Selling oil from the flowers south India grows
Which when sniffed are like paintings you see through your nose...
Jasmine and ylang-ylang which have the effect
Of igniting the fire of the opposite sex
Lemongrass for energy, lavender for burns
Geraniums, lotuses, basil and ferns
And after I'd spent my fat stack of rupees
(my fragrance-filled nose on the brink of a sneeze)
The oil man had one last bottle to show me
The essence of the black-blossomed jacaranda tree...
And he took the glass stopper out of that jar
Said, "This is the base of the perfume Drakkar"
I said, "What's it good for, Baba oil-czar?"
And he shrugged said, "Attracts the French girls from afar..."

Flash forward to Goa, to Palolem beach
My celibate stretch in its twentieth week
And after my swim and after my shower
(a quarter past sunset o'clock was the hour)

I unzipped my bag of plant-extract power
And applied the oil of the jacaranda flower...
To third eye and temples, earlobes, chest and nape
No woman who smelled me tonight could escape
My tentacular clutches, my heart's off its crutches
On the prowl looking for daughter or duchess
And I join English Al to go get some eats
With another Brit bloke he'd met on the beach
Who happens to be a big name and big spender
The director of the British TV show East Enders
The most popular soap in his island nation
In Palolem chillin', a two-week vacation
And wouldn't you know, he'd love to hear poetry
(have his agent contact my agent, get back to me)
And that's when she walked in and sat down like a dream
The most beautiful French woman I've ever seen...

Green eyes like a cat that hunts for its meals
Buxom, tan flesh to my body appeals
Honey hair falling over soft, sinewy shoulders
She speaks her own truth with a smile, my heart smolders
It's the Osho sannyasin, Ma Deva Anugraha
Could this be the end of my heart's Kaliyuga?
"But she's cult sheep from Rajneeshpuram," I mutter
English Al says, "I reckon she's a bit of a nutter
And mate, seeing how much you rubbished maroon
Why don't you read her that stuff from the commune?"
I say, "Al if you mention those poems I wrote?
I'll take this nutter-butter knife to your English throat —
Je m'excuse, mademoiselle, would you care to sit here?
I have a few poems, je suis prêt à lire"

And I pick seven non-Osho poems and read
Seducing Anugraha with word, scent and deed
And after Director Man says keep in touch
After the tea, bill, lights, handshakes and such
When the moment of action and no more words looms
Anugraha says, "Let's go out under the moon..."

We walk to my hut...
Fireflies in my gut...
Turns out she knows oils and she smells each one but...
When she reaches jacaranda and samples a whiff?
She turns up her nose and says, "Yuck, what is this?"
And I laugh 'cause I know the black-blossom's use
To attract and repulse, an octopus truth
And I ask if there's something she'd like to apply
She says, "Certainement, but I'll let you decide"
And I let my decision a few moments hang...
Before giving her drops of jasmine and ylang-ylang
And we kiss, languid bliss, brahmacharya at risk
And her sannyasin name means Divine Gratefulness
And I promise to be grateful, oh Kama, God of Love
Rain down with your honeybee bolts from above
And we laugh and swap stories, metaphors, allegories
She kisses my shoulder and oh, how she lures me
To a simple, thatch cabin up high on a hill
Beckons me into her lair for the kill
The bed under a tent of white linen gauze
Fingertips itch at the end of my paws
And we rinse in cold water, warm tropic perfection
And, "Oh," she says, "by the way, do you have...
Con...
Tra...
Cep..

Tion?"

Next thing I'm sprinting down midnight's beach
To Shiva I pray that my cabin I'll reach
"And if," I pray, "it's not my place to be found
In this woman's arms then, Lord, strike me down!"
'Cause it's dark, I can't see, the sand ahead of me
Could slip-fall-trip-break jawbone, ankle or knee
But I'll run for that latex as fast as I can
Offer my vow on this white, moonlit sand
While the crabs, they scurry, under my feet
Or into their tiny crab burrows retreat
And when the Hindus, they bathe in the holy Ganges
They offer themselves to death by disease
Saying Shiva, this body is yours, don't you see?
And like this I offer my celibacy...

And when I get back, she says, "That was fast."
Welcomes me into her arms at long last
And she's strong and she's sweet, challenging, not demure
(a bit of a nutter, that's for damn sure)
Who won't let me lie, looks deep in my eye
We share our big fears, then share a good cry...
And I don't wake for yoga, instead I sleep in
To the slowest, best breakfast that I've ever eaten
To a day filled with laughter, new love and affection
(deserted beach running while sporting erection?)
And she's thirty-four which is seven years older
Seven years wiser, seven years bolder
And my seven poems, they leave her elated
Seven days, seven nights that the earth was created

Seven continents, seven visible planets
And Anugraha she's in cabin seven, I can't stand it!
One night stand? Future wife? Right now I don't care
As we walk down the beach breathing rarefied air...

MIKE'S WEED

Say my goodbyes, pack up my things
To Anugraha's abode I delightedly bring
My oils, my clothes, my shrine to Ganesh
'Cause her change of heart means my change of address
A girl whose big fear is about being claimed —
But would I move in with her? Lioness tamed!
Shacking-up in the truest true sense of the word
In an open-air, thatch bamboo hut, how absurd
"After only three days," says Canadian Mike
Who's leaving tomorrow and asks if I'd like
The rest of his stash, just what everyone needs
A plump, ziplock bag of tobacco and weed

Move into her cabin, throw my shit down
Open it up, spread it around
Light some Nag Champa, make some good love
Much more from a day, I can't ask or dream of
But afterward "Hey," she says, "fancy a 'j'?"
So I roll, get it going and pass it her way
Her tentative draw, cough-cough and exhale
Me, the big booyah, smoke ring, French inhale
Knowing that if I can handle my trip
Enjoy it, then what's the use trying to quit?
Cause Anugraha, I love her, love getting to know her
She wants high adventure? Well that I can show her

The mushrooms that make the machine elves come close
Five grams, look no hands, man, a psychonaut's dose
Opium, just to lie down and feel good
White powder chowder from bad neighborhoods
Which I'd given up...
And now I'm stoned but...
My high has gone down when it shoulda gone up!
Paranoia again, like a tiger come stalking
"Je m'excuse, ma petite was that you I heard talking?
A tok you had during your art college days?
How 'Fumer de l'herbe' always seemed like a phase?
"Well let me tell you, my phase lasted ten years
You never caught me in no bar drinking beers
'Cause we got a war going on in the States
Where people who didn't say no are called inmates
And I risked it all by growing the chronic —
Got high as my stance, man, against Reaganomics..."

Anugraha frowns up at me, looking concerned
"Çava?" she inquires
"Yeah, I'm just burned."
And suddenly the French girl, she looks not so fine
A spark, but no longer a blaze of Divine
Then she says, "Yan — I don't like this new tone
Don't think I like how you get when you're stoned."
"Then you don't like me," I snap back. "Is that clear?
"'Cause this is the way that it's been for ten years."

Sit in the restaurant, waiting for food
Silently fuming, with bad attitudes
What kind of mistake have we made? I think frowning
Fall-in-love-shack in three days — but who's counting?

And what am I doing in Goa, by god?
Anugraha can't eat, gives her plate to the dog
Spin back to our cabin —more argument maybe?
"Bon nuit," she says, curtly.
"Whatever, ma cherie."
Light a few candles then lay down to sleep
A roach in the ash tray that reeks of defeat
"I need to get out of here — out for some air"
"Are you coming back?"
I pretend not to care
 — and I know what my stoner friends stateside would say:
"Just shut the fuck up, man, and pass that shit my way…"
But I want to feel like I did yesterday
Falling in love on Palolem Bay
With a gem from the rough of the Osho commune
Who's naked inside of our thatch, bamboo room
While I'm on the beach in a tropical rain
Then a coconut whizzes a foot from my brain!
Practically kills me and — am I insane?
No, no, hold up: you just need to explain…

Curl up to a beautiful, relative stranger
Fall asleep with a sense of emotional danger
Of her being gone before the sun rises
Instead I wake up to her brilliant, green eyeses
And the girl tucks a dreadlock behind my left ear
Leans her lips close to make sure I can hear,
Says "Yan, I'm sorry I asked to smoke pot
After you said you were trying to stop
And I love that you did it, and did it for me
But jamais you should compromise truth for somebody!

You promise yourself pas de plus cigarettes
You follow ta coeur — pas te bite ou ta tête!"
And I kiss her because she's a guide on my path
"That's twice now I've quit," I reply with a laugh
And we yawn, stretch and rise and find to our surprise
The truth of the matter has shed its disguise
With a stoned oversight that almost spelt doom
To the night I moved into Anugraha's thatch room
A structure made mostly of coir and bamboo
Cotton netting draped over the featherbed too
Because there, on the nightstand, a half-melted lighter
(a shiver crawls over my neck like a spider)
A blackened alarm clock, a puddle of wax
A water glass empty because it had cracked
For it seems while we slept, the candles burned low
And set fire to Mike's bag of weed and tobacco…

THE DREAM AND THE DREAMCATCHER

Anugraha's asleep when my feet touch the sand
Of this idyllic beach in this faraway land
Hoping to capture this part of the globe
In a craft good enough for her Paris abode
Made of flotsam and jetsam and coconut beads
Found treasures and feathers, holed seashells and seeds
Not something you'd find in a souvenir shop
Or some dyed piece of crap from an Albuquerque truck stop…
Made how I was shown by a Cherokee girl
From the Native American Indian world
Who taught me to weave the dreamcatcher's web
Made of willow and sinew and waxed-linen thread
A girl who said dreams are what make you unique
What separates One from the Tribe, so to speak
And the dreamcatcher? Some say it catches those dreams
Filters them out of the land Inbetween
Binding nightmares forever in seashells and leather
Allowing the ancestor's blessings through feathers
Or tell certain someones, "We make a good match."
But is this a dream I'm trying to catch?

Wade, crawl and swim through the tidal lagoon
Past mangroves and herons and tropical blooms
Trying to find the perfect coiled vine

That bends but won't break — and I haven't much time
One day to create my best dreamcatcher ever
One day for one gift for one woman, forever
'Cause tomorrow we're leaving this place by the sea
And what will become of Anugraha and me?

They say that romance isn't love but a dream
Catch that rare bird and you'll see what I mean
Because after the kiss, fuck and fall, you know what?
Reality dawns like the sun, you wake up
You rise from the bliss of your holiday bed
And another fine woman walks by, turns your head
And the condoms you picked up in town aren't as good
As the ones from that shop out in West Hollywood…
And the guru, he laughs, says, "True love's full of shit —
An impossible dream and we all fall for it."
And last night an enlightened young woman from Israel
Blew into our lives like a tropical gale
Lay hands on Anugraha, let energy pour
Until she fell back and convulsed on the floor
Rolled whites of her eyes while the crowd watched in awe
(I had both mine open, don't know what I saw)
But when she awoke from that trance she was higher
Higher than yesterday's passionate fire
Sayin' "Sleep with that fox in cabin number six
No more jealous bullshit attachment love tricks."
But we slept on the beach last night, under the stars
I held her so close but felt her so far
And to reach her, well, I had to ascend
Past being partners or lovers or friends
Past poem and koan, into the unknown

To that high, holy place where you're always alone...

Soak the vine in freshwater, bend into a hoop
Tie it in place, wrap it in jute
Head to the market, pick up some beads
Malachite, fish bone and lapis lazuli
Collect raven feathers along the way back
To the palm-shaded peace of our Palolem shack
Where I weave in the breeze while Anugraha, she reads
The Bhagwan Rajneesh's advice no-one heeds
The vibrations between us grown easy and subtle
While around us small children laugh, play, shriek and scuttle
And she paints all their hands, one after another
With henna — she would make an excellent mother
But tomorrow we move it, we pack it away
To meet with her husband in Calingut Sunday...
Why do I keep forgetting she's married?
A hatchet somewhere that needs to be buried
In her heart, her husband's, quite possibly mine
As I weave the shell-lotus in place with my twine
Wondering if one day's enough time
To capture a romance as rare and as fine
As this dream we have lived and woken up from
Under enlightenment's candlelit sun...

The sunset turns orange and twilight descends
"One last swim?" she proposes, invoking the end
And I wonder, a blunder, what was and will be
As we entwine our fingers and enter the sea
The last light of day igniting her eyes
As we stare, spin and kiss and watch Venus rise
And back in our cabin I pick up the thread

Mix shells from her cache in the dreamcatcher's web
Weaving the lapis and malachite dense
To expose the square-rose Fibonacci sequence...
The mathematical pattern which also describes
How a finger uncurls or a fern frond arrives
The Golden Ratio some people call it
(the cephalopods do it inside a nautilus)
A series of bisected lines in a spiral
A pattern more powerful than that of my rival
Whose ring she'll be wearing for worse or for better
But I tie my knot on a raven's tail feather...

Tighten the web with the point of a needle
Affix the found, emerald green wings of a beetle
And just as the hour of midnight draws close
A tear soaks its way through a fibre of rope
A la prochain, says the lotus of shells
Dripping black magic and Cherokee spells
And I hang the dreamcatcher in front of the candle
Wait for Anugraha to turn the door handle
And when she appears in her small, lacy whites
Strips off and comes toward me, unsure in the light
I gesture above to the rotating the craft
Empty handed once more
For now the dream has passed.

X. THE SERPENT

Spring Equinox, New Delhi

Airports are the same all over the world, a place to kill time, watch clocks and change money. For me, they have always held an air of unreality, sterile interstices between cultures and continents. I think I've experienced psychic airports too — hubs of tunnels connecting different levels of consciousness — and while I remember seeing other beings in those places, it's always in passing.
Nobody lives there.
 Tonight I arrive at the New Delhi airport having cashed in my original voucher from Bombay. This morning, I caught a catamaran from Calingut, central Goa. Anugraha and I left Palolem yesterday. Along the way we stopped at a travel agency where I purchased a ticket to London, flying *west* — the most reckless thing I've done in my life — to "give it a go" on the performance poetry circuit. Again, I had sobbed, just like with the cobras, while Anugraha stroked my head and we became friends.
 "I'm going to Britain with five hundred bucks. It's the worst plan in history — I don't even have a coat."
 "*Formidable, mon amor*, you have nothing to lose."
 "Easy for you to say."
 "Truth is *never* easy."

Anugraha's husband had met us in Calingut, a pleasant, surprisingly bland Dutch *sannyasin*. He understood my anguish and even consoled me, for he had a lover in my same situation. He'd married Anugraha a decade before, first for love, then convenience then devotion to Osho. Now, they seemed more like brother and sister, more inclined than not to spending their lives together. In many ways, I admire their lifestyle; their open and mostly Platonic relationship. They would fight and tear out their hair like most couples but they had their cake and were also eating it. When they told me last night over dinner — their treat — they'd decided to head back to our cabin in Palolem, I'd felt such a powerful sense of betrayal it was either detachment or murderous rampage.

Learn to transform your poisons into hon-ey...

Anugraha and I had a three-year relationship within the space of less than two weeks. We met, fell in love, came out the other side, fought through jealousy, drugs, became friends and traded e-mail.

The craziest thing was her *Osho Zen Tarot* deck, from which we would each pick a card every morning and for ten consecutive days — ten consecutive — one of us would pick out a card called *The Dream*. It pictures a young woman staring into the night sky at a prince and a princess embracing in the heavens. By the time I picked the card yesterday morning, it was no longer necessary to read from the handbook:

Some enchanted evening, it reads, *you're going to meet your soulmate, the perfect person who will meet all your needs and fulfill all your dreams. Right? Wrong! This fantasy that songwriters and poets are so fond of perpetuating has its roots in memories of the womb... You were going to fall. You were going to avoid yourself somehow or other...*

More blocks. Anugraha is everything I want in a woman, save being married to a polyamorous *sannyasin:* attractive, professional, satisfies my francophilia, forthright, spiritual, independent and adventurous. And I was going to fall. Away from the self. To find someone with whom to be loving and cling. Solitude is the hardest lesson of all, but once you hack that one, brother, then you are truly free.

Last night, after dinner and an awkward last kiss in a tawdry rave town in the middle of Goa, I waved goodbye to Divine Gratefulness as she and her husband hit the highway on his motorcycle. She'd learn her own lessons back in Palolem, I was sure, about when to let go and when to hold on. She and I lived The Dream and woke up and you, Mr. Man, have a tough act to follow.

I linger a few minutes inside the terminal, watching the numbers flash up on the screen. I could fly to Manchester in less than an hour. Back to Cairo in two. Johannesburg in three. My ticket to London, Heathrow is good for six months — enough time to head into Nepal on my credit card, finagle a visa and cross into China. Bus into Lhasa. Hitchhike. Walk. Pilgrimage.

The Hindus say all the world is Maya, the Goddess of Illusion, the folds of her dress. All the world except for Mount Kailash, the abode of Lord Shiva, the destroyer of illusion. I'm at a crossroads in the New Delhi Airport, torn between these opposite paths. To join or exit the world of illusion. To establish an identity or shed one like snakeskin.

There've been times in my life — after free-basing DMT, my first night with Jaime, or walking away from a seventy-mile-an-hour car wreck, unscathed — when all the facades have melted away, leaving me breathless to face the big questions: *Who am I? What is this place? Have I done good? Whose name would be on my lips if I died?* Right now I'm stuck on question number one: Am I the Techno-Pagan Octopus Messiah?

It's going to be my stage name, that much is certain, but who am I kidding? I'm just some Californian dude who went to India. To find himself on the hippie trail, like millions before him — but every cliché has a nugget of truth to it. "Looking only at the teachings," to use Sammy's words. "Forget the astrology, remember the lesson," to use Jimmy's. Osho said, "Look where I'm pointing, don't look at my finger." India has untold millions of gods but they're each just a facet of the gemstone called *brahma* and, in that spirit, we're all the Messiah, only mine is of the Techno-Pagan Octopus variety.

Outside the airport I hail a Maruti Suzuki, a utilitarian bubble-framed model of cottage industry. The driver is Sikh with a smartly-wrapped turban and a mustache that disappears into his sideburns. He takes me across town to the main Delhi bus station, offers to watch my pack while I queue but I tell him I'm cool with just being alone — sardined between thousands of Muslims and Hindus. I could spend a whole day in New Delhi, or a year, but I have a thousand kilometers' momentum. The heat and mosquitoes and crowds are unbearable but *this too will pass* — which is bulletproof fortune telling.

I check my bag at the station cloakroom, fill out the baggage claim form in triplicate and make my way through the usual suspects: arm-grabbers, beggars, hard-sleepers on cardboard.

Out on the streets, *samosa* in hand, I notice an Asian man clutching a lamppost. His shirt is torn, his hair wild and lousy, he's missing front teeth but his eyes are no junkie's.

"What are you so damn happy about?" I ask.

"Freedom," he says, in unaccented English.

With time on my hands, I find out that Shukri, from Singapore, used to manage hotels in nearby Kuala Lumpur. Three years ago he'd been caught partying in Goa with a marble-sized nugget of hash on his person. He'd been thrown into prison to rot, awaiting trial, lost eight teeth in fights — "Like an animal," he tells me. Never got charged, never saw a lawyer and the guards never once forwarded his mail.

"I called my wife yesterday," he says, still in shock. "She says, 'Who is this?' I say, 'It's Shukri.' She says, 'Shukri's dead.' I say, 'I'm in Goa. Do you still love me?'" He mists up. "She said yes."

Shukri was released without warning yesterday about the same time I woke up with Anugraha. The authorities had issued him a temporary passport, two hundred rupees and the clothes he's now wearing. After calling his wife — who hadn't remarried — he hopped coaches to Delhi, the cheapest way possible. Arrived at the bus station the same time I did. Tomorrow his wife arrives with their daughter.

He refuses me twice before finally accepting my offer of dinner and a glass of champagne.

"And you, what's your story? You're the first person who's spoken to me tonight. I feel invisible out here on the street."

"Me? I'm just a traveller, passing through. Campfire to campfire as long as I can stretch it — but hey, you know what, dude? I'm really glad I met you. This morning I woke up and thought I had problems."

Riding the overnight bus out of Delhi, my bag on the roof with the rice sacks and cooking oil, I practice Hindi with the people around me, happy to answer their what-name-what-countrys. It's a government bus with hard, wooden seats, and packed so full I can't see the front windshield. The Indians sit so close it's a comfort. It feels good to be part of the swarm, like I belong here. As the night wears on and the detours grow treacherous, I find myself drifting in and out of sleep, thinking about two guys Shukri got busted with who got eleven years for a pipe of brown powder.

The bus arrives in Rishikesh at dawn — much warmer in March than it was in December. The Ganges has risen a foot since my last visit. A much darker green than what I remember. The Kumbh Mela has finished by two weeks though the *saddhu*s still take their ablutions on the *ghats*. I climb to the roof to help unload baggage, much to the amusement of my fellow passengers. When I'm done, an Indian man with a cane makes a show of giving me two rupes *baksheesh*. The bill is creased and unreadable, near confetti. I tuck it in my wallet: my new favorite keepsake.

On my way to the foot-bridge I buy some bananas and notice an old puppeteer on the pavement. He's performing the Ramayana with chapati-dough puppets, delighting a gaggle of uniformed schoolchildren. I recognize Krishna, playing the flute, charming a songbird for a blushing milkmaid. The puppets are crude and colored with crayons. It's a two-thousand-five-hundred-year old entertainment.

And if you experience life as a play
Then somebody *had to write it, didn't they?*
And whoever, whatever made up this dance
Was an artist, une artiste, *who gave us a chance*
To be just like them and create works of beauty
Be they puppets or paintings, software or symphonies
And when you translate to art the things that you're seeing?
You become a more perfect human being...

The mystic, of course, makes himself into art but I'm not a mystic and not here to quibble. I'm here to hire a Jeep to Neel Kanth and finally get rid of Naga Baba's *lingam*. I cross the Shivajhula footbridge wearing my pack, declining the entrepreneurs with their wheelbarrows. At the end of the bridge I buy pellets for the catfish, give pens to the children and bananas to the monkeys. It'd be nice to have a shower, get a room, take a nap, eat a few meals, hit the temple tomorrow, but after Anugraha had left me in Goa I got it in my head not to stop until Neel Kanth.

Luckily there's room in a Jeep of young Brits who happen to be taking a day trip to the temple. Two couples from Leeds, all soon-to-be students. Carefree, young and in love. On their gap year. They're grateful to have me to cut down on costs, though not exactly thrilled to make room for my pack.

"You going to be staying up there?" one girl asks, a wide-eyed brunette in a Tibetan skullcap. "The book says the temple has no on-site accommodation."

"Oy, sod the book," says her strapping, blonde boyfriend.

I chew on the tip of my tongue until there's blood, wondering how much I should tell them. Would they believe I woke up in Goa yesterday? The series of events that led me to Naga Baba? Not far from here, Barry said not to talk about the Serpent, or anything else having to do with DMT.

I decide they probably would if I told it right. But now is not the time.

"I'm playing it by ear, mate."

Our driver is a jocular, musclebound Indian who's seen one-too-many Bollywood action movies. He wears a tight-fitting tank top and wrap-around sunglasses. Between Marlboro Reds, he chews on a matchstick. As we rumble along the pitted, dirt road, tossing the monkeys and cows our banana peels, the Brits say they *cannot believe* all the trash here. This, I discover, is their fourth day in India.

The road veers east, away from the river and angles itself up a forested hill. We zoom past the site of the Silly Straw shoot and the place where Lars had made us turn around. None but the driver have been past this point before, which makes the next leg a descent into novelty.

"*An ascent* into a descent into novelty," I like to imagine McKenna correcting me.

After an hour of nauseating switchbacks, much of it stuck behind a cement truck, the road terminates at a sheer wall of granite. End of the road, in the literal sense. We pile from the Jeep and bang dust from our clothing. Leaving my pack, I disengage from the Brits; slip past the stands selling flowers and other offerings. I find a dirt path between candy-colored outbuildings and follow it into a grove of old banyans.

Encircled with *murtis* and ornately-painted columns, Neel Kanth is a steep-sided, square-bottomed trapezoid — a multi-tiered riot of colorful plaster, four stories tall and as wide as a bus-length. I notice the figure of a five-headed cobra being wrestled away from a statue of Shiva. The scales on the underside run parallel like a real snake's but the scales on its back are polkadot round — much like the suction-cups of an octopus. I mount the stairs to the temple's side entrance, toss my boots onto a pile at the threshold. The floor is wet inside. *Saddhu*s are emptying large metal urns, most likely water brought up from the Ganges. The temple doesn't strike me as ancient or spectacular but, then again, what was I expecting? Outside, the Brits arrive waving their cameras but an Indian voice tells them sternly, "No photos."

I reach into my pocket and take out the *lingam*, a golfball-sized gravy boat carved in gray stone. It symbolizes the creative force of the universe, what the French call the little death, *le petit mort.* The orgasm.

I head for the shrine at the center of the temple, ringing iron prayer bells along the way. Stepping between pillars I find a small dais, upon which sits a *saddhu* in front of a gold cobra statue. He wears the orange robes and red *tika* of his order, has wild, unkempt hair and ash on his skin.

"*Naga Baba told me to come here*," I say.

He Hindu headshakes and stares at me vacantly.

When I show him the *lingam*, he gestures to a platter full of flowers, other offerings and similar *lingams*. I set down my carving along with the others. The *saddhu* nods solemnly, dabs a *tika* on my forehead.

That's it. No lightning flash. No transcendental bliss. A *lingam* among dozens in front of a gold cobra.

"*Naga Baba is a friend of mine. Have you seen him?*"

He enunciates slowly. "*I am Naga Baba.*"

The first Hindu temple I ever visited was across the road from Malibu Creek State Park. I noticed it after taking a school group through the chaparral. This was about two weeks after my first DMT trip. Knowing nothing of Hinduism, I'd taken off my hiking boots and spent a few minutes in front of each *murti*, trying to verify which one I'd seen. Without question, the many-armed entity had been Shiva.

At the time, there was a visiting priest from India, a saffron-robed bald man with fierce, bloodshot eyes. An intimidating figure but I was on a mission.

"Excuse me, I was wondering if you could help me? I had this… dream."

Before he could reply four Indian men in suits, with excited expressions, rushed to his side. They told me the priest was a powerful holy man and they were his disciples, tour guides and translators. The priest packed his cheek with some suspicious-looking snuff then asked for the men to translate my story. Afterward he shot me a few words in Hindi.

"He is asking you how many arms did it have?"

"Eight. Although it could have been sixteen — definitely not twelve — but a multiple of four."

The priest nodded brusquely and grunted more Hindi.

"Now he is asking you what is the sex?"

I thought for a moment then threw up my hands. This made him smile, perhaps even curious. He spoke the Queen's English now, albeit curried: "Yes? And?"

"What do you mean '*and*'?"

"And you've told us your story. What do you want to know?"

"I want to know... what it *means*," I exploded. "I just saw Shiva in a freakin' UFO! He was floating with other gods over pyramids. Bright as the sun, I could barely even look."

The saffron-robed priest huffed a short little laugh, tossed his disciples another few words, sidestepped around me smacking his lips and continued along in the direction of the dining hall.

"Well?" I demanded.

The smallest of the men stepped forward, apologetically. "He said you're in the grace of God. Just keep praying and you'll get whatever you want."

What kind of fortune-cookie crap is that? I laced my boots and headed to the parking lot. *Blessing Number Four,* is what it had felt like. Dude, I just saw the most incredible — "Yes? And?"

And now, on the opposite side of the planet, two years later, putting on the same pair of boots, here I am.

Shaking my head, I cross the temple and leave from the opposite door I came in. Outside, all the Brits are inspecting the *murtis* carved on the temple's exterior by the dozen.

"Oy, what do you make of that one?" says the blond

guy. I turn, shield my eyes from the afternoon sun. And there, at the feet of a towering Shiva, coiled upon itself with its abdomen exposed, stands a six-foot blue cobra with a human head and torso, beckoning me with four outstretched arms.

EPILOGUE

So you caught me halfway on my round-the-world ticket
How's that for a story, my friend, pretty wicked?
Now I'm off to Mt. Kailash in western Tibet
To meet the Destroyer and hope he will let
Me save the good people from the world's coming fire
Me being the Techno-Pagan Octopus Messiah!
And I see your head shakin', sayin', "That boy, he's crazy!"
But that kind of shit, man, it don't even phase me
'Cause the truth don't require belief to be true
It is the truth, traveller, and there's nothing you can do.

POSTSCRIPT/ACKNOWLEDGEMENTS

It was chucking sleet when I returned to Heathrow, where this book began, in March of '98. I arrived from India on Emirates Air, via Dubai, with roughly a thousand dollars, a backpack full of journals and a ratty, Nepalese "jumper" to my name. The rest of my life would not be possible without the synchronicity, support and vicious barbs I found in London, my favorite city, which has become my home. To her and to the following people I extend my gratitude: to Alayne, the English girl in Hampi who recommended I perform at a pub called the Enterprise in Camden; to Liam, the Irish guy I met on the plane who put me up my first three nights in London on his floor in Hounslow West, two whole tube stops from the airport; to Enterprise performance poetry promoter Paul Lyalls who said I could do five minutes on his open mic, £5 entry fee, non-negotiable -- "Don't give a monkey's where you been, geez"-- before inviting me back to become a regular and eventually to headline; to books' editor Maja Prausnitz who spotted me that fateful first mic and invited me to housesit her flat for six weeks and there transcribe my journals; to the audiences of poetry events and slams across Britain for their heckles, cheers and gongs; to the Electric Ballroom for letting me work under the table serving snakebite-and-blacks to ravers on the weekends; to John Citizen, Jem Rolls, Asher, Victoria Mosley and all the other slam poets and productions who put me on their stages; to "big name comedian" Dan Antopolski for giving me a shot at stand-up at Kool Eddy's, and for hosting me at the Edinburgh Fringe; to former East Enders *director Chris Fallon for his friendship and support; to housemate Sandra Tharumalingam for all those walks on all those short and dreary winter days; to Manoj and Lakshmi Tiwari for having the courtesy to end up around the corner from me in North London after their honeymoon; and to Kaye and Martin Roach of Independent Music Press for giving me my first break as an author. To them, Terence McKenna, David Holthouse, the Naturalists and everyone else who helped kick my ridiculous can down the road: to them, I say, namaste. Not me. You.*

For this 20th anniversary edition I must thank and kiss the feet of Mrs. Cathy Winn who dropped a signed copy of the first edition off a longtail boat in Thailand, had to replace it for a mutual friend — thank you Linda Thorne — tracked me down, exchanged e-mails with me for eighteen months and, long story short, when I asked her to marry me said, "Absolutely." We were married first by Sakalava crocodile shaman in Madagascar and officially by Moorlock and the late, great Greg Junell, in their capacity as mail-order ministers, on a beach in California. I would also like to thank Jasmin Kirkbride, the hacktacular Robert Kaye, editor-in-kindness Rebekah Lattin-Rawstrone and Justine Solomons, founder of global publishing network Byte the Book (dot com!) for her savvy and encouragement.

Gratitude,
Ian

For news about my upcoming memoir*, Californian, *please check octopusmessiah.com.

Made in the USA
Columbia, SC
16 November 2023